Poetry

Recent American
poetry in
open forms

edited by

Stephen Berg and *Robert Mezey*

Indianapolis and New York

© 1969 by The Bobbs-Merrill Company, Inc.
Printed in the United States of America
ISBN-0-672-60669-0 (pbk)
Library of Congress Catalog Card Number 69-16527
ISBN 0-672-51158-4
Fifth Printing

Naked Poetry

Naked

And sketching open forms
with the arcs of the sailing regatta
space plays half awake—
a child who's not known the cradle.

—Osip Mandelstam

The Bobbs-Merrill Company, Inc.

ACKNOWLEDGMENTS

STEPHEN BERG. "Ollie, Answer Me" first appeared in *Poetry*, May 1966, copyright 1966 by the Modern Poetry Association. Reprinted with permission of the author and of the editor of *Poetry*. "People Trying to Love" and "The Survivor" originally appeared in *New American Review #3*. "To My Friends" and "A Wife Talks to Herself" (1965), "Between Us" (1967), "Dreaming with a Friend," and "The Holes" (1969) copyrighted ©, in the respective years shown, by The New Yorker Magazine, Inc. "A Glimpse of the Body Shop" first appeared in *The North American Review*. "The Animals" first appeared in *TriQuarterly*. "Gooseberries" first appeared in *December*.

JOHN BERRYMAN. Reprinted from *77 Dream Songs* by John Berryman, by permission of Farrar, Straus & Giroux, Inc. Copyright © 1959, 1962, 1963, 1964 by John Berryman.

ROBERT BLY. "After Drinking All Night with a Friend, We Go Out in a Boat at Dawn to See Who Can Write the Best Poem," "Surprised by Evening," "Driving Toward the Lac Qui Parle River," "Poem in Three Parts," "Awakening," "Driving to Town Late to Mail a Letter," "Getting Up Early," "Afternoon Sleep," "Watering the Horse," "In a Train," "After Working," "Night," "Old Boards," "The Clear Air of October," "Depression," and "Silence" are reprinted from *Silence in the Snowy Fields*, Wesleyan University Press, 1962. Copyright 1959, 1960, 1961, 1962 by Robert Bly and reprinted with the permission of Robert Bly. "Looking at New-Fallen Snow from a Train," "Hurrying Away from the Earth," "Those Being Eaten by America," "The Executive's Death," "Counting Small-Boned Bodies," "Asian Peace Offers Rejected without Publication," "A Dream of Suffocation," "Written in Dejection near Rome," and "Looking at Some Flowers" are reprinted from *The Light Around the Body*, Harper & Row, 1967. Copyright 1967 by Robert Bly, reprinted with the permission of Robert Bly. "Hatred of Men with Black Hair" is reprinted from *A Poetry Reading Against The Viet Nam War*, by permission of Robert Bly.

ROBERT CREELEY. The poems by Robert Creeley are reprinted by permission of Charles Scribner's Sons from *For Love* (Copyright © 1959, 1962 Robert Creeley) and from *Words* (Copyright © 1962, 1963, 1964, 1967 Robert Creeley), by Robert Creeley.

ALLEN GINSBERG. "Death to Van Gogh's Ear!" and "Ignu" reprinted from *Kaddish*, by Allen Ginsberg. "Howl, Part 1," "In the Baggage Room at Greyhound," "A Supermarket in California," and "America" reprinted from *Howl*, by Allen Ginsberg. "Wichita Vortex Sutra" reprinted from *Planet News*, by Allen Ginsberg. All copyright © 1968 by Allen Ginsberg. "Love Poem on Theme by Whitman" reprinted from *Reality Sandwiches*, copyright © 1963, by Allen Ginsberg. Reprinted by permission of City Lights Books.

WELDON KEES. All poems reprinted from *The Collected Poems of Weldon Kees*, by permission of University of Nebraska Press and the Stone Wall Press. Copyright © 1943, 1947, 1954 by Weldon Kees; copyright © 1960 by John A. Kees.

GALWAY KINNELL. "The Poem" and "The Porcupine" are reprinted with the permission of Galway Kinnell. "Freedom, New Hampshire" and "The Avenue Bearing the Initial of Christ into the New World" are reprinted from *What a Kingdom It Was*, copyright © 1960 by Galway Kinnell. Reprinted by permission of the publisher, Houghton Mifflin Company. "The Homecoming of Emma Lazarus," "Spindrift," "Poems of Night," "Cells Breathe in the Emptiness," "Flower Herding on Mount Monadnock," and "Ruins under the Stars" reprinted from *Flower Herding on Mount Monadnock*, copyright © 1964 by Galway Kinnell. Reprinted with the permission of the publisher, Houghton Mifflin Company. "How Many Nights" reprinted from *Body Rags*, copyright © 1967 by Galway Kinnell. Reprinted with the permission of the publisher, Houghton Mifflin Company.

DENISE LEVERTOV. "The Absence," "The Presence," " '. . . Else a Great Prince in Prison Lies," "Come into Animal Presence," "The Depths," Partial Resemblance" from Denise Levertov, *The Jacob's Ladder*. Copyright © 1958, 1959, 1960, 1961 by Denise Levertov Goodman. Reprinted with the permission of the publisher, New Directions Publishing Corporation. "Our Bodies," "The Secret," "The Novices," "Song for Ishtar," "Losing Track," "The Breathing," and "The Old Adam" from Denise Levertov, *O Taste and See*. "The Breathing" © 1966 by Steuben Glass. Others © 1964 by Denise Levertov Goodman. Reprinted by permission of New Directions Publishing Corporation. "Bedtime," "A Day Begins," "The Mutes," and "Two Variations" from Denise Levertov, *The Sorrow Dance*. Copyright © 1966, 1967 by Denise Levertov Goodman. Reprinted by permission of New Directions Publishing Corporation. "Some Notes on Organic Form" by Denise Levertov was first published in *Poetry*, September 1965. Copyright 1965 by the Modern Poetry Association; reprinted by permission of Denise Levertov and Henry Rago, editor of *Poetry*.

PHILIP LEVINE. "Silent in America" was first published by the Shaw Avenue Press, Iowa City 1965. "Silent in America," "The Cemetery at Academy, California" (parts of which originally appeared in *The New Yorker*), "Sunday Afternoon," "Baby Villon," "Commanding Elephants," "Heaven," "The Midget," "The Businessman of Alicante," "Winter Rains: Cataluña," "Waking an Angel," and "The Second Angel" are reprinted from *Not This Pig*, by Philip Levine. Copyrights © 1964, 1966, 1967, 1968 by Philip Levine. Reprinted by permission of the Wesleyan University Press. "The Children's Crusade" was first published in *Northwest Review* and is reprinted by permission of *Northwest Review*.

ROBERT LOWELL. "For the Union Dead," "The Mouth of the Hudson," "July in Washington" are reprinted from *For the Union Dead* by Robert Lowell, by permission of Farrar, Straus & Giroux, Inc. Copyright © 1960, 1964 by Robert

Lowell. "Memories of West Street and Lepke" is reprinted from *Life Studies* by Robert Lowell, by permission of Farrar, Straus & Giroux, Inc. Copyright © 1958 by Robert Lowell. All other poems in the Robert Lowell selection are reprinted from *Imitations* by Robert Lowell, by permission of Farrar, Straus & Giroux, Inc. Copyright © 1958, 1959, 1960, 1961 by Robert Lowell.

W. S. MERWIN. "Air," "Sire," "The Indigestion of the Vampire," "The Students of Justice," "For Now," and "Spring" appear in *The Moving Target* by W. S. Merwin, published by Atheneum in 1963, and are reprinted by permission of the publisher. "Sire" (was previously published in *The New Yorker*), "Air," "Students of Justice," and "Spring" (were previously published in *Poetry*) copyright © 1962, 1963 by W. S. Merwin. "The Indigestion of the Vampire," "For Now" copyright © 1963 by W. S. Merwin. "The Asians Dying," "The Herds," "Looking for Mushrooms at Sunrise," "Come Back" (have also all appeared in *The New Yorker*), "The Gods," "Whenever I Go There" (have also appeared in *Poetry*), "Avoiding News by the River," "The Room," "Dusk in Winter," "For the Anniversary of My Death," "Watchers," "Caesar," "It is March," and "December among the Vanished" appear in *The Lice* by W. S. Merwin, published by Atheneum in 1967 and reprinted with permission of the publisher. Copyright © 1963, 1964, 1965, 1966, 1967 by W. S. Merwin.

ROBERT MEZEY. "Touch It," "A Confession," "There," "Night on Clinton," "My Mother," "The Underground Gardens," "The Friendship," "After Hours," "You Could Say," "To Her," "White Blossoms," and "Reaching the Horizon" are from *White Blossoms*, published by the Cummington Press and reprinted by permission of Cummington Press and the author. The selection from "Theresienstadt Poems," "New Year's Eve in Solitude," "An Evening," and "In the Soul Hour" are reprinted by permission of *kayak* and the author. "April Fourth" is reprinted by permission of the author.

KENNETH PATCHEN. From *Selected Poems:* "And What with the Blunders," "The Character of Love Seen as a Search for the Lost," "Fog," "Behold, One of Several Little Christs," copyright 1939 and © 1957 by New Directions. "Gautama in the Deer Park at Benares" copyright 1943 by Kenneth Patchen; © 1957 by New Directions. "The Reason for Skylarks" and "Pastoral" copyright 1953 by New Directions and © 1957 by New Directions. "The Everlasting Contenders," "The Constant Bridegrooms," © 1957 by New Directions. "The Orange Bears" copyright 1949 and © 1957 by New Directions. "In Order To," copyright 1954 by New Directions. Reprinted by permission of the publisher, New Directions Publishing Company. From *First Will and Testament:* "Elegy for the Silent Voices and the Joiners of Everything" and "The Hunted City" copyright 1939, © 1965 by New Directions. Reprinted by permission of the publisher, New Directions Publishing Corporation. From *Because It Is:* "Because They Were Very Poor That Winter," "Because Sometimes You Can't Always Be So," "Because Going Nowhere Takes a Long Time," "Because in This Sorrowing Statue of Flesh," "Because He Liked to Be at Home" copyright © 1960 by New Directions. Reprinted by permission of the publisher, New Directions Publishing Corporation. The selections from *The Journal of Albion Moonlight* copyright 1941 by Kenneth Patchen. Reprinted by permission of the publisher, New Directions Publishing Corporation.

TO THE MEMORY OF ROBERT OCKENE
1934–1969

FOREWORD

We feel like intruders here. Two years ago, when we first decided that
there was a need for a book like this, we planned to start it off with
a long essay on the theory and practice of . . . of what? There wasn't
even a satisfactory name for the kinds of poetry we were gathering and
talking about, and still isn't. Some people said "Free Verse" and others
said "Organic Poetry" (and a few old ones said "That's not poetry!"),
and we finally came up with Open Forms, which isn't bad but isn't all
that good either. And we took a phrase from Jiménez for a title which
expresses what we feel about the qualities of this poetry as no technical
label could do. But what does it matter what you call it? Here is a book
of nineteen American poets whose poems don't rhyme (usually) and
don't move on feet of more or less equal duration (usually). That
nondescription gropes toward the only technical principle they all
have in common. But we had in mind, among other things,
to show a wide gamut of rhythmic styles and so we wanted the
work of a few poets who, though often working close to the limits
of the old accentuals and accentual-syllabics, have often broken those
limits and in fact broken down the distinctions between "strict" and
"free" verse. There are also three poets whose contributions are mostly
in syllabics, which, in our view, employs a single arbitrary restriction to
shape or control what is really a kind of free verse. And there are some
others here who sometimes, in their "free verse," freely write lines,
stanzas, even whole sections, in the old iambic mode. So, what to say of
these nineteen poets? Everything we thought to ask about their formal
qualities has come to seem more and more irrelevant, and we find we
are much more interested in what they say, in their dreams, visions, and
prophecies. Their poems take shape from the shapes of their emotions,
the shapes their minds make in thought, and certainly don't need
interpreters. In any case, we soon grew bored with our original plan to
discuss the theory and practice of what. Our job, we now see, was
to imagine the anthology (for there was nothing like it), put it
together, and get out of the way. This is an act of silent criticism, is it
not? and even a way of theorizing.

A few words, before we get out of the way, about the kind of book
we imagined and the one we finally made. We began with the firm
conviction that the strongest and most alive poetry in America had
abandoned or at least broken the grip of traditional meters and had
set out, once again, into "the wilderness of unopened life." We decided
to stay with contemporary work, which is always the most interesting
if it's good, and by contemporary we mean more or less from the end
of World War II to this afternoon, sometime before World War III. (That

doesn't mean there aren't a few poems here which fall on either side of those rough limits.) We decided to keep it American because we knew American, and because, with a few exceptions (mainly Ted Hughes), nothing much new has happened in English poetry since Lawrence laid down his pen and died. We decided to cut across the schools, ignoring all feuds and other ugliness of literary life, and simply pick the best poets writing (and three who died untimely and who if this world were better would be living and writing today) and present them in rich and varied selections. Accordingly, we would include only those poets who had more than a handful of good poems. There are many lovely poets around who have written poems as good as any anthologist could want, but we did not see how they could fill ten or fifteen pages or more without using a lot of fill. We hoped also that no poet in the book would be very much like any other poet in the book, that each would have his own voice, his own distinct flavor, and so, regretfully, we left out several fine poets who seemed to us too much like this or that more interesting writer already included. In the case of two poets, we used mostly translations because we felt them to be among their best work in open forms.

Having ditched our idea of a definitive essay, we invited each poet, everyone that had an address this side the grave, to write an essay or statement or letter to accompany his poems, and most of them responded, talking about their notion of poetry, about open forms, what they were doing, how they felt, why they considered themselves to be etc. In some cases, only a vicious persistence on our part persuaded a poet to surrender and write a little prose; we apologize for our pestering. Others preferred to say nothing more than their poems, and why not?

As is the case with most anthologies of poetry, poets are excluded from this first edition because of costs and space, who should be here and who, we hope, will be in the second edition: St. Geraud, Alan Dugan, C. K. Williams, LeRoi Jones, John Ashberry, Michael Harper, Bert Meyers, Charles Simic, and others. Still, there will be the usual complaints that one poet or another has been left out, that one or another has been put in. Most of our reasons for putting in and leaving out are clearly set forth above; please check them before complaining. Naturally, there are other reasons. There are a few poets who would seem to demand inclusion by virtue of their enormous and dazzling reputations, not to mention the openness of their forms, but they are not here because they are not good enough, or worse. And without a doubt, some poets are missing because they are writing unknown in a room in St. Louis or Oakland or Tampa and we don't know them, or, if they are known, because we have not had the sense to recognize their power and originality. But we will put aside all the traditional modesties and say plainly what we think, that much of the best poetry written in America during the last two decades is collected in this book.

Stephen Berg
Philadelphia, Pennsylvania

Robert Mezey
Tollhouse, California

December 1968

We owe thanks to the following people for help, encouragement, criticism, and many other acts of good will—Linda Norton, Beatrice Roethke, Alice Powley, C. K. Williams, Dianne Wildman, Robert Bly, Galway Kinnell, Gary Johnson, S. J. Marks, Sydney Schenk, Philip Levine, Robert Ockene and William Hackett, Jr.—and to our wives, for the usual, and unusual.

CONTENTS

KENNETH PATCHEN

WILLIAM STAFFORD

PHILIP LEVINE

SYLVIA PLATH

Naked Poetry

KENNETH REXROTH

Kenneth Rexroth was born in 1905 in South Bend, Indiana, and grew up in Chicago. He quit school at 16, and worked at various jobs, as reporter, labor organizer, logger, etc. His books of verse include The Phoenix and the Tortoise, The Art of Worldly Wisdom, The Signature of All Things, The Homestead Called Damascus, In Defense of the Earth, *and* Natural Numbers. *He is also the author of several distinguished books of translations, among them* 100 Poems from the Chinese *and* Poems from the Greek Anthology; *of two essay collections,* Bird in the Bush *and* Assays; *and of* An Autobiographical Novel.

SNOW STORM

Tumult, weeping, many new ghosts.
Heartbroken, aging, alone, I sing
To myself. Ragged mist settles
In the spreading dusk. Snow skurries
In the coiling wind. The wineglass
Is spilled. The bottle is empty.
The fire has gone out in the stove.
Everywhere men speak in whispers.
I brood on the uselessness of letters.

Tu Fu

MOON FESTIVAL

The Autumn constellations
Begin to rise. The brilliant
Moonlight shines on the crowds.
The moon toad swims in the river
And does not drown. The moon rabbit
Pounds the bitter herbs of the
Elixir of eternal life.
His drug only makes my heart
More bitter. The silver brilliance
Only makes my hair more white.
I know that the country is
Overrun with war. The moonlight
Means nothing to the soldiers
Camped in the western deserts.

Tu Fu

WRITTEN ON THE WALL AT
CHANG'S HERMITAGE

It is Spring in the mountains.
I come alone seeking you.
The sound of chopping wood echos
Between the silent peaks.

The streams are still icy.
There is snow on the trail.
At sunset I reach your grove
In the stony mountain pass.
You want nothing, although at night
You can see the aura of gold
And silver ore all around you.
You have learned to be gentle
As the mountain deer you have tamed.
The way back forgotten, hidden
Away, I become like you,
An empty boat, floating, adrift.

Tu Fu

THE WILLOW

My neighbor's willow sways its frail
Branches, graceful as a girl of
Fifteen. I am sad because this
Morning the violent
Wind broke its longest bough.

Tu Fu

JADE FLOWER PALACE

The stream swirls. The wind moans in
The pines. Grey rats scurry over
Broken tiles. What prince, long ago,
Built this palace, standing in
Ruins beside the cliffs? There are
Green ghost fires in the black rooms.
The shattered pavements are all
Washed away. Ten thousand organ
Pipes whistle and roar. The storm
Scatters the red autumn leaves.
His dancing girls are yellow dust.
Their painted cheeks have crumbled

Away. His gold chariots
And courtiers are gone. Only
A stone horse is left of his
Glory. I sit on the grass and
Start a poem, but the pathos of
It overcomes me. The future
Slips imperceptibly away.
Who can say what the years will bring?

Tu Fu

NIGHT IN THE HOUSE BY THE RIVER

It is late in the year;
Yin and Yang struggle
In the brief sunlight.
On the desert mountains
Frost and snow
Gleam in the freezing night.
Past midnight,
Drums and bugles ring out,
Violent, cutting the heart.
Over the Triple Gorge the Milky Way
Pulsates between the stars.
The bitter cries of thousands of households
Can be heard above the noise of battle.
Everywhere the workers sing wild songs.
The great heroes and generals of old time
Are yellow dust forever now.
Such are the affairs of men.
Poetry and letters
Persist in silence and solitude.

Tu Fu

NIGHT THOUGHTS WHILE TRAVELLING

A light breeze rustles the reeds
Along the river banks. The
Mast of my lonely boat soars
Into the night. Stars blossom

Over the vast desert of
Waters. Moonlight flows on the
Surging river. My poems have
Made me famous but I grow
Old, ill and tired, blown hither
And yon; I am like a gull
Lost between heaven and earth.

Tu Fu

GREEN JADE PLUM TREES IN SPRING

Spring comes early to the gardens
Of the South, with dancing flowers.
The gentle breeze carries the sound
Of horses whinnying. The blue
Green plums are already as large
As beans. The willow leaves are long,
And really are curved like a girl's
Eyebrows. Butterflies whirl in the
Long sunlight. In the evening the
Mist lies heavy on the flowers.
The grass is covered with dew.
Girls in their transparent dresses,
Indolent and lascivious,
Lounge in their hammocks. Swallows, two
By two, nest under the painted eaves.

Ou Yang Hsiu

THE WILD FLOWER MAN

Do you know the old man who
Sells flowers by the South Gate?
He lives on flowers like a bee.
In the morning he sells mallows,
In the evening he has poppies.
His shanty roof lets in the

Blue sky. His rice bin is
Always empty. When he has
Made enough money from his
Flowers, he heads for a teahouse.
When his money is gone, he
Gathers some more flowers.
All the spring weather, while the
Flowers are in bloom, he is
In bloom, too. Every day he
Is drunk all day long. What does
He care if new laws are posted
At the Emperor's palace?
What does it matter to him
If the government is built
On sand? If you try to talk
To him, he won't answer but
Only give you a drunken
Smile from under his tousled hair.

Lu Yu

THE TERRACE IN THE SNOW

In the golden twilight the rain
Was like silk threads. During the night
It cleared. The wind fell. It grew
Colder. My covers felt damp
And cold. Without my knowing it,
The snow had drifted into
The room like heaps of salt. At
The fifth watch, in the first flush
Of dawn, I close the curtain
Of the study. During the
Rest of the night I listen
To the ice, warping the colored
Tiles of the roof. In the morning
I sweep the Northern terrace
And look out at Saddle Peak.
It is clear of clouds and I
Can see both summits. Above

The village in the morning
Sunlight, crows begin to circle.
The mud of the streets is covered
With white. No cart track has marked it.
Ice has turned the shop roofs to
White jade. Snow has filled the doorways
With rice. The last cicadas
Have long since gone to earth. Now
They will have to dig a thousand
Feet deeper. Some clouds pile up,
The color of dried moss. My
Chest bothers me again.
I feel I have lost the
Ability to write.
The icicles on the eaves
Drone in the wind like the swords
Of murderers.

                    Su Tung P'o

MOON, FLOWERS, MAN

I raise my cup and invite
The moon to come down from the
Sky. I hope she will accept
Me. I raise my cup and ask
The branches, heavy with flowers,
To drink with me. I wish them
Long life and promise never
To pick them. In company
With the moon and the flowers,
I get drunk, and none of us
Ever worries about good
Or bad. How many people
Can comprehend our joy? I
Have wine and moon and flowers.
Who else do I want for drinking companions?

                    Su Tung P'o

HYSTERIA

When I look in the mirror
My face frightens me. I am
Afraid of myself. Every
Spring weakness overcomes me like
A mortal sickness. I am too
Weary to arrange the flowers
Or paint my face. Everything
Bothers me. All the old sorrows
Flood back and make the present worse.
The crying nightjars terrify me.
The mating swallows embarrass me,
Flying two by two outside
My window. Plucked eyebrows,
Weary eyes—that have grown hard
With loneliness. Swallows chirp
In the painted eaves—but I
Have lost the ability
Even to dream of happiness.
Each new Spring finds me deeper
Tangled and snarled in bitterness.
As all the world grows more lovely
My bowels are torn with sorrow.
Peach blossoms quiver in the
Light of the new moon on the first
Nights of the Season of Cold Food.
Huge willows in the golden
Twilight wave their long shadows
In the clear bright winds of Spring.
Surrounded by flowers, trapped in
Pain, I watch the sun set beyond
The roofs of the women's quarters.

Chu Shu Chen

ON THE DEATH OF A NEW BORN CHILD

The flowers in bud on the trees
Are pure like this dead child.
The East wind will not let them last.
It will blow them into blossom,

And at last into the earth.
It is the same with this beautiful life
Which was so dear to me.
While his mother is weeping tears of blood,
Her breasts are still filling with milk.

Mei Yao Ch'en

THE BOATS ARE AFLOAT

Last night along the river banks
The floods of Spring have risen.
Great warships and huge barges
Float as lightly as feathers.
Before, nothing could move them from the mud.
Today they swim with ease in the swift current.

Chu Hsi

ROGATION DAYS

Under the orchards, under
The tree strung vines, little blue
Figures are making hay, high
On the steep hillsides above
Palladio's drowsy villas
And Tiepolo's swirling walls.
On the highest field they are
Still cutting with swinging scythes;
Down below they are tossing
The long swathes of hay to cure
In the sun; further down they
Are cocking it, or carrying
It off in two wheeled donkey carts.
The Venetian plain vanishes
In haze. The nearby Alps are
Indefinite blue smudges,
Capped with faint streaks of orange
Snow. Clouds of perfume roll up

The hillside in waves. All the birds
Sing. All the flowers bloom. Here
At a stone table like this,
On a little hill like this,
In a circle of cypress
And olive like this, the infinite
Visited Leopardi,
And ravished him and carried
Him off in the deep summer.
It would carry me off, too,
If I knew where I wanted
To go, or if I just wanted
To go nowhere at all.

KINGS RIVER CANYON

My sorrow is so wide
I cannot see across it;
And so deep I shall never
Reach the bottom of it.
The moon sinks through deep haze,
As though the Kings River Canyon
Were filled with fine, warm, damp gauze.
Saturn gleams through the thick light
Like a gold, wet eye; nearby,
Antares glows faintly,
Without sparkle. Far overhead,
Stone shines darkly in the moonlight—
Lookout Point, where we lay
In another full moon, and first
Peered down into this canyon.
Here we camped, by still autumnal
Pools, all one warm October.
I baked you a bannock birthday cake.
Here you did your best paintings—
Innocent, wondering landscapes.
Very few of them are left
Anywhere. You destroyed them
In the terrible trouble
Of your long sickness. Eighteen years
Have passed since that autumn.

There was no trail here then.
Only a few people knew
How to enter this canyon.
We were all alone, twenty
Miles from anybody,
A young husband and wife,
Closed in and wrapped about
In the quiet autumn,
In the sound of quiet water,
In the turning and falling leaves,
In the wavering of innumerable
Bats from the caves, dipping
Over the odorous pools
Where the great trout drowsed in the evenings.

Eighteen years have been ground
To pieces in the wheels of life.
You are dead. With a thousand
Convicts they have blown a highway
Through Horseshoe Bend. Youth is gone,
That only came once. My hair
Is turning grey and my body
Heavier. I too move on to death.
I think of Henry King's stilted
But desolated Exequy,
Of Yuan Chen's great poem,
Unbearably pitiful;
Alone by the Spring river
More alone than I had ever
Imagined I would ever be,
I think of Frieda Lawrence,
Sitting alone in New Mexico,
In the long drought, listening
For the hiss of the milky Isar,
Over the cobbles, in a lost Spring.

THEODORE ROETHKE

Theodore Roethke was born in 1908 in Saginaw, Michigan. He was educated at the University of Michigan; he taught at Penn State and then for many years at the University of Washington. He died of a heart attack in 1964. His books of verse include Open House, The Lost Son and Other Poems, Praise to the End, The Waking, Words for the Wind, *and* The Far Field. *Some of his essays and papers on poetry were gathered after his death and published in a book,* On the Poet and His Craft.

North American Sequence

THE LONGING

1

On things asleep, no balm:
A kingdom of stinks and sighs,
Fetor of cockroaches, dead fish, petroleum,
Worse than castoreum of mink or weasels,
Saliva dripping from warm microphones,
Agony of crucifixion on barstools.
    Less and less the illuminated lips,
    Hands active, eyes cherished;
    Happiness left to dogs and children—
    (Matters only a saint mentions!)
Lust fatigues the soul.
How to transcend this sensual emptiness?
(Dreams drain the spirit if we dream too long.)
In a bleak time, when a week of rain is a year,
The slag-heaps fume at the edge of the raw cities:
The gulls wheel over their singular garbage;
The great trees no longer shimmer;
Not even the soot dances.

And the spirit fails to move forward,
But shrinks into a half-life, less than itself,
Falls back, a slug, a loose worm
Ready for any crevice,
An eyeless starer.

2

A wretch needs his wretchedness. Yes.
O pride, thou art a plume upon whose head?

How comprehensive that felicity! . . .
A body with the motion of a soul.
What dream's enough to breathe in? A dark dream.
The rose exceeds, the rose exceeds us all.
Who'd think the moon could pare itself so thin?
A great flame rises from the sunless sea;

The light cries out, and I am there to hear—
I'd be beyond; I'd be beyond the moon,
Bare as a bud, and naked as a worm.

To this extent I'm a stalk.
   —How free; how all alone.
Out of these nothings
   —All beginnings come.

3

I would with the fish, the blackening salmon, and the mad lemmings,
The children dancing, the flowers widening.
Who sighs from far away?
I would unlearn the lingo of exasperation, all the distortions of
    malice and hatred;
I would believe my pain: and the eye quiet on the growing rose;
I would delight in my hands, the branch singing, altering the
    excessive bird;
I long for the imperishable quiet at the heart of form;
I would be a stream, winding between great striated rocks in late
    summer;
A leaf, I would love the leaves, delighting in the redolent disorder
    of this mortal life,
This ambush, this silence,
Where shadow can change into flame,
And the dark be forgotten.
I have left the body of the whale, but the mouth of the night is still
    wide;
On the Bullhead, in the Dakotas, where the eagles eat well,
In the country of few lakes, in the tall buffalo grass at the base
    of the clay buttes,
In the summer heat, I can smell the dead buffalo,
The stench of their damp fur drying in the sun,
The buffalo chips drying.

    Old men should be explorers?
    I'll be an Indian.
    Ogalala?
    Iroquois.

MEDITATION AT OYSTER RIVER

1

Over the low, barnacled, elephant-colored rocks,
Come the first tide-ripples, moving, almost without sound, toward
    me,
Running along the narrow furrows of the shore, the rows of dead
    clam shells;
Then a runnel behind me, creeping closer,
Alive with tiny striped fish, and young crabs climbing in and out
    of the water.

No sound from the bay. No violence.
Even the gulls quiet on the far rocks,
Silent, in the deepening light,
Their cat-mewing over,
Their child-whimpering.

At last one long undulant ripple,
Blue-black from where I am sitting,
Makes almost a wave over a barrier of small stones,
Slapping lightly against a sunken log.
I dabble my toes in the brackish foam sliding forward,
Then retire to a rock higher up on the cliff-side.
The wind slackens, light as a moth fanning a stone:
A twilight wind, light as a child's breath
Turning not a leaf, not a ripple.
The dew revives on the beach-grass;
The salt-soaked wood of a fire crackles;
A fish raven turns on its perch (a dead tree in the rivermouth),
Its wings catching a last glint of the reflected sunlight.

2

The self persists like a dying star,
In sleep, afraid. Death's face rises afresh,
Among the shy beasts, the deer at the salt-lick,
The doe with its sloped shoulders loping across the highway,
The young snake, poised in green leaves, waiting for its fly,
The hummingbird, whirring from quince-blossom to morning-glory—
With these I would be.

And with water: the waves coming forward, without cessation,
The waves, altered by sand-bars, beds of kelp, miscellaneous
　　　driftwood,
Topped by cross-winds, tugged at by sinuous undercurrents
The tide rustling in, sliding between the ridges of stone,
The tongues of water, creeping in, quietly.

3

In this hour,
In this first heaven of knowing,
The flesh takes on the pure poise of the spirit,
Acquires, for a time, the sandpiper's insouciance,
The hummingbird's surety, the kingfisher's cunning—
I shift on my rock, and I think:
Of the first trembling of a Michigan brook in April,
Over a lip of stone, the tiny rivulet;
And that wrist-thick cascade tumbling from a cleft rock,
Its spray holding a double rain-bow in early morning,
Small enough to be taken in, embraced, by two arms,—
Or the Tittebawasee, in the time between winter and spring,
When the ice melts along the edges in early afternoon.
And the midchannel begins cracking and heaving from the pressure
　　　beneath,
The ice piling high against the iron-bound spiles,
Gleaming, freezing hard again, creaking at midnight—
And I long for the blast of dynamite,
The sudden sucking roar as the culvert loosens its debris of branches
　　　and sticks,
Welter of tin cans, pails, old bird nests, a child's shoe riding a log,
As the piled ice breaks away from the battered spiles,
And the whole river begins to move forward, its bridges shaking.

4

Now, in this waning of light,
I rock with the motion of morning;
In the cradle of all that is,
I'm lulled into half-sleep
By the lapping of water,
Cries of the sandpiper.
Water's my will, and my way,
And the spirit runs, intermittently,

In and out of the small waves,
Runs with the intrepid shorebirds—
How graceful the small before danger!

In the first of the moon,
All's a scattering,
A shining.

JOURNEY TO THE INTERIOR

1

In the long journey out of the self,
There are many detours, washed-out interrupted raw places
Where the shale slides dangerously
And the back wheels hang almost over the edge
At the sudden veering, the moment of turning.
Better to hug close, wary of rubble and falling stones.
The arroyo cracking the road, the wind-bitten buttes, the canyons,
Creeks swollen in midsummer from the flash-flood roaring into the
        narrow valley.
Reeds beaten flat by wind and rain,
Gray from the long winter, burnt at the base in late summer.
—Or the path narrowing,
Winding upward toward the stream with its sharp stones,
The upland of alder and birchtrees,
Through the swamp alive with quicksand,
The way blocked at last by a fallen fir-tree,
The thickets darkening,
The ravines ugly.

2

I remember how it was to drive in gravel,
Watching for dangerous down-hill places, where the wheels whined
        beyond eighty—
When you hit the deep pit at the bottom of the swale,
The trick was to throw the car sideways and charge over the hill,
        full of the throttle.
Grinding up and over the narrow road, spitting and roaring.

A chance? Perhaps. But the road was part of me, and its ditches,
And the dust lay thick on my eyelids,—Who ever wore goggles?—
Always a sharp turn to the left past a barn close to the roadside,
To a scurry of small dogs and a shriek of children,
The highway ribboning out in a straight thrust to the North,
To the sand dunes and fish flies, hanging, thicker than moths,
Dying brightly under the street lights sunk in coarse concrete,
The towns with their high pitted road-crowns and deep gutters,
Their wooden stores of silvery pine and weather-beaten red
    courthouses,
An old bridge below with a buckled iron railing, broken by some
    idiot plunger;
Underneath, the sluggish water running between weeds, broken
    wheels, tires, stones.
And all flows past—
The cemetery with two scrubby trees in the middle of the prairie,
The dead snakes and muskrats, the turtles gasping in the rubble,
The spikey purple bushes in the winding dry creek bed—
The floating hawks, the jackrabbits, the grazing cattle—
I am not moving but they are,
And the sun comes out of a blue cloud over the Tetons,
While, farther away, the heat-lightning flashes.
I rise and fall in the slow sea of a grassy plain,
The wind veering the car slightly to the right,
Whipping the line of white laundry, bending the cottonwoods apart,
The scraggly wind-break of a dusty ranch-house.
I rise and fall, and time folds
Into a long moment;
And I hear the lichen speak,
And the ivy advance with its white lizard feet—
On the shimmering road,
On the dusty detour.

3

I see the flower of all water, above and below me, the never receding,
Moving, unmoving in a parched land, white in the moonlight:
The soul at a still-stand,
At ease after rocking the flesh to sleep,
Petals and reflections of petals mixed on the surface of a glassy
    pool,
And the waves flattening out when the fishermen drag their nets over
    the stones.

In the moment of time when the small drop forms, but does not fall,
I have known the heart of the sun,—
In the dark and light of a dry place,
In a flicker of fire brisked by a dusty wind.
I have heard, in a drip of leaves,
A slight song,
After the midnight cries.
I rehearse myself for this:
The stand at the stretch in the face of death,
Delighting in surface change, the glitter of light on waves,
And I roam elsewhere, my body thinking,
Turning toward the other side of light,
In a tower of wind, a tree idling in air,
Beyond my own echo,
Neither forward nor backward,
Unperplexed, in a place leading nowhere.

As a blind man, lifting a curtain, knows it is morning,
I know this change:
On one side of silence there is no smile;
But when I breathe with the birds,
The spirit of wrath becomes the spirit of blessing,
And the dead begin from their dark to sing in my sleep.

THE LONG WATERS

1

Whether the bees have thoughts, we cannot say,
But the hind part of the worm wiggles the most,
Minnows can hear, and butterflies, yellow and blue,
Rejoice in the language of smells and dancing.
Therefore I reject the world of the dog
Though he hear a note higher than C
And the thrush stopped in the middle of his song.

And I acknowledge my foolishness with God,
My desire for the peaks, the black ravines, the rolling mists
Changing with every twist of wind,
The unsinging fields where no lungs breathe,
Where light is stone.
I return where fire has been,

To the charred edge of the sea
Where the yellowish prongs of grass poke through the blackened ash,
And the bunched logs peel in the afternoon sunlight,
Where the fresh and salt waters meet,
And the sea-winds move through the pine trees,
A country of bays and inlets, and small streams flowing seaward.

2

Mnetha, Mother of Har, protect me
From the worm's advance and retreat, from the butterfly's havoc,
From the slow sinking of the island peninsula, the coral efflorescence,
The dubious sea-change, the heaving sands, and my tentacled
     sea-cousins.

But what of her?—
Who magnifies the morning with her eyes,
That star winking beyond itself,
The cricket-voice deep in the midnight field,
The blue jay rasping from the stunted pine.

How slowly pleasure dies!—
The dry bloom splitting in the wrinkled vale,
The first snow of the year in the dark fir.
Feeling, I still delight in my last fall.

3

In time when the trout and young salmon leap for the low-flying
     insects,
And the ivy-branch, cast to the ground, puts down roots into the
     sawdust,
And the pine, whole with its roots, sinks into the estuary,
Where it leans, tilted east, a perch for the osprey,
And a fisherman dawdles over a wooden bridge,
These waves, in the sun, remind me of flowers:
The lily's piercing white,
The mottled tiger, best in the corner of a damp place,
The heliotrope, veined like a fish, the persistent morning-glory,
And the bronze of a dead burdock at the edge of a prairie lake,
Down by the muck shrinking to the alkaline center.

I have come here without courting silence,
Blessed by the lips of a low wind,
To a rich desolation of wind and water,

To a landlocked bay, where the salt water is freshened
By small streams running down under fallen fir trees.

4

In the vaporous grey of early morning,
Over the thin, feathery ripples breaking lightly against the irregular
       shoreline—
Feathers of the long swell, burnished, almost oily—
A single wave comes in like the neck of a great swan
Swimming slowly, its back ruffled by the light cross-winds,
To a tree lying flat, its crown half broken.

I remember a stone breaking the eddying current,
Neither white nor red, in the dead middle way,
Where impulse no longer dictates, nor the darkening shadow,
A vulnerable place,
Surrounded by sand, broken shells, the wreckage of water.

5

As light reflects from a lake, in late evening,
When bats fly, close to slightly tilting brownish water,
And the low ripples run over a pebbly shoreline,
As a fire, seemingly long dead, flares up from a downdraft of air
       in a chimney,
Or a breeze moves over the knees from a low hill,
So the sea wind wakes desire.
My body shimmers with a light flame.

I see in the advancing and retreating waters
The shape that came from my sleep, weeping:
The eternal one, the child, the swaying vine branch,
The numinous ring around the opening flower,
The friend that runs before me on the windy headlands,
Neither voice nor vision.

I, who came back from the depths laughing too loudly,
Become another thing;
My eyes extend beyond the farthest bloom of the waves;
I lose and find myself in the long water;
I am gathered together once more;
I embrace the world.

THE FAR FIELD

1

I dream of journeys repeatedly:
Of flying like a bat deep into a narrowing tunnel,
Of driving alone, without luggage, out a long peninsula,
The road lined with snow-laden second growth,
A fine dry snow ticking the windshield,
Alternate snow and sleet, no on-coming traffic,
And no lights behind, in the blurred side-mirror,
The road changing from glazed tarface to a rubble of stone,
Ending at last in a hopeless sand-rut,
Where the car stalls,
Churning in a snowdrift
Until the headlights darken.

2

At the field's end, in the corner missed by the mower,
Where the turf drops off into a grass-hidden culvert,
Haunt of the cat-bird, nesting-place of the field-mouse,
Not too far away from the ever-changing flower-dump,
Among the tin cans, tires, rusted pipes, broken machinery,—
One learned of the eternal;
And in the shrunken face of a dead rat, eaten by rain and
        ground-beetles
(I found it lying among the rubble of an old coal bin)
And the tom-cat, caught near the pheasant-run,
Its entrails strewn over the half-grown flowers,
Blasted to death by the night watchman.

I suffered for birds, for young rabbits caught in the mower,
My grief was not excessive.
For to come upon warblers in early May
Was to forget time and death:
How they filled the oriole's elm, a twittering restless cloud,
        all one morning,
And I watched and watched till my eyes blurred from the bird
        shapes,—
Cape May, Blackburnian, Cerulean,—
Moving, elusive as fish, fearless,
Hanging, bunched like young fruit, bending the end branches,

Still for a moment,
Then pitching away in half-flight,
Lighter than finches,
While the wrens bickered and sang in the half-green hedgerows,
And the flicker drummed from his dead tree in the chicken-yard.

—Or to lie naked in sand,
In the silted shallows of a slow river,
Fingering a shell,
Thinking:
Once I was something like this, mindless,
Or perhaps with another mind, less peculiar;
Or to sink down to the hips in a mossy quagmire;
Or, with skinny knees, to sit astride a wet log,
Believing:
I'll return again,
As a snake or a raucous bird,
Or, with luck, as a lion.

I learned not to fear infinity,
The far field, the windy cliffs of forever,
The dying of time in the white light of tomorrow,
The wheel turning away from itself,
The sprawl of the wave,
The on-coming water.

3

The river turns on itself,
The tree retreats into its own shadow.
I feel a weightless change, a moving forward
As of water quickening before a narrowing channel
When banks converge, and the wide river whitens;
Or when two rivers combine, the blue glacial torrent
And the yellowish-green from the mountainy upland,—
At first a swift rippling between rocks,
Then a long running over flat stones
Before descending to the alluvial plain,
To the clay banks, and the wild grapes hanging from the elmtrees.
The slightly trembling water
Dropping a fine yellow silt where the sun stays;

And the crabs bask near the edge,
The weedy edge, alive with small snakes and bloodsuckers,—

I have come to a still, but not a deep center,
A point outside the glittering current;
My eyes stare at the bottom of a river,
At the irregular stones, iridescent sandgrains,
My mind moves in more than one place,
In a country half-land, half-water.

I am renewed by death, thought of my death,
The dry scent of a dying garden in September,
The wind fanning the ash of a low fire.
What I love is near at hand,
Always, in earth and air.

    4

The lost self changes,
Turning toward the sea,
A sea-shape turning around,—
An old man with his feet before the fire,
In robes of green, in garments of adieu.

A man faced with his own immensity
Wakes all the waves, all their loose wandering fire.
The murmur of the absolute, the why
Of being born fails on his naked ears.
His spirit moves like monumental wind
That gentles on a sunny blue plateau.
He is the end of things, the final man.

All finite things reveal infinitude:
The mountain with its singular bright shade
Like the blue shine on freshly frozen snow,
The after-light upon ice-burdened pines;
Odor of basswood on a mountain-slope,
A scent beloved of bees;
Silence of water above a sunken tree:
The pure serene of memory in one man,—
A ripple widening from a single stone
Winding around the waters of the world.

THE ROSE

1

There are those to whom place is unimportant,
But this place, where sea and fresh water meet,
Is important—
Where the hawks sway out into the wind,
Without a single wingbeat,
And the eagles sail low over the fir trees,
And the gulls cry against the crows
In the curved harbors,
And the tide rises up against the grass
Nibbled by sheep and rabbits.

A time for watching the tide,
For the heron's hieratic fishing,
For the sleepy cries of the towhee,
The morning birds gone, the twittering finches,
But still the flash of the kingfisher, the wingbeat of the scoter,
The sun a ball of fire coming down over the water,
The last geese crossing against the reflected afterlight,
The moon retreating into a vague cloud-shape
To the cries of the owl, the eerie whooper.
The old log subsides with the lessening waves,
And there is silence.

I sway outside myself
Into the darkening currents,
Into the small spillage of driftwood,
The waters swirling past the tiny headlands.
Was it here I wore a crown of birds for a moment
While on a far point of the rocks
The light heightened,
And below, in a mist out of nowhere,
The first rain gathered?

2

As when a ship sails with a light wind—
The waves less than the ripples made by rising fish,
The lacelike wrinkles of the wake widening, thinning out,
Sliding away from the traveler's eye,

The prow pitching easily up and down,
The whole ship rolling slightly sideways,
The stern high, dipping like a child's boat in a pond—
Our motion continues.

But this rose, this rose in the sea-wind,
Stays,
Stays in its true place,
Flowering out of the dark,
Widening at high noon, face upward,
A single wild rose, struggling out of the white embrace of the
     morning-glory,
Out of the briary hedge, the tangle of matted underbrush,
Beyond the clover, the ragged hay,
Beyond the sea pine, the oak, the wind-tipped madrona,
Moving with the waves, the undulating driftwood,
Where the slow creek winds down to the black sand of the shore
With its thick grassy scum and crabs scuttling back into their
     glistening craters.

And I think of roses, roses,
White and red, in the wide six-hundred-foot greenhouses,
And my father standing astride the cement benches,
Lifting me high over the four-foot stems, the Mrs. Russells, and his
     own elaborate hybrids,
And how those flowerheads seemed to flow toward me, to beckon
     me, only a child, out of myself.

What need for heaven, then,
With that man, and those roses?

3

What do they tell us, sound and silence?
I think of American sounds in this silence:
On the banks of the Tombstone, the wind-harps having their say,
The thrush singing alone, that easy bird,
The killdeer whistling away from me,
The mimetic chortling of the catbird
Down in the corner of the garden, among the raggedy lilacs,
The bobolink skirring from a broken fencepost,
The bluebird, lover of holes in old wood, lilting its light song,
And that thin cry, like a needle piercing the ear, the insistent cicada,
And the ticking of snow around oil drums in the Dakotas,
The thin whine of telephone wires in the wind of a Michigan winter,

The shriek of nails as old shingles are ripped from the top of a roof,
The bulldozer backing away, the hiss of the sandblaster,
And the deep chorus of horns coming up from the streets in early
        morning.
I return to the twittering of swallows above water,
And that sound, that single sound,
When the mind remembers all,
And gently the light enters the sleeping soul,
A sound so thin it could not woo a bird,

Beautiful my desire, and the place of my desire.

I think of the rock singing, and light making its own silence,
At the edge of a ripening meadow, in early summer,
The moon lolling in the close elm, a shimmer of silver,
Or that lonely time before the breaking of morning
When the slow freight winds along the edge of the ravaged hillside,
And the wind tries the shape of a tree,
While the moon lingers,
And a drop of rain water hangs at the tip of a leaf
Shifting in the wakening sunlight
Like the eye of a new-caught fish.

    4

I live with the rocks, their weeds,
Their filmy fringes of green, their harsh
Edges, their holes
Cut by the sea-slime, far from the crash
Of the long swell,
The oily, tar-laden walls
Of the toppling waves,
Where the salmon ease their way into the kelp beds,
And the sea rearranges itself among the small islands.

Near this rose, in this grove of sun-parched, wind-warped madronas,
Among the half-dead trees, I came upon the true ease of myself,
As if another man appeared out of the depths of my being,
And I stood outside myself,
Beyond becoming and perishing,
A something wholly other,
As if I swayed out on the wildest wave alive,
And yet was still.
And I rejoiced in being what I was:
In the lilac change, the white reptilian calm,

In the bird beyond the bough, the single one
With all the air to greet him as he flies,
The dolphin rising from the darkening waves;

And in this rose, this rose in the sea-wind,
Rooted in stone, keeping the whole of light,
Gathering to itself sound and silence—
Mine and the sea-wind's.

Meditations of an Old Woman

FIRST MEDITATION

1

On love's worst ugly day,
The weeds hiss at the edge of the field,
The small winds make their chilly indictments.
Elsewhere, in houses, even pails can be sad;
While stones loosen on the obscure hillside,
And a tree tilts from its roots,
Toppling down an embankment.

The spirit moves, but not always upward,
While animals eat to the north,
And the shale slides an inch in the talus,
The bleak wind eats at the weak plateau,
And the sun brings joy to some.
But the rind, often, hates the life within.

How can I rest in the days of my slowness?
I've become a strange piece of flesh,
Nervous and cold, bird-furtive, whiskery,
With a cheek soft as a hound's ear.
What's left is light as a seed;
I need an old crone's knowing.

2

Often I think of myself as riding—
Alone, on a bus through western country.

I sit above the back wheels, where the jolts are hardest,
And we bounce and sway along toward the midnight,
The lights tilting up, skyward, as we come over a little rise,
Then down, as we roll like a boat from a wave-crest.

All journeys, I think, are the same:
The movement is forward, after a few wavers,
And for a while we are all alone,
Busy, obvious with ourselves,
The drunken soldier, the old lady with her peppermints;
And we ride, we ride, taking the curves
Somewhat closer, the trucks coming
Down from behind the last ranges,
Their black shapes breaking past;
And the air claps between us,
Blasting the frosted windows,
And I seem to go backward,
Backward in time:

    Two song sparrows, one within a greenhouse,
    Shuttling its throat while perched on a wind-vent,
    And another, outside, in the bright day,
    With a wind from the west and the trees all in motion.
    One sang, then the other,
    The songs tumbling over and under the glass,
    And the men beneath them wheeling in dirt to the cement
        benches,
    The laden wheelbarrows creaking and swaying,
    And the up-spring of the plank when a foot left the runway.

Journey within a journey:
The ticket mislaid or lost, the gate
Inaccessible, the boat always pulling out
From the rickety wooden dock,
The children waving;
Or two horses plunging in snow, their lines tangled,
A great wooden sleigh careening behind them,
Swerving up a steep embankment.
For a moment they stand above me,
Their black skins shuddering:
Then they lurch forward,
Lunging down a hillside.

3

As when silt drifts and sifts down through muddy pond-water,
Settling in small beads around weeds and sunken branches,
And one crab, tentative, hunches himself before moving along the
    bottom,
Grotesque, awkward, his extended eyes looking at nothing in
    particular,
Only a few bubbles loosening from the ill-matched tentacles,
The tail and smaller legs slipping and sliding slowly backward—
So the spirit tries for another life,
Another way and place in which to continue;
Or a salmon, tired, moving up a shallow stream,
Nudges into a back-eddy, a sandy inlet,
Bumping against sticks and bottom-stones, then swinging
Around, back into the tiny maincurrent, the rush of brownish-white
    water,
Still swimming forward—
So, I suppose, the spirit journeys.

4

I have gone into the waste lonely places
Behind the eye; the lost acres at the edge of smoky cities.
What's beyond never crumbles like an embankment,
Explodes like a rose, or thrusts wings over the Caribbean.
There are no pursuing forms, faces on walls:
Only the motes of dust in the immaculate hallways,
The darkness of falling hair, the warnings from lint and spiders,
The vines graying to a fine powder.
There is no riven tree, or lamb dropped by an eagle.

There are still times, morning and evening:
The cerulean, high in the elm,
Thin and insistent as a cicada,
And the far phoebe, singing,
The long plaintive notes floating down,
Drifting through leaves, oak and maple,
Or the whippoorwill, along the smoky ridges,
A single bird calling and calling;
A fume reminds me, drifting across wet gravel;
A cold wind comes over stones;
A flame, intense, visible,
Plays over the dry pods,

Runs fitfully along the stubble,
Moves over the field,
Without burning.
    In such times, lacking a god,
    I am still happy.

I'M HERE

1

Is it enough?—
The sun loosening the frost on December windows,
The glitter of wet in the first of morning?
The sound of voices, young voices, mixed with sleighbells,
Coming across snow in early evening?

Outside, the same sparrows bicker in the eaves.
I'm tired of tiny noises:
The April cheeping, the vireo's insistence,
The prattle of the young no longer pleases.
Behind the child's archness
Lurks the bad animal.

    —How needles and corners perplex me!
      Dare I shrink to a hag,
      The worst surprise a corner could have,
      A witch who sleeps with her horse?
      Some fates are worse.

2

I was queen of the vale—
For a short while,
Living all my heart's summer alone,
Ward of my spirit,
Running through high grasses,
My thighs brushing against flower-crowns;
Leaning, out of all breath,
Bracing my back against a sapling,
Making it quiver with my body;
At the stream's edge, trailing a vague finger;
Flesh-awkward, half-alive,
Fearful of high places, in love with horses;

In love with stuffs, silks,
Rubbing my nose in the wool of blankets;
Bemused; pleased to be;
Mindful of cries,
The meaningful whisper,
The wren, the catbird.

So much of adolescence is an ill-defined dying,
An intolerable waiting,
A longing for another place and time,
Another condition.

I stayed: a willow to the wind.
The bats twittered at noon.
The swallows flew in and out of the smokeless chimneys.
I sang to the edges of flame,
My skin whiter in the soft weather,
My voice softer.

3

I remember walking down a path,
Down wooden steps toward a weedy garden;
And my dress caught on a rose-brier.
When I bent to untangle myself,
The scent of the half-opened buds came up over me.
I thought I was going to smother.

In the slow coming-out of sleep,
On the sill of the eyes, something flutters,
A thing we feel at evening, and by doors,
Or when we stand at the edge of a thicket,
And the ground-chill comes closer to us,
From under the dry leaves,
A beachy wetness.

The body, delighting in thresholds,
Rocks in and out of itself.
A bird, small as a leaf,
Sings in the first
Sunlight.

And the time I was so sick—
The whole place shook whenever I got a chill—
I closed my eyes, and saw small figures dancing,

A congress of tree-shrews and rats,
Romping around a fire,
Jumping up and down on their hind feet,
Their forepaws joined together, like hands—
They seemed very happy.

    In my grandmother's inner eye,
    So she told me when I was little,
    A bird always kept singing.
    She was a serious woman.

4

My geranium is dying, for all I can do,
Still leaning toward the last place the sun was.
I've tried I don't know how many times to replant it.
But these roses: I can wear them by looking away.
The eyes rejoice in the act of seeing and the fresh after-image;
Without staring like a lout, or a moping adolescent;
Without commotion.
Look at the far trees at the end of the garden.
The flat branch of that hemlock holds the last of the sun,
Rocking it, like a sun-struck pond,
In a light wind.

    I prefer the still joy:
    The wasp drinking at the edge of my cup;
    A snake lifting its head;
    A snail's music.

5

What's weather to me? Even carp die in this river.
I need a pond with small eels. And a windy orchard.
I'm no midge of that and this. The dirt glitters like salt.
Birds are around. I've all the singing I would.
I'm not far from a stream.
It's not my first dying.
I can hold this valley,
Loose in my lap,
In my arms.

    If the wind means me,
    I'm here!
    Here.

HER BECOMING

1

I have learned to sit quietly,
Watching the wind riffle the backs of small birds,
Chirping with fleas in the sand,
My shape a levity—Yes!—
A mad hen in a far corner of the dark,
Still taking delight in nakedness,
In the sun, busy at a young body,
In the rain, slackening on a summer field;
In the back of my mind, running with the rolling water,
My breast wild as the waves.

> I see a shape, lighted with love,
> Light as a petal falling upon stone.
> From the folds of my skin, I sing,
> The air still, the ground alive,
> The earth itself a tune.

How sweetly I abide. Am I a bird?
Soft, soft, the snow's not falling. What's a seed?
A face floats in the ferns. Do maimed gods walk?
A voice keeps rising in my early sleep,
A muffled voice, a low sweet watery noise.
Dare I embrace a ghost from my own breast?
A spirit plays before me like a child,
A child at play, a wind-excited bird.

> A ghost from the soul's house?
> I'm where I always was.
> The lily broods. Who knows
> The way out of a rose?

2

Is it the sea we wish? The sleep of the changeless?
In my left ear I hear the loud sound of a minor collapse.
Last night I dreamt of a jauntier principle of order;
Today I eat my usual diet of shadows.
Dare I speak, once more, in the monotony of great praise,
In the wild disordered language of the natural heart?
What else can I steal from sleep?

We start from the dark. Pain teaches us little.
I can't laugh from a crater of burning pitch,
Or live the dangerous life of an insect.
Is there a wisdom in objects? Few objects praise the Lord.
The bulks cannot hide us, or the bleak sheds of our desolation,
I know the cold fleshless kiss of contraries,
The nerveless constriction of surfaces—
Machines, machines, loveless, temporal;
Mutilated souls in cold morgues of obligation.

3

There are times when reality comes closer:
In a field, in the actual air,
I stepped carefully, like a new-shod horse,
A raw tumultuous girl
Making my way over wet stones.
And then I ran—
Ran ahead of myself,
Across a field, into a little wood.

And there I stayed until the day burned down.

My breath grew less. I listened like a beast.
Was it the stones I heard? I stared at the fixed stars.

The moon, a pure Islamic shape, looked down.
The light air slowed: It was not night or day.
All natural shapes became symbolical.
The only thing alive in heaven's eye,
I shed my clothes to slow my daemon down.
And then I ran again.

Where was I going? Where?
What was I running from?
To these I cried my life—
The loved fox, and the wren.

Speech passed between small birds;
Silence became a thing;
Echo itself consumed;
The scene shrank to a pin.

Did my will die? Did I?
I said farewell to sighs,
Once to the toad,
Once to the frog,
And once to my flowing thighs.

Who can believe the moon?
I have seen! I have seen!—
The line! The holy line!
A small place all in flame.

Out, out, you secret beasts,
You birds, you western birds.
One follows fire. One does.
My breath is more than yours.

What lover keeps his song?
I sigh before I sing.
I love because I am
A rapt thing with a name.

4

Ask all the mice who caper in the straw—
I am benign in my own company.
A shape without a shade, or almost none,
I hum in pure vibration, like a saw.
The grandeur of a crazy one alone!—
By swoops of bird, by leaps of fish, I live.
My shadow steadies in a shifting stream;
I live in air; the long light is my home;
I dare caress the stones, the field my friend;
A light wind rises: I become the wind.

FOURTH MEDITATION

1

I was always one for being alone,
Seeking in my own way, eternal purpose;
At the edge of the field waiting for the pure moment;

Standing, silent, on sandy beaches or walking along green
      embankments;
Knowing the sinuousness of small waters:
As a chip or shell, floating lazily with a slow current,
A drop of the night rain still in me,
A bit of water caught in a wrinkled crevice,
A pool riding and shining with the river,
Dipping up and down in the ripples,
Tilting back the sunlight.

Was it yesterday I stretched out the thin bones of my innocence?
O the songs we hide, singing only to ourselves!
Once I could touch my shadow, and be happy;
In the white kingdoms, I was light as a seed,
Drifting with the blossoms,
A pensive petal.

But a time comes when the vague life of the mouth no longer suffices;
The dead make more impossible demands from their silence;
The soul stands, lonely in its choice,
Waiting, itself a slow thing,
In the changing body.

    The river moves, wrinkled by midges,
    A light wind stirs in the pine needles.
    The shape of a lark rises from a stone;
    But there is no song.

  2

What is it to be a woman?
To be contained, to be a vessel?
To prefer a window to a door?
A pool to a river?
To become lost in a love,
Yet remain only half aware of the intransient glory?
To be a mouth, a meal of meat?
To gaze at a face with the fixed eyes of a spaniel?

I think of the self-involved:
The ritualists of the mirror, the lonely drinkers,
The minions of benzedrine and paraldehyde,
And those who submerge themselves deliberately in trivia,

Women who become their possessions,
Shapes stiffening into metal,
Match-makers, arrangers of picnics—
What do their lives mean,
And the lives of their children?—
The young, brow-beaten early into a baleful silence,
Frozen by a father's lip, a mother's failure to answer.
Have they seen, ever, the sharp bones of the poor?
Or known, once, the soul's authentic hunger,
Those cat-like immaculate creatures
For whom the world works?

What do they need?
O more than a roaring boy,
For the sleek captains of intuition cannot reach them;
They feel neither the tearing iron
Nor the sound of another footstep—
How I wish them awake!
May the high flower of the hay climb into their hearts;
May they lean into light and live;
May they sleep in robes of green, among the ancient ferns;
May their eyes gleam with the first dawn;
May the sun gild them a worm;
May they be taken by the true burning;
May they flame into being!—

I see them as figures walking in a greeny garden,
Their gait formal and elaborate, their hair a glory,
The gentle and beautiful still-to-be-born;
The descendants of the playful tree-shrew that survived the archaic
        killers,
The fang and the claw, the club and the knout, the irrational edict,
The fury of the hate-driven zealot, the meanness of the human weasel;
Who turned a corner in time, when at last he grew a thumb;
A prince of small beginnings, enduring the slow stretches of change,
Who spoke first in the coarse short-hand of the subliminal depths,
Made from his terror and dismay a grave philosophical language;
A lion of flame, pressed to the point of love,
Yet moves gently among the birds.

3

Younglings, the small fish keep heading into the current.
What's become of care? This lake breathes like a rose.

Beguile me, change. What have I fallen from?
I drink my tears in a place where all light comes.
I'm in love with the dead! My whole forehead's a noise!
On a dark day I walk straight toward the rain.
Who else sweats light from a stone?
By singing we defend;
The husk lives on, ardent as a seed;
My back creaks with the dawn.

Is my body speaking? I breathe what I am:
The first and last of all things.
Near the graves of the great dead,
Even the stones speak.

WHAT CAN I TELL MY BONES?

1

Beginner,
Perpetual beginner,
The soul knows not what to believe,
In its small folds, stirring sluggishly,
In the least place of its life,
A pulse beyond nothingness,
A fearful ignorance.

    Before the moon draws back,
    Dare I blaze like a tree?

In a world always late afternoon,
In the circular smells of a slow wind.
I listen to the weeds' vesperal whine,
Longing for absolutes that never come.
And shapes make me afraid:
The dance of natural objects in the mind,
The immediate sheen, the reality of straw,
The shadows crawling down a sunny wall.

    A bird sings out in solitariness
    A thin harsh song. The day dies in a child.
    How close we are to the sad animals!
    I need a pool; I need a puddle's calm.

O my bones,
Beware those perpetual beginnings,
Thinning the soul's substance;
The swan's dread of the darkening shore,
Or these insects pulsing near my skin,
The songs from a spiral tree.

> Fury of wind, and no apparent wind,
> A gust blowing the leaves suddenly upward,
> A vine lashing in dry fury,
> A man chasing a cat,
> With a broken umbrella,
> Crying softly.

2

It is difficult to say all things are well,
When the worst is about to arrive;
It is fatal to woo yourself,
However graceful the posture.

> Loved heart, what can I say?
> When I was a lark, I sang;
> When I was a worm, I devoured.

> The self says, I am;
> The heart says, I am less;
> The spirit says, you are nothing.

Mist alters the rocks. What can I tell my bones?
My desire's a wind trapped in a cave.
The spirit declares itself to these rocks.
I'm a small stone, loose in the shale.
Love is my wound.

The wide streams go their way,
The pond lapses back into a glassy silence.
The cause of God in me—has it gone?
Do these bones live? Can I live with these bones?
Mother, mother of us all, tell me where I am!
O to be delivered from the rational into the realm of pure song,

My face on fire, close to the points of a star,
A learned nimble girl,
Not drearily bewitched,
But sweetly daft.

> To try to become like God
> Is far from becoming God.
> O, but I seek and care!

> I rock in my own dark,
> Thinking, God has need of me.
> The dead love the unborn.

3

Weeds turn toward the wind weed-skeletons.
How slowly all things alter.
Existence dares perpetuate a soul,
A wedge of heaven's light, autumnal song.
I hear a beat of birds, the plangent wings
That disappear into a waning moon;
The barest speech of light among the stones.

> To what more vast permission have I come?
> When I walk past a vat, water joggles.
> I no longer cry for green in the midst of cinders,
> Or dream of the dead, and their holes.
> Mercy has many arms.

Instead of a devil with horns, I prefer a serpent with scales;
In temptation, I rarely seek counsel;
A prisoner of smells, I would rather eat than pray.
I'm released from the dreary dance of opposites.
The wind rocks with my wish; the rain shields me;
I live in light's extreme; I stretch in all directions;
Sometimes I think I'm several.

> The sun! The sun! And all we can become!
> And the time ripe for running to the moon!
> In the long fields, I leave my father's eye;
> And shake the secrets from my deepest bones;
> My spirit rises with the rising wind;

I'm thick with leaves and tender as a dove,
I take the liberties a short life permits—
I seek my own meekness;
I recover my tenderness by long looking.
By midnight I love everything alive.
Who took the darkness from the air?
I'm wet with another life.
Yea, I have gone and stayed.

What came to me vaguely is now clear,
As if released by a spirit,
Or agency outside me.
Unprayed-for,
And final.

THE MEADOW MOUSE

1

In a shoe box stuffed in an old nylon stocking
Sleeps the baby mouse I found in the meadow,
Where he trembled and shook beneath a stick
Till I caught him up by the tail and brought him in,
Cradled in my hand,
A little quaker, the whole body of him trembling,
His absurd whiskers sticking out like a cartoon-mouse,
His feet like small leaves,
Little lizard-feet,
Whitish and spread wide when he tried to struggle away,
Wriggling like a miniscule puppy.

Now he's eaten his three kinds of cheese and drunk from his bottle-cap
        watering-trough—
So much he just lies in one corner,
His tail curled under him, his belly big
As his head; his bat-like ears
Twitching, tilting toward the least sound.

Do I imagine he no longer trembles
When I come close to him?
He seems no longer to tremble.

But this morning the shoe-box house on the back porch is empty.
Where has he gone, my meadow mouse,
My thumb of a child that nuzzled in my palm?—
To run under the hawk's wing,
Under the eye of the great owl watching from the elm-tree,
To live by courtesy of the shrike, the snake, the tom-cat.

I think of the nestling fallen into the deep grass,
The turtle gasping in the dusty rubble of the highway,
The paralytic stunned in the tub, and the water rising,—
All things innocent, hapless, forsaken.

ALL MORNING

Here in our aging district the wood pigeon lives with us,
His deep-throated cooing part of the early morning,
Far away, close-at-hand, his call floating over the on-coming traffic,
The lugubriously beautiful plaint uttered at regular intervals,
A protest from the past, a reminder.

They sit, three or four, high in the fir-trees back of the house,
Flapping away heavily when a car blasts too close,
And one drops down to the garden, the high rhododendron,
Only to fly over to his favorite perch, the cross-bar of a telephone pole;
Grave, hieratic, a piece of Assyrian sculpture,
A thing carved of stone or wood, with the dull iridescence of
        long-polished wood,
Looking at you without turning his small head,
With a round vireo's eye, quiet and contained,
Part of the landscape.

And the Stellar jay, raucous, sooty headed, lives with us,
Conducting his long wars with the neighborhood cats,
All during mating season,
Making a racket to wake the dead,
To distract attention from the short-tailed ridiculous young ones
Hiding deep in the blackberry bushes—
What a scuttling and rapping along the drainpipes,
A fury of jays, diving and squawking,

THEODORE ROETHKE 45

When our spayed female cat yawns and stretches out in the sunshine—
And the wrens scold, and the chickadees frisk and frolic,
Pitching lightly over the high hedgerows, dee-deeing,
And the ducks near Lake Washington waddle down the highway
        after a rain,
Stopping traffic, indignant as addled old ladies,
Pecking at crusts and peanuts, their green necks glittering;
And the hummingbird dips in and around the quince tree,
Veering close to my head,
Then whirring off sideways to the top of the hawthorn,
Its almost-invisible wings, buzzing, hitting the loose leaves
        intermittently—

A delirium of birds!
Peripheral dippers come to rest on the short grass,
Their heads jod-jodding like pigeons;
The gulls, the gulls far from their waves
Rising, wheeling away with harsh cries,
Coming down on a patch of lawn:

It is neither spring nor summer: it is Always,
With towhees, finches, chickadees, California quail, wood doves,
With wrens, sparrows, juncos, cedar waxwings, flickers,
With Baltimore orioles, Michigan bobolinks,
And those birds forever dead,
The passenger pigeon, the great auk, the Carolina paraquet,
All birds remembered, O never forgotten!
All in my yard, of a perpetual Sunday,
All morning! All morning!

KENNETH PATCHEN

Kenneth Patchen was born in 1911 in Niles, Ohio, and educated at the University of Wisconsin's Experimental College. For over thirty years he has been afflicted with a painful and disabling spinal disease and has been bedridden since 1960. He lives with his wife in Palo Alto, California. He is the author of many books of verse, including When We Were Here Together, Cloth of the Tempest, Sleepers Awake, Red Wine and Yellow Hair, The Famous Boating Party, Because It Is, Teeth of the Lion, Poems of Humor and Protest, *and* The Collected Poems of Kenneth Patchen. *He is also the author of two prose classics,* The Journal of Albion Moonlight *and* Memoirs of a Shy Pornographer.

THE EVERLASTING CONTENDERS

Of the beast . . . an angel
Creatures of the earth
It is good
Any who praise not grandly

O but they should

But they should
Death waits for everything that lives
Beast of the wood
Grim beast of the wood

Who praise not grandly

Should should
Heart weeps for all things
Here
And is greatly comforted
For heart is the angel
Of all
Who praise not grandly

But wish they could

from THE HUNTED CITY

V

The little hill climbs up to the village and puts its green hands
tenderly round it; women have their days in the cider-
sharp sun and men their work riding over the infested land
of the fogwidowed sea and lowering nets that convulse like
stomachs.

> The earth has its milk to give.
> Beautiful horsemen bathe the immortal slopes with the rich
> yellow blood of wheat and men say as I continue to say
> This is a battle worthy of our weapons.

But a different sort of soldier is seen prowling about
like a pod holding death's fat grub . . .
Purer than a man's first girl the sky floats in virginal peace
above the pallid snouts that jut from the stone of the warstatues
     I have seen the crippled lark rise like a dream
       to the fugitive kiss of the wind's delirious mouth . . .
      and there is no report whatever that fish have ceased
to have their admirable babies deep down in the sea.
I have heard the noiseless talking of our graves
and the worms have evolved a very effective way of writing history.
     Man is all around the things that men do
      but there is little enough to be happy about . . .
I do not accuse you, little fellows, I only declare
that instead of drums to beat you consider your miserable
breasts, and I caution you to know now that this world is
fashioned of pain and of murder. You will not recognize the
hangman until your own poor human head is in his noose.
The poet should wear comfortable shoes and see a lot of children

Listen! is that the third throat of the cock?
Has the mariner built his last desolate fire on this coast?
The moon rubs his great clean face against the roofs of the city
and harlots display their green sores which are the slum flowers . . .
O pity the backward ape who has no flute, who has no Christ,
who has no civilization and no poison gas to protect it with;
pity those in asylums whose fists cannot reach faces to smash;
pity the dead for their weight is not measured in military pounds.

Evidently those are deathbells keening through the night
and there are no horses saddled in the inn yard
there is no light at any window, no warmth, no hope . . .
This is indeed a battle worthy of our weapons.

ELEGY FOR THE SILENT VOICES AND
THE JOINERS OF EVERYTHING

The featureless ghost under the wall cannot jerk out at us,
     like a pig would, or shriek, like the guns will,
      or be our own fallen human face, as madness is

(Therefore) And he cannot have tense, wakeful girls and fall
   vaguely into heaven, like Shelley did, the sexual balloon
   coming down to spend its gas in his baby-blue eyes

These are the survivors: a drunkard, two shepherds
With tan beards, an office force consisting of bookkeeper,
Typist and errandboy, several scrubwomen, a rapist,
Four Germans, a whore's union, a signpainter, no boxers,
Wrestlers or policemen, one gunman and one half of a Japanese
How soon can we expect Murphy, the Snag-Tooth they asked eagerly

Therefore: (They took a quick gander at the steam readings:

                    DANGER   ZERO,

   and saw that some twenty or more sailors with big skins
   and endless ribs had brought the ship, *Lonedeath,* up fast
   to a shivering dock: hove-to: and it all going God-high,
   town, engine room, skipper, cripples, spotted dogs, with
      a diamond
   of thunderous sound, splitting the sky up like a fat fish's belly)

(People hurry along like pictures taken through milk)
A pretty girl gave birth to a child in a muddy field
And the ragged wonder of it was featured on the radio,
A pleasing description being given of what the mother
               wanted her son to be
'Castrated,' she said simply and somebody is very likely to

With dignity, continuously pure and fortunate,
something lives and taunts that disappearing ghost,
as Melville did, intangible as an idiot's dream

Behind shouting trees the figure glides like blood in a mouse's
         side
Within our faces the poor move their awful hands in desolate
         proverbs
Jesus Joseph and Mary it is not thus, it is not thus, it is not thus
That the whole round world is broken

There is nothing to be afraid of
Our houses need holes for new air and we will get them through
         our heads.

IN ORDER TO

Apply for the position (I've forgotten now for what) I had
to marry the Second Mayor's daughter by twelve noon. The
order arrived at three minutes of.

I already had a wife; the Second Mayor was childless: but I
did it.

Next they told me to shave off my father's beard. All right.
No matter that he'd been a eunuch, and had succumbed in
early childhood: I did it, I shaved him.

Then they told me to burn a village; next, a fair-sized town;
then, a city; a bigger city; a small, down-at-heels country;
then one of "the great powers"; then another (another, another)—In fact, they went right on until they'd told me to
burn up every man-made thing on the face of the earth! And
I did it, I burned away every last trace, I left nothing, nothing
of any kind whatever.

Then they told me to blow it all to hell and gone! And I blew
it all to hell and gone (oh, didn't I) . . .

Now, they said, put it back together again; put it all back the
way it was when you started.

Well . . . it was my turn to tell *them* something! Shucks,
I didn't want any job that bad.

THE CONSTANT BRIDEGROOMS

Far down the purple wood
Coats of a company
Of silent soldiers
Flap idly in the wind.
There they have stood
Since early day—
Faces turned incuriously to the sound

Of the dry rustling
Of leaves in the wind.
No command has reached
Them there;
All silent have they stood
As
Though they were asleep—
Now night darkens their coats.
Far away
Their names are spoken

Somewhere at world's end

PASTORAL

The dove walks with sticky feet
Upon the green crowns of the almond tree,
Its feathers smeared over with warmth
Like honey
That drips lazily down into the shadow . . .

Anyone standing in that orchard,
So filled with peace and sleep,
Would hardly have noticed the hill
Nearby
With its three strange wooden arms
Lifted above a throng of motionless people
—Above the helmets of Pilate's soldiers
Flashing like silver teeth in the sun.

FOG

Rain's lovely gray daughter has lost her tall lover.
He whose mouth she knew; who was good to her.

I've heard her talk of him when the river lights
Scream 'Christ! it's lonely; Christ! it's cold.'

Heard the slug cry of her loneliness calling him
When the ship's mast points to no star in the North.

Many men have thought they were he;
Feeling her cold arms as they held death in theirs—

The woman-face in the frame of nothingness;
As the machinery of sleep turned its first wheel;

And they slept, while angels fell in colored sound
Upon the closing waters. Child and singing cradle one.

O sorrowful lady whose lover is that harbor
In a heaven where all we of longing lie, clinging together
        as it gets dark.

BEHOLD, ONE OF SEVERAL LITTLE CHRISTS, *with
a curiously haunted ugly face, crouched beneath the first and
the last, embracing you in its horrible arms, blowing its fetid
breath in your face and using fearful threats of death and of
judgment*

Their war-boots said big shots to the plank floor.
*I am the timorous mouse, brother mortal, take aim
at my wee brown eye and you will hit William T. God.*
Bring her in Leather Face said: he is my leader, a strong boy
And the dirt of many marches is on his soul; swarms of camp fires
In the bush-country, lions like bastard druids, telling us
To come out and give them a taste, and the dust and the sand
When the water is gone and you wonder what you are there for,
Not believing the stuff about flags after you have seen a man dance
Rope-necked on a dirty platform and the pretty girls yelling like mad
Moving their thighs as though Death were coming into them too.
*I am the crafty Caesar and my baby sister shall one day
be whore to all the world, tastefully gowned in your guts.*
Beautiful my heart said when I saw her.
She was very young and everything good was in her face.
I could have been Christ if she had touched me.
Nail her to the door my leader said and they put knives
Through her hands and knives through her feet, but
I did not turn my face away
*I am a singer of songs and there is no one
listening now*

Flame of all the world, honor of the wounded tiger,
There is something that has not been said,
There is something that can not be said,
To The Word which is the girl who hangs here,
To the one upon whom her eyes now are
For her pain, for her innocence, for her pigeon-mouthed death
That coos and trills over the fogsweet deeps of her flesh,
For those who killed her and for the strange planet of her dying,
For all the mockery of the just and for the battlements of salt
That man has against the howling dark
There is nothing, there is no voice, no quiet hand,
There is the sneer of the bat and the gull's fang,
There is a lobster beating his breast and singing,
Yea, singing, I am the answer to your prayer, sugar,
I am the one to come to your window in the first stinking sweat
Of night and I shall bed thee down in star-manure,
A pot of green paint for thy Jerusalem, believe me,
Babe, till the seas gang gok my rod shall comfort thee
I am of the first thing and of the last thing
Mine is the face in your dream
Mine is the body beside you in the night
Why isn't she dead grumbled the leader
It was getting later than the night had room for
And the lanterns were beginning to look silly
(Birds pleading with something out in the swamp)
Our faces hunched over our brains like tight pods.
We looked again at the maps and a little stream of her blood
Had made a river that we had no fit equipment to cross
And her hand had fallen over the city that we hoped to take
Her hair went over us praying here all of us not the least
Nor the greatest not the pure alone but those who are most bent
On murder the evil more than the good over the lost and the hunted
Over the gambler and the bitch followed by the whole human pack

THE ORANGE BEARS

The orange bears with soft friendly eyes
Who played with me when I was ten,
Christ, before I left home they'd had
Their paws smashed in the rolls, their backs
Seared by hot slag, their soft trusting
Bellies kicked in, their tongues ripped

Out, and I went down through the woods
To the smelly crick with Whitman
In the Haldeman-Julius edition,
And I just sat there worrying my thumbnail
Into the cover—What did he know about
Orange bears with their coats all stunk up with soft coal
And the National Guard coming over
From Wheeling to stand in front of the millgates
With drawn bayonets jeering at the strikers?

I remember you could put daisies
On the windowsill at night and in
The morning they'd be so covered with soot
You couldn't tell what they were anymore.

A hell of a fat chance my orange bears had!

THE REASON FOR SKYLARKS

It was nearly morning when the giant
Reached the tree of children.
Their faces shone like white apples
On the cold dark branches
And their dresses and little coats
Made sodden gestures in the wind.
He did not laugh or weep or stamp
His heavy feet. He set to work at once
Lifting them tenderly down
Into a straw basket which was fixed
By a golden strap to his shoulder.
Only one did he drop—a soft pretty child
Whose hair was the color of watered milk.
She fell into the long grass
And he could not find her
Though he searched until his fingers
Bled and the full light came.

He shook his fist at the sky and called
God a bitter name.

But no answer was made and the giant
Got down on his knees before the tree
And putting his hands about the trunk
Shook
Until all the children had fallen
Into the grass. Then he pranced and stamped
Them to jelly. And still he felt no peace.
He took his half-full basket and set it afire,
Holding it by the handle until
Everything had been burned. He saw now
Two men on steaming horses approaching
From the direction of the world.
And taking a little silver flute
Out of his pocket he played tune
After tune until they came up to him.

GAUTAMA IN THE DEER PARK AT BENARES

In a hut of mud and fire
Sits this single man—"Not to want
Money, to want a life in the world,
To want no trinkets on my name"—
And he was rich; his life lives where
Death cannot go; his honor stares
At the sun.

The fawn sleeps. The little winds
Ruffle the earth's green hair. It is
Wonderful to live. My sword rusts
In the pleasant rain. I shall not think
Anymore. I touch the face of my friend;
He shows his dirty teeth as he scratches
At a flea—and we grin. It is warm
And the rice stirs usefully in our bellies.

The fawn raises its head—the sun floods
Its soft eye with the kingdoms of life—
I think we should all go to sleep now,
And not care anymore.

AND WHAT WITH THE BLUNDERS, *what with the*
real humor of the address, the end is sure to be attained, that
of roarous fun in the roused hamlet or mountain village which
pours forth its whole population in a swarm round the
amorous orator, down to the baby that can but just tottle and
the curs that join in the clamor, mad with ecstasy at the novelty
of some noise besides that of trees and the horrible clamor
of the grass

We talked of things but all the time we wanted each other
and finally we were silent and I knelt above your body

a closing of eyes
and falling unfalteringly
over a warm pure country and something crying

when I was a child things being hurt made me sorry
for them but it seemed the way men and women did
and we had not made the world

coming into it crying
(I wanted so not to hurt you)
and going out of it like a sudden pouring of salt

later, being tired and overflowing with tenderness
girl's body to boy's body lying there and wondering what it had been
we got to our feet very quietly so that they would not waken
but we felt their shy sorrowful look on us as we left them alone
        there

    *   *   *   *   *

All things are one thing to the earth
rayless as a blind leper Blake lies with everyman
and the fat lord sleeps beside his bastard at last
and it doesn't matter, it doesn't mean what we think it does
for we two will never lie there
we shall not be there when death reaches out his sparkling
        hands

there are so many little dyings that it doesn't matter which of
        them is death.

BECAUSE *THEY WERE VERY POOR THAT WINTER*

The only mother he could afford was a skinny old man
Who sat on the roof all day drinking champagne—
(The real stuff of course was much too expensive);
Previous to that, about a year later,
She joined the Society For The Placating
Of Polar Giraffes—and almost immediately discovered
That by earnestly pronouncing "Your coat's wet"
In Arabic, great numbers of drowned sailors
Would drop from the sky and dance
Through the streets until shot by cops.
So, being just turned three, little Coralou
Naturally bristled at her grandfather's suggestion that
They go together to the stationhouse and
Try the new lavatory facilities there. "Conscientious taxpayer,
Are you!" she snorted. "I suppose that's why you've
Got your overcoat pockets stuffed with snapshots
Of Martha Washington playing basketball on rollerskates!"
Obscure indeed are the vestments of destiny:
In the end, rose and ostrich smell much
Alike; and only the thinking of clouds
Keeps the world on its untroubled course.

BECAUSE *SOMETIMES YOU CAN'T ALWAYS BE SO*

I never read of any enforceable regulation
Against removing orangeskins from apples in private;
But when my brother tried to buy
A sandwich in the Lodi post office yesterday,
One of the town's leading social blights
Bit him in the leg! Why, only last
Week an aunt of mine had a horse
Named Sesroh fall asleep on her shoulder
In the subway! The fifth Friday in July
A flagload of my cousins were arrested for pulling
A rowboat down the main drag in Yonkers—
Despite the fact it had cost them sixty bucks
To get the governor's grandmother drunk enough
To ride nude in it! Talk about patriotism!—
Is civic mindedness to be an empty catchsword
For every schoolboy to sneak his first shave with?

Are the hallowed drawers of our forefathers to be bulged
Thus shamelessly forth above every pawnshop in the land?
I believe it was Old Mother Frietchie who said:
"Shoot, son, even if I could dance,
There are a lot better ways to have a ball
Than scraping the hair off your own head."

BECAUSE *GOING NOWHERE TAKES A LONG TIME*

Something in the climate of a hammer
Struck him when young. Call a
Sparrow a lamp, you'll still need
The liking of chairs to settle
What is at bottom only painted over
Cloth; and that flat cunning of plates,
How little it speaks above the soup's
So roundly directional bravura. Count the sky
A pan, you'll still be hard put to find
Any flash in its like. But ah, alas, alas,
Lottipo . . . the mushy marshes, those tree-lined woods,
The so-small journeying, and the trivial occupants thereof . . .
These, too, and all else, alas, are only real. So may we
Remember once again how the grasses cause the wind to move . . .
Ah, alas, dear Toppilo, what then is this realm that seems
So like a cell, without jailor or judge, or witness even . . .?
And that we love! is this not a proof of something!
No, I admit—not necessarily of heaven . . .

BECAUSE *IN THIS SORROWING STATUE OF FLESH*

They were hopeful of a curtain raiser
That would not sputter off in walls
And worklands instinct with shadows before gates
Where all helmets and orders eventually collect;
But none went to himself fully or
Made his might little enough to bear
The green loaves in his hand of leaves.
"All memory is piecemeal murder;
The hater in the mirror, it has a mother's impersonal gaze . . ."
"I do not think of the shorelights blurring out,
Or of the gray and raging glee

That slates these waves; but only
Of her tiny delicacy, of the strange gentleness of her fingers . . .
And of how very odd it is
That my man's heart should now be torn right out of me!"
"But the event itself, it has no speech; nor has it
Any meaning or purpose outside its own being. For existence
Is an animal substance, indivisible, and hence, unknowable;
And all things—stars, brides, and apple boughs—
And non-things, too—such as "history's happenings"—
Are but its cells and bones and tissues."
"And the voice of the father, there is no mercy in it;
All that vast chemistry of the sun . . . and little birds freeze!"
"I do not now think so much of what may only be idly argued;
For it seems a fact still of some importance, that I am dying."

BECAUSE *HE LIKED TO BE AT HOME*

He usually managed to be there when
He arrived. A horse, his name was
Hunry Fencewaver Walkins—he'd sometimes
Be almost too tired to make it;
Because, since he also hated being alone,
He was always on the alert to pop forth
At a full run whenever the door opened.
Then one day it happened—
He didn't get there in time!
Of course he couldn't risk opening the door—
So, panting, he just stood there in the hall—
And listened to the terrible sound of himself weeping
In that room he could never, never enter again.

THE CHARACTER OF LOVE SEEN AS A SEARCH FOR THE LOST

You, the woman; I, the man; this, the world:
And each is the work of all.

There is the muffled step in the snow; the stranger;
The crippled wren; the nun; the dancer; the Jesus-wing

Over the walkers in the village; and there are
Many beautiful arms about us and the things we know.

See how those stars tramp over heaven on their sticks
Of ancient light: with what simplicity that blue
Takes eternity into the quiet cave of God, where Caesar
And Socrates, like primitive paintings on a wall,
Look, with idiot eyes, on the world where we two are.

You, the sought for; I, the seeker; this, the search:
And each is the mission of all.

For greatness is only the drayhorse that coaxes
The built cart out; and where we go is reason.
But genius is an enormous littleness, a trickling
Of heart that covers alike the hare and the hunter.

How smoothly, like the sleep of a flower, love,
The grassy wind moves over night's tense meadow:
See how the great wooden eyes of the forest
Stare upon the architecture of our innocence.

You, the village; I, the stranger; this, the road:
And each is the work of all.

Then, not that man do more, or stop pity; but that he be
Wider in living; that all his cities fly a clean flag . . .
We have been alone too long, love; it is terribly late
For the pierced feet on the water and we must not die now.

Have you wondered why all the windows in heaven were broken?
Have you seen the homeless in the open grave of God's hand?
Do you want to acquaint the larks with the fatuous music of war?

There is the muffled step in the snow; the stranger;
The crippled wren; the nun; the dancer; the Jesus-wing
Over the walkers in the village; and there are
Many desperate arms about us and the things we know.

from THE JOURNAL OF ALBION MOONLIGHT

                              I
                        want you
                        to listen
                        to
                        me
                                    it is growing dark
      Without the despondency of the garlic-rose for the nun's cot
      Without the bone in Pedro's lard tub which has been reported
      Without the sacrifice of the executioner's widow in the lake
country
      Without the passion of the snail for the female strawberry
      Without the mastery of the sly nightingale in the rose's womb
      Without the treachery of the virgin who pronounces a low vow
      Without the pride of the naked beast on the snow's breast
      Without the nightmare as the rag is wiped the thighs along
      Without the violence of the elastic pillar which prods the hen
      Without the lechery of the bullet which studs a soldier
      Without the fury in the honeysuckle's allowing root
      Without the desire of the yellow bear for Carol's scented arms
      Without the memory of the chaste child for the pot of snake-
gods
      Without the hunger of the master for the slave's dried snot
      Without the energy of the shutter which bangs on the no-house
      Without the murder of the stranger who stands eternally alone
      Without the harmony of the star in the order of phosphorescent
gardens
      Without the mockery of the lunatic who has been deftly warned
      Without the disappearance of the last useless spitting landmark
      Without the agony of the angels of resignation
      Without the warning which bursts through the sucking circle
      Without the disorder in the brain of the whirling death-man
      Without the silence in the bitter teat of the whale
      Without the depravity in the horizon's oily black stare
      Without the torment in the crush of water-bulls bellowing at
sea
      Without the boast of the cyclone to the butterfly and the wren
      How could we be expected to live and sweat and take wives?
      Yet with all the endless bright furniture of the sky
      And that war of shadows in the morphological clown-flesh
      And that obsession for the object which is always God

And that arcade where the statues couple in horrible privacy
And that detail which must be forgotten but which was never
known
And that slim gray fish whose ancestors were old before man
came

*The subject of the attack admits of two natural divisions;
(from A Treatise on Field Fortification, by D. H. Mahan) the
first of which comprehends all the preliminary steps taken
before the troops are brought into action; the second all the
subsequent operations of the troops.*

And that whip about which it is better not to go on record at all
And that nursemaid concerning whom many treatises were
written
And that alligator which mated with a certain queen of renown
And that contrived glance which does not go back to the eyes
And that fashion of childbirth which was the rage in Arabia
And that assassin whose fingerprints could not be taken in
daylight

*An attack is made either by surprise, or openly. In both cases
exact information should be obtained of the approaches to
the works; their strength; the number and character of the
garrison; and also the character of the commander. This information may be obtained through spies, deserters, prison-
ers, and others who have access to the works; but implicit
faith ought not to be placed in the relations of such persons,
as they may be in the interests of the enemy; and in all cases
they should be strictly cross-examined and their different
representations be carefully compared with each other.*

And that city where the innocents were mercifully slaughtered
And that grace of walk which puts birds singing between a
man's thighs
And that far-heralded feast where girl children were raped and
eaten
And that cathedral's gate upon which many fat Popes have
swung
And that remarkable millionaire who gave money for asylums
And that feature of a death which never fails to surprise
And that swan's disease which men contract in the black
swamps

And that march for salt which left the plains a chalk bog of
skeletons
And that famous design which Leonardo gave his life to have

*The best source of information is an examination, or recon-
naissance, made by one or more intelligent officers.*

And that plague from which everyone now is dying
And that mansion where our fathers once so quaintly stood
And that wrench for which no bolt was ever invented
And that science of murder in which they would have us excel
And that devil-lark whose wings span the seven disorders
And that comedian upon whom the curse of Christ fell
And that intensity of wakefulness from which there is no re-
covery
And that blood-sick beast which tracks man to his cave
And that hooting and screaming and stamping and barking
And with the nose and the eye and the leg and the cock and the
folding bed
We are still not able to tame that fabulous kingdom of the Word
For the word is to put it plainly unlettered
The word is NOT deed
The word is the way something floats which cannot be seen
The word is the call of the tribe from down under the water
The word is the thing the wind says to the dead
The word is the white candle at the foot of the throne

*This investigation should, if possible, be made secretly; but
as this will not be practicable if the enemy show even or-
dinary vigilance, it will be necessary to protect the recon-
noitering officer by small detachments, who drive in the out-
posts of those attacked.*

The word is the saying
The word is the echo of our dreaming
The word is the web we take from the womb

from THE JOURNAL OF ALBION MOONLIGHT

But there is no black jaw which cannot be broken by our word
But there is a sadness which rots our souls
But there is a simplicity which turns us mad

KENNETH PATCHEN 65

So it is the duty of the artist to discourage all traces of shame
To extend all boundaries   *I hit*
To fog them in right over the plate   *the undertaker*
To kill only what is ridiculous   *in the eye*
To establish problems   *with a wet*
To ignore solutions   *snowball*
To listen to no one   *Ha. Ha. You*
To omit nothing   *are frightened*
To contradict everything   *and you no*
To generate the free brain   *longer want*
To bear no cross   *me to get*
To take part in no crucifixion   *into bed*
To tinkle a warning when mankind strays   *with you.*
To explode upon all parties
To wound deeper than the soldier
To heal this poor obstinate monkey once and for all
To have kids with pretty angels
To display his dancing seed   *My soul*
To sail only in polar seas   *and I*
To laugh at every situation   *both*
To besiege all their cities   *wish*
To exhaust the primitive   *you*
To follow every false track   *a good mark*
To verify the irrational   *in God's*
To exaggerate all things   *little school.*
To inhabit everyone   *Our weeping*
To lubricate each proportion   *is for*
To experience only experience   *everybody*
To deviate at every point   *but*
To offer no examples   *especially*
To dismiss all support   *for you.*
To make one monster at least   *I feel*
To go underground immediately   *your hand*
To smell the shark's ass   *on my arm . . .*
To multiply all opinions
To work only in the distance
To extend all shapes
To acquire a sublime reputation
To consort forever with the runaway
To sport the glacial eye   *I am the love.*
To direct all smouldering ambitions   *I am the hate.*
To frequent only the exterminating planets   *I am the pain.*
To kidnap the phantom's first-born   *I am the tears.*

To forego no succulent filth
To masquerade as the author of every platitude
To overwhelm the mariner with improper charts *I* ...
To expose himself to every ridicule *I* ...
To ambush their blow-nose Providence *I* ... *help me!*
To set a flame in the high air *I am*
To exclaim at the commonplace alone *afraid* ...
To cause the unseen eyes to open *Please! !*
To advance with the majesty of the praying serpent
To contrive always to be caught with his pants down
To sprinkle mule-milk on the lifted brows of virgins
To attach no importance whatever to his activity
To admire only the absurd
To be concerned with every profession save his own
To raise a fortuitous stink on the boulevards of truth and beauty
To desire an electrifiable intercourse with a female alligator
To lift the flesh above the suffering
To forgive the beautiful its disconsolate deceit
To send the world away to crawl under his discarded pedestals
To have the cunning of the imperilled wave
To hide his lamentations in the shredded lungs of the tempest
To recommend stone eyelashes for all candid lookers
To attribute every magnificence to himself
To maintain that the earth is neither round nor flat but a scoma-
phoid
To flash his vengeful badge at every abyss
To be revolted by only the sacred cow which piddles at the toes
of the swamp
To kneel with the blind and drunk brigands and learn their
songs
To *happen*
To embrace the intemperate hermaphrodite of memory
It is the artist's duty to be alive
To drag people into glittering occupations
To return always to the renewing stranger
To observe only the funereal spectator
To assume the ecstasy in all conceivable attitudes
To follow the plundering whirlpool to its source
To cry out nervously with every knock
To stock his shelves with plaintive confessions and pernicious
diaries
To outflow the volcano in semen and phlegm
To be treacherous when nothing is to be gained

To enrich himself at the expense of everyone   *I have no desire*
To reel in an exquisite sobriety   *to be intelligent*
To blush perpetually in gaping innocence
To drift happily through the ruined race-intelligence
To burrow beneath the subconscious
To defend the unreal at the cost of his reason   *I have*
To obey each outrageous impulse   *no money*
To commit his company to all enchantments   *whatever.*
To rage against the sacrificing shepherds   *I can't*
To return to a place remote from his native land   *make a*
To pursue the languid executioner to his hall bedroom *living*
To torment the spirit-lice   *at all*
To cover the mud with distinguished vegetation
To regain the emperor's chair   *I am*
To pass from one world to another in carefree devotion *hungry*
To withdraw only when all have been profaned   *and cold*
To contract every battering disease   *. . . tired*
To peel off all substances from the face of horror
To glue himself to every lascivious breast
To hurl his vigorous cone into every trough
To unroll the hide from that repugnant rhinoceros Time
To refrain from no ownership
To crowd the squat-rumped centuries into his own special resi-
dence
To plunge beyond their smoking armpits

I am   Night   *alone—*
sick   that   *and yet not alone,*
as a buggered pig   great   *for reaching out my hand*
with all this   black   *I touch the cold*
mess. I can't   she-dog   *still face*
go on with the   squatting   *but there is too much*
farce. "Quality"—   up there   *BLOOD I don't care*
I hope some   above us   *what the hell difference*
smart fool tears   with   *does it make—God!*
this book apart   all   *what do you suppose*
and throws it   her   *they can do to make*
in the toilet and   white   *me get back into line*
then does his little   tits
function even as   showing
you and I

from A NOTE ON *THE HUNTED CITY,* 1939–1967

A note on structure: so much nonsense has been written about "structure" of late (usually by schoolmaster-poets), that a great many people have forgotten that the way to build a house is to build it. Those who work with their hands know that the proper method for moving a heavy stone is to get a good firm hold, brace your feet, kick it into motion with the nubs of your fists, and ride it to where you want it to go. Make the stone work. (I have no bone to pick with the critics; their dryasdust bones don't interest me; give me an ounce of Melville's meat and blood; I have no time for the sawdust they manage to pull out of the heads of tenth-rate poets, mostly deceased—whether dead or not.) I believe that Hart Crane's *Bridge* failed because he didn't think enough about its structure as it had to do with *his own structure as a man.*

I am not sure but that our whole conception of the verse-line is wrong. Words have distinct values of relationship that have no bearing whatever on the relationship of line to line; if this is remembered, of course, we get a perfect relationship of line to line *over the whole poem.* There is such a thing as weight in words. A rhythm felt is a rhythm that has its own laws. It is an absolute mistake to ladle out stress like a cook measuring off the ingredients for a cake. We've got a country full of cake-baking poets now, one just as good and just as bad as the next.

Poetry is writing. Maybe what I'm talking about is not poetry (the stuff the critics are yammering about). In whose name is the criterion? Dante's, I think. Dostoievski's, I think. They were writers, and they wrote.

Kenneth Patchen
Palo Alto, California

WILLIAM STAFFORD

William Stafford was born in 1914 in Hutchinson, Kansas. He was educated at Kansas, Wisconsin, and Iowa. He has taught at Lewis and Clark College for the past twenty years. His books of verse are Down in My Heart, West of Your City, Traveling Through the Dark, *and* The Rescued Year.

Kit Stafford

RETURNED TO SAY

When I face north a lost Cree
on some new shore puts a moccasin down,
rock in the light and noon for seeing,
he in a hurry and I beside him.

It will be a long trip; he will be a new chief;
we have drunk new water from an unnamed stream;
under little dark trees he is to find a path
we both must travel because we have met.

Henceforth we gesture even by waiting;
there is a grain of sand on his knifeblade
so small he blows it and while his breathing
darkens the steel his eyes become set

And start a new vision: the rest of his life.
We will mean what he does. Back of this page
the path turns north. We are looking for a sign.
Our moccasins do not mark the ground.

BEFORE THE BIG STORM

You are famous in my mind.
When anyone mentions your name
all the boxes marked "1930's"
fall off the shelves;
and the orators on the Fourth of July
all begin shouting again.
The audience of our high school commencement
begin to look out of the windows at the big storm.

And I think of you in our play—
oh, helpless and lonely!—crying,
and your father is dead again.
He was drunk; he fell.

When they mention your name,
our houses out there in the wind

creak again in the storm;
and I lean from our play, wherever I am,
to you, quiet at the edge of that town:
"All the world is blowing away."
"It is almost daylight."
"Are you warm?"

TORNADO

First the soul of our house left, up the chimney,
and part of the front window went outward—pursued
whatever tore at the chest. Part of the lake
on top guyed around the point, bellied
like a tent; and fish like seeds ripened felt
a noiseless Command around their gills, while
the wheatfields crouched, reminded with a hand.

That treble talk always at the bottom of the creek
at the mouth, where the lake leaned away from the rock
at the mouth, rose above water. Then Command moved
away again and our town spread, ruined
but relieved, at the bottom of its remembered air.
We weren't left religion exactly (the church
was ecumenical bricks), but a certain tall element:
a pulse beat still in the stilled rock
and in the buried sound along the buried mouth of the creek.

REQUIEM

Mother is gone. Bird songs wouldn't let her breathe.
The skating bug broke through the eternal veil.
A tree in the forest fell; the air remembered.
Two rocks clinked in the night to signal some meaning.

Traveler north, beyond where you can return,
hearing above you the last of the razor birds whizz
over the drift of dust that bore your name,
there's a kind of waiting you teach us—the art of not knowing.

Suicidal gestures of nobility driven to the wrist,
our molten bodies remembering some easier form,
we feel the bones assert the rites of yesterday
and the flow of angular events becoming destiny.

Summer and locusts own the elm part of town;
on the millpond moss is making its cream.
Our duty is just a certain high kind of waiting;
beyond our hearing is the hearing of the community.

FALL JOURNEY

Evening came, a paw, to the gray hut by the river.
Pushing the door with a stick, I opened it.
Only a long walk had brought me there,
steps into the continent they had placed before me.

I read weathered log, stone fireplace, broken chair,
the dead grass outside under the cottonwood tree—
and it all stared back. We've met before, my memory
started to say, somewhere. . . .

And then I stopped: my father's eyes were gray.

CHICKENS THE WEASEL KILLED

A passerby being fair about sacrifice,
with no program but walking,
no acrobat of salvation,
I couldn't help seeing the weasel
fasten on the throat.

Any vision isolates:
those chickens the weasel killed—
I hear them relax years from now,
subsiding while they threaten,
and then appeal to the ground with their wings.

LAKE CHELAN

They call it regional, this relevance—
the deepest place we have: in this pool forms
the model of our land, a lonely one,
responsive to the wind. Everything we own
has brought us here: from here we speak.

The sun stalks among these peaks to sight
the lake down aisles, long like a gun;
a ferryboat, lost by a century, toots
for trappers, the pelt of the mountains
rinsed in the sun and that sound.

Suppose a person far off to whom this lake
occurs: told a problem, he might hear a word
so dark he drowns an instant, and stands dumb
for the centuries of his country and the suave
hills beyond the stranger's sight.

Is this man dumb, then, for whom Chelan lives
in the wilderness? On the street you've seen
someone like a trapper's child pause,
and fill his eyes with some irrelevant flood—
a tide stops him, delayed in his job.

Permissive as a beach, he turns inland,
harks like a fire, glances through the dark
like an animal drinking, and arrives along that line
a lake has found far back in the hills
where what comes finds a brim gravity exactly requires.

AT COVE ON THE CROOKED RIVER

At Cove at our camp in the open canyon
it was the kind of place where you might look out
some evening and see trouble walking away.

And the river there meant something
always coming from snow and flashing around boulders
after shadow-fish lurking below the mesa.

We stood with wet towels over our heads for shade,
looking past the Indian picture rock and the kind of trees
that act out whatever has happened to them.

Oh civilization, I want to carve you like this,
decisively outward the way evening comes
over that kind of twist in the scenery

When people cramp into their station wagons
and roll up the windows, and drive away.

IN DEAR DETAIL, BY IDEAL LIGHT

1

Night huddled our town,
plunged from the sky.
You moved away.
I save what I can of the time.

In other towns, calling my name,
home people hail me, dazed;
those moments we hold,
reciting in the evening,

Reciting about you, receding
through the huddle of any new town.
Can we rescue the light
that happened, and keeps on happening, around us?

Gradually we left you there
surrounded by the river curve
and the held-out arms,
elms under the streetlight.

These vision emergencies come
wherever we go—
blind home
coming near at unlikely places.

2

One's duty: to find a place
that grows from his part of the world—
it means leaving
certain good people.

Think: near High Trail, Colorado,
a wire follows cottonwoods
helping one to know—
like a way on trust.

That lonely strand leaves the road
depending on limbs or little poles,
and slants away,
hunting a ranch in the hills.

There, for the rest of the years,
by not going there, a person could believe
some porch looking south,
and steady in the shade—maybe you,

Rescued by how the hills
happened to arrive where they are,
depending on that wire
going to an imagined place

Where finally the way the world feels
really means how things are,
in dear detail,
by ideal light all around us.

THE CONCEALMENT: ISHI, THE LAST WILD INDIAN

A rock, a leaf, mud, even the grass
Ishi the shadow man had to put back where it was.
In order to live he had to hide that he did.
His deep canyon he kept unmarked for the world,
and only his face became lined, because no one saw it
and it therefore didn't make any difference.

If he appeared, he died; and he was the last. Erased
footprints, berries that purify the breath, rituals
before dawn with water—even the dogs roamed a land
unspoiled by Ishi, who used to own it, with his aunt
and uncle, whose old limbs bound in willow bark finally
stopped and were hidden under the rocks, in sweet leaves.

We ought to help change that kind of premature suicide,
the existence gradually mottled away till the heartbeat
blends and the messages all go one way from the world
and disappear inward: Ishi lived. It was all right
for him to make a track. In California now where his opposites
unmistakably dwell we wander their streets

And sometimes whisper his name—
"Ishi."

RIGHT NOW

Tonight in our secret town
wires are down. Black
lights along the street blow
steady in a wind held still.
A deaf dog listens. A girl
retreats from her gaze: her eyes
go endlessly back, a spool of shadow.

Led by my own dark I go
my unmarked everlasting round
frozen in this moment: Now
smooths all the smother, held,
wild but still. I know
so well nothing moves, arrived:
my glimpse, this town, our time.

IN THE DEEP CHANNEL

Setting a trotline after sundown
if we went far enough away in the night
sometimes up out of deep water
would come a secret-headed channel cat,

Eyes that were still eyes in the rush of darkness,
flowing feelers noncommittal and black,
and hidden in the fins those rasping bone daggers,
with one spiking upward on its back.

We would come at daylight and find the line sag,
the fishbelly gleam and the rush on the tether:
to feel the swerve and the deep current
which tugged at the tree roots below the river.

LETTER FROM OREGON

Mother, here there are shadowy salmon;
ever their sides argue up the falls.
Watching them plunge with fluttering gills,
I thought back through Wyoming where I came from.

The gleaming sides of my train glimmered
up over passes and arrowed through shoals
of aspen fluttering in a wind of yellow.
Only the sky stayed true; I turned,

Justifying space through those miles of Wyoming
till the wave of the land was quelled by the stars;
then tunnels of shadow led me far
through doubt, and I was home.

Mother, even home was doubtful;
many slip into the sea and are gone for years,
just as I boarded the six-fifteen there.
Over the bar I have leaped outward.

Somewhere in the ocean beyond Laramie
when that grass folded low in the dark
a lost fin waved, and I felt the beat
of the old neighborhood stop, on our street.

MY FATHER: OCTOBER 1942

He picks up what he thinks is
a road map, and it is
his death: he holds it easily, and
nothing can take it from his firm hand.
The pulse in his thumb on the map
says, "1:19 P.M. next Tuesday, at
this intersection." And an ambulance
begins to throb while his face looks tired.

Any time anyone may pick up something
so right that he can't put it down:
that is the problem for all who travel—they
fatally own whatever is really theirs,
and that is the inner thread, the lock,
what can hold. If it is to be, nothing breaks
it. Millions of observers guess all the
time, but each person, once, can say, "Sure."

Then he's no longer an observer. He isn't right,
or wrong. He just wins or loses.

WALKING THE WILDERNESS

God is never sure He has found
the right grass. It never forgets Him.
My mother in a dream dreamed
this place, where storms drown
down or where God makes it arch to mountains,
flood with winter, stare upward at His
eye that freezes people, His zero breath
their death. In the night they lie, she
dreamed, sealed with lips to earth, who wait
at last with confidence for justice
or such firm coming as the wolverine's.

All the way into her dream and back
I walk and guard the day, since daylight broke
past guards of trees and streamed away.

WILLIAM STAFFORD **79**

Hear me, full sky, all your
lines I do not know, the roads
birds fly, the channels their lives make—
my mother in the dream dreamed
even deeper: people drowned awake,
each one staring, alone, pitiable,
come to all at once in that
dream, welcomed the more, the more
they trembled. God never notices opposition;
the deep of that dream always waits.

Snowflake designs lock; they clasp in the sky,
hold their patterns one by one, down,
spasms of loneliness, each one God's answer.
Warm human representatives may vote and
manage man; but last the blizzard will dignify
the walker, the storm hack trees to cyclone
groves, he catch the snow, his brave eye
become command, the whole night howl against
his ear, till found by dawn he
reach out to God no trembling hand.

THE WELL RISING

The well rising without sound,
the spring on a hillside,
the plowshare brimming through deep ground
everywhere in the field—

The sharp swallows in their swerve
flaring and hesitating
hunting for the final curve
coming closer and closer—

The swallow heart from wing beat to wing beat
counseling decision, decision:
thunderous examples. I place my feet
with care in such a world.

THE EPITAPH ENDING IN AND

In the last storm, when hawks
blast upward and a dove is
driven into the grass, its broken wings
a delicate design, the air between
wracked thin where it stretched before,
a clear spring bent close too often
(that Earth should ever have such wings
burnt on in blind color!), this will be
good as an epitaph:

Doves did not know where to fly, and

FINDING THE LANGUAGE

Speaking of writing, I usually welcome all kinds of impulses and ideas, not making an effort, during that first moment of encounter, to restrict the cadence or pace or flow of the language. The feel of composition is more important than any rule or prescribed form. Swimmers after much practice can achieve a sense of catching hold of the water; the hand enters quickly and quickly adjusts to "the catch," the optimum angle and sweep for propulsion. I believe that the speaker and writer can cultivate that kind of readiness to accept and use the feel of the language.

Once anything is said or written, once the speaker or writer turns back to look at it, he may theorize in a number of ways about what he has done, in his freedom. And two such ways occur to me now.

One way focuses on syllables. Instead of assuming that the language has syllables with many sounds, only certain ones matched for rhyme or equivalent duration or emphasis, I assume that all syllables rhyme, sort of. That is, any syllable sounds more like any other syllable than it sounds like silence. This assumption confronts me with a whole torrent of immediate opportunities, in which the responsibility of the writer is not restricted to intermittent requirements of sound repetition or variation: the writer or speaker enters a constant, never-ending flow and variation of gloriously seething changes of sound. His responsibility is total—and his opportunities are also total. Once the writer accepts this total relation to the language, most discussions about meter and form (in regard to sound) become inadequate. The discussions may not be irrelevant, but they inevitably come as a series of distortions of the way writing *feels*. Like the swimmer, the practiced writer *finds* the material, an experience too rich for sequential explanation.

The other way of considering how it feels to write freely comes to me by way of a gradually sharpening awareness that the language—any language a speaker knows well—is really two languages at once. It is the language ordinarily identified by listless users, a temporarily fixed combination of words and denotations. But it is also stealthily and irresistibly a set of incipient meanings and influences which impose themselves on readers or listeners (or speakers or writers) by virtue of certain reinforcing patterns of sound which the language, as if by chance, has taken up into itself. That is, all syllables tend to slide by inherent quality toward certain meanings, either because of varying demands on the throat in utterance, or because of relations among clusters of syllables which have become loaded with associated meanings, and so on. I believe that this clustering of meanings operates everywhere in the language, but that its presence is easily evident to us only where its effect has become unusually marked. Words like slide, slick, slither, slime, sludge, etc. embody an *sl* sound which will steadily induce something of its potential meaning into any other words it gets itself into. Skid, ski, skate, scat, skull, etc. would immediately come to mind as another cluster. My belief is that the language is continuously under the influence of such currents or tendencies, and that alert or lucky speakers and writers ride such currents, with corresponding enhancements in their language. As a poet I am interested in living with such influences and benefiting from them. These influences are much more pervasive and subtle and helpful than any set of rules or verse forms could embody or anticipate.

The attitudes and beliefs expressed above make me, not an enemy of form or rule, but at least occasionally a roamer. And in writing I find that my practice initially is to roam forward through experience, finding the way as the process unfolds. This way with the language is interesting to me, and I believe such readiness is valid for living the language as we use it. Relying on forms or rules is always possible—is always one of the possible directions to take. But it is also possible that the everlasting process which led to discovery of forms and rules in the first place will continue to be worthy. Our experience with the language explores and validates and discovers. And that ever-new confrontation is essential for writing, even for effective writing in the strictest of forms.

So, respect for the achieved, along with readiness for a new achievement, is the attitude I would cultivate, and is in fact my prevalent feeling when I write.

William Stafford
Lake Oswego, Oregon

WELDON KEES

William Heick

Weldon Kees was born in 1914 in Beatrice, Nebraska. He spent his youth in New York, where he wrote poetry, painted, made films, and played jazz piano. In 1955 he disappeared, probably having leapt to his death from the Golden Gate Bridge. His books of verse are The Last Man, The Fall of the Magicians, Poems 1947–1954, *and* The Collected Poems of Weldon Kees.

CRIME CLUB

No butler, no second maid, no blood upon the stair.
No eccentric aunt, no gardener, no family friend
Smiling among the bric-a-brac and murder.
Only a suburban house with the front door open
And a dog barking at a squirrel, and the cars
Passing. The corpse quite dead. The wife in Florida.

Consider the clues: the potato masher in a vase,
The torn photograph of a Wesleyan basketball team,
Scattered with check stubs in the hall;
The unsent fan letter to Shirley Temple,
The Hoover button on the lapel of the deceased,
The note: "To be killed this way is quite all right with me."

Small wonder that the case remains unsolved,
Or that the sleuth, Le Roux, is now incurably insane,
And sits alone in a white room in a white gown,
Screaming that all the world is mad, that clues
Lead nowhere, or to walls so high their tops cannot be seen;
Screaming all day of war, screaming that nothing can be solved.

ASPECTS OF ROBINSON

Robinson at cards at the Algonquin; a thin
Blue light comes down once more outside the blinds.
Gray men in overcoats are ghosts blown past the door.
The taxis streak the avenues with yellow, orange, and red.
This is Grand Central, Mr. Robinson.

Robinson on a roof above the Heights; the boats
Mourn like the lost. Water is slate, far down.
Through sounds of ice cubes dropped in glass, an osteopath,
Dressed for the links, describes an old Intourist tour.
—Here's where old Gibbons jumped from, Robinson.

Robinson walking in the Park, admiring the elephant.
Robinson buying the *Tribune*, Robinson buying the *Times*.
    Robinson

Saying, "Hello. Yes, this is Robinson. Sunday
At five? I'd love to. Pretty well. And you?"
Robinson alone at Longchamps, staring at the wall.

Robinson afraid, drunk, sobbing Robinson
In bed with a Mrs. Morse. Robinson at home;
Decisions: Toynbee or luminol? Where the sun
Shines, Robinson in flowered trunks, eyes toward
The breakers. Where the night ends, Robinson in East Side bars.

Robinson in Glen plaid jacket, Scotch-grain shoes,
Black four-in-hand and oxford button-down,
The jeweled and silent watch that winds itself, the brief-
Case, covert topcoat, clothes for spring, all covering
His sad and usual heart, dry as a winter leaf.

ROBINSON

The dog stops barking after Robinson has gone.
His act is over. The world is a gray world,
Not without violence, and he kicks under the grand piano,
The nightmare chase well under way.

The mirror from Mexico, stuck to the wall,
Reflects nothing at all. The glass is black.
Robinson alone provides the image Robinsonian.

Which is all of the room—walls, curtains,
Shelves, bed, the tinted photograph of Robinson's first wife,
Rugs, vases, panatellas in a humidor.
They would fill the room if Robinson came in.

The pages in the books are blank,
The books that Robinson has read. That is his favorite chair,
Or where the chair would be if Robinson were here.

All day the phone rings. It could be Robinson
Calling. It never rings when he is here.

Outside, white buildings yellow in the sun.
Outside, the birds circle continuously
Where trees are actual and take no holiday.

RELATING TO ROBINSON

Somewhere in Chelsea, early summer;
And, walking in the twilight toward the docks,
I thought I made out Robinson ahead of me.

From an uncurtained second-story room, a radio
Was playing *There's a Small Hotel;* a kite
Twisted above dark rooftops and slow drifting birds.
We were alone there, he and I,
Inhabiting the empty street.

Under a sign for Natural Bloom Cigars,
While lights clicked softly in the dusk from red to green,
He stopped and gazed into a window
Where a plaster Venus, modeling a truss,
Looked out at Eastbound traffic. (But Robinson,
I knew, was out of town: he summers at a place in Maine,
Sometimes on Fire Island, sometimes the Cape,
Leaves town in June and comes back after Labor Day.)
And yet, I almost called out, "Robinson!"

There was no chance. Just as I passed,
Turning my head to search his face,
His own head turned with mine
And fixed me with dilated, terrifying eyes
That stopped my blood. His voice
Came at me like an echo in the dark.

"I thought I saw the whirlpool opening.
Kicked all night at a bolted door.
You must have followed me from Astor Place.
An empty paper floats down at the last.
*And then a day as huge as yesterday in pairs
Unrolled its horror on my face
Until it blocked—*" Running in sweat
To reach the docks, I turned back
For a second glance. I had no certainty,
There in the dark, that it was Robinson
Or someone else.
                    The block was bare. The Venus,

Bathed in blue fluorescent light,
Stared toward the river. As I hurried West,
The lights across the bay were coming on.
The boats moved silently and the low whistles blew.

PROBLEMS OF A JOURNALIST

"I want to get away somewhere and re-read Proust,"
Said an editor of *Fortune* to a man on *Time*.
But the fire roared and died, the phoenix quacked like a goose,
And all roads to the country fray like shawls
Outside the dusk of suburbs. Pacing the halls
Where mile-high windows frame a dream with witnesses,
You taste, fantast and epicure, the names of towns along the coast,
Black roadsters throbbing on the highways blue with rain
Toward one lamp, burning on those sentences.

"I want to get away somewhere and re-read Proust,"
Said an editor of *Newsweek* to a man on *Look*.
Dachaus with telephones, Siberias with bonuses.
One reads, as winter settles on the town,
The evening paper, in an Irving Place café.

EARLY WINTER

Memory of summer is winter's consciousness.
Sitting or walking or merely standing still,
Earning a living or watching the snow fall,
I am remembering the sun on sidewalks in a warmer place,
A small hotel and a dead girl's face;
I think of these in this higher altitude, staring West.

But the room is cold, the words in the books are cold;
And the question of whether we get what we ask for
Is absurd, unanswered by the sound of an unlatched door
Rattling in wind, or the sound of snow on roofs, or glare
Of the winter sun. What we have learned is not what we were told.
I watch the snow, feel for the heartbeat that is not there.

THE SMILES OF THE BATHERS

The smiles of the bathers fade as they leave the water,
And the lover feels sadness fall as it ends, as he leaves his love.
The scholar, closing his book as the midnight clocks strike, is
      hollow and old;
The pilot's relief on landing is no release.
These perfect and private things, walling us in, have imperfect
      and public endings—
Water and wind and flight, remembered words and the act of love
Are but interruptions. And the world, like a beast, impatient and
      quick,
Waits only for those that are dead. No death for you. You are
      involved.

THE COMING OF THE PLAGUE

September was when it began.
Locusts dying in the fields; our dogs
Silent, moving like shadows on a wall;
And strange worms crawling; flies of a kind
We had never seen before; huge vineyard moths;
Badgers and snakes, abandoning
Their holes in the field; the fruit gone rotten;
Queer fungi sprouting; the fields and woods
Covered with spiderwebs; black vapors
Rising from the earth—all these,
And more, began that fall. Ravens flew round
The hospital in pairs. Where there was water,
We could hear the sound of beating clothes
All through the night. We could not count
All the miscarriages, the quarrels, the jealousies.
And one day in a field I saw
A swarm of frogs, swollen and hideous,
Hundreds upon hundreds, sitting on each other,
Huddled together, silent, ominous,
And heard the sound of rushing wind.

THE PATIENT IS RALLYING

Difficult to recall an emotion that is dead,
Particularly so among these unbelieved fanfares
And admonitions from a camouflaged sky.

I should have remained burdened with destinations
Perhaps, or stayed quite drunk, or obeyed
The undertaker, who was fairly charming, after all.

Or was there a room like that one, worn
With our whispers, and a great tree blossoming
Outside blue windows, warm rain blowing in the night?

There seems to be some doubt. No doubt, however,
Of the chilled and empty tissues of the mind
—Cold, cold, a great gray winter entering—
Like spines of air, frozen in an ice cube.

HOMAGE TO ARTHUR WALEY

Seattle weather: it has rained for weeks in this town,
The dampness breeding moths and a gray summer.
I sit in the smoky room reading your book again,
My eyes raw, hearing the trains steaming below me
In the wet yard, and I wonder if you are still alive.
Turning the worn pages, reading once more:
"By misty waters and rainy sands, while the yellow dusk thickens."

WET THURSDAY

To Lindley Williams Hubbell

A stiff wind off the channel
Linking the chimney's mutterings
With rain; the shaken trees,
Mile after mile, greening the sand.
Turn to the fire as the afternoon

Turns gray. Then suddenly
The locked door opens without a sound,
Thunder shaking the sky, to usher in
A monstrous cat that seems
Far older than the oldest carp
In the waters under the earth,
Moving like a shadow over the floor
To warm its frozen paws
Before the fire. He turns,
Smiling into the woodbox,
And says, *"Felis libyca domestica*
They call me, kept by man for catching
Rats and mice. Of Eastern or
Egyptian origin. Now to be
Your spiteful and envenomed shadow. Here
Will I live out my nine and evil lives
Before your very interesting fire.
And the days, months, years, are endless."

Wind pounds along the coast.
The trees bend double to the sand.
The cat sleeps like an old campaigner
During this season of the long rains.

COLLOQUY

In the broken light, in owl weather,
Webs on the lawn where the leaves end,
I took the thin moon and the sky for cover
To pick the cat's brains and descend
A weedy hill. I found him groveling
Inside the summerhouse, a shadowed bulge,
Furred and somnolent.—"I bring,"
I said, "besides this dish of liver, and an edge
Of cheese, the customary torments,
And the usual wonder why we live
At all, and why the world thins out and perishes
As it has done for me, sieved
As I am toward silences. Where
Are we now? Do we know anything?"

—Now, on another night, his look endures.
"Give me the dish," he said.
I had his answer, wise as yours.

BACK

Much cry and little wool:
I have come back
As empty-handed as I went.

Although the woods were full,
And past the track
The heavy boughs were bent

Down to my knees with fruit
Ripe for a still life, I had meant
My trip as a search for stones.

But the beach was bare
Except for the drying bones
Of a fish, shells, an old wool

Shirt, a rubber boot,
A strip of lemon rind.
They were not what I had in mind:

It was merely stones.
Well, the days are full.
This day at least is spent.

Much cry and little wool:
I have come back
As empty-handed as I went.

THE CATS

What the cats do
To amuse themselves
When we are gone
I do not know.

They have the yard
And the fences
Of the neighbors,
And, occasionally,
May arrive at the door, miaowing,
With drops of milk
On their chins,
Waving their shining tails
And exhibiting signs of alarm
When the light inside
The refrigerator
Goes on. But what
They do all day
Remains a mystery.
It is a dull neighborhood.
Children scream
From the playground.
The cats go by in a bluish light.
At six o'clock the cats run out
When we come home from work
To greet us, crying, dancing,
After the long day.

ROUND

"Wondrous life!" cried Marvell at Appleton House.
Renan admired Jesus Christ "wholeheartedly."
But here dried ferns keep falling to the floor,
And something inside my head
Flaps like a worn-out blind. Royal Cortissoz is dead,
A blow to the *Herald-Tribune*. A closet mouse
Rattles the wrapper on the breakfast food. Renan
Admired Jesus Christ "wholeheartedly."

Flaps like a worn-out blind. Cézanne
Would break out in the quiet streets of Aix
And shout, "Le monde, c'est terrible!" Royal
Cortissoz is dead. And something inside my head
Flaps like a worn-out blind. The soil
In which the ferns are dying needs more Vigoro.
There is no twilight on the moon, no mist or rain,
No hail or snow, no life. Here in this house

Dried ferns keep falling to the floor, a mouse
Rattles the wrapper on the breakfast food. Cézanne
Would break out in the quiet streets and scream. Renan
Admired Jesus Christ "wholeheartedly." And something inside my head
Flaps like a worn-out blind. Royal Cortissoz is dead.
There is no twilight on the moon, no hail or snow.
One notes fresh desecrations of the portico.
"Wondrous life!" cried Marvell at Appleton House.

SARATOGA ENDING

1

Iron, sulphur, steam: the wastes
Of all resorts like this have left their traces.
Old canes and crutches line the walls. Light
Floods the room, stripped from the pool, broken
And shimmering like scales. Hidden
By curtains, women dry themselves
Before the fire and review
The service at hotels,
The ways of dying, ways of sleep,
The blind ataxia patient from New York,
And all the others who were here a year ago.

2

Visconti, mad with pain. Each day,
Two hundred drops of laudanum. Hagen, who writhes
With every step. The Count, a shrunken penis
And a monocle, dreaming of horses in the sun,
Covered with flies.—Last night I woke in sweat
To see my hands, white, curled upon the sheet
Like withered leaves. I thought of days
So many years ago, hauling driftwood up from the shore,
Waking at noon, the harbor birds following
Boats from the mainland. And then no thoughts at all.
Morphine at five. A cold dawn breaking. Rain.

3

I lie here in the dark, trying to remember
What my life has taught me. The driveway lights blur
In the rain. A rubber-tired metal cart goes by,

Followed by a nurse; and something rattles
Like glasses being removed after
A party is over and the guests have gone.
Test tubes, beakers, graduates, thermometers—
Companions of these years that I no longer count.
I reach for a cigarette and my fingers
Touch a tongue depressor that I use
As a bookmark; and all I know
Is the touch of this wood in the darkness, remembering
The warmth of one bright summer half a life ago—
A blue sky and a blinding sun, the face
Of one long dead who, high above the shore,
Looked down on waves across the sand, on rows of yellow jars
In which the lemon trees were ripening.

THE CONTOURS OF FIXATION

The stoned dogs crawl back through the blood,
Through the conquered weather, through the wet silk light,
To disenchanted masters who are not quite dead.

Like severed heads of a dead age
They gasp in the square, in the alleys of dusk.
Explanations are posted on the shattered walls.

The moon illuminates a cenotaph.
"All is insanity," the dogs conclude,
Yet the odor of blood has a certain appeal.

Their pain soaks eyes on every balcony.
"Forebear, refrain, be scrupulous"—dogs' admonitions,
Sad and redundant, paraphernalia of goodbye,

Hang in the sulphured air like promises of girls.
Then silence. Down the street the lights go dead.
One waits, one waits. And then the guns sound on another hill.

1926

The porchlight coming on again,
Early November, the dead leaves
Raked in piles, the wicker swing
Creaking. Across the lots
A phonograph is playing *Ja-Da*.

An orange moon. I see the lives
Of neighbors, mapped and marred
Like all the wars ahead, and R.
Insane, B. with his throat cut,
Fifteen years from now, in Omaha.

I did not know them then.
My airedale scratches at the door.
And I am back from seeing Milton Sills
And Doris Kenyon. Twelve years old.
The porchlight coming on again.

JOHN BERRYMAN

John Berryman was born in 1914 in McAlester, Oklahoma. He was educated at Columbia, Princeton, and Oxford, and has taught at several universities, including Iowa and Minnesota. His books of verse are The Disposessed, Homage to Mistress Bradstreet, 77 Dream Songs, *and* Berryman's Sonnets; *he is also the author of* Stephen Crane, *a critical biography.*

from 77 Dream Songs

14

Life, friends, is boring. We must not say so.
After all, the sky flashes, the great sea yearns,
we ourselves flash and yearn,
and moreover my mother told me as a boy
(repeatingly) 'Ever to confess you're bored
means you have no

Inner Resources.' I conclude now I have no
inner resources, because I am heavy bored.
Peoples bore me,
literature bores me, especially great literature,
Henry bores me, with his plights & gripes
as bad as achilles,

who loves people and valiant art, which bores me.
And the tranquil hills, & gin, look like a drag
and somehow a dog
has taken itself & its tail considerably away
into mountains or sea or sky, leaving
behind: me, wag.

15

Let us suppose, valleys & such ago,
one pal unwinding from his labours in
one bar of Chicago,
and this did actual happen. This was so.
And many graces are slipped, & many a sin
even that laid man low

but this will be remembered & told over,
that she was heard at last, haughtful & greasy,
to bawl in that low bar:
'You can biff me, you can bang me, get it you'll never.
I may be only a Polack   broad but I don't lay easy.
Kiss my ass, that's what you are.'

Women is better, braver. In a foehn of loss
entire, which too they hotter understand,
having had it,
we struggle. Some hang heavy on the sauce,
some invest in the past, one hides in the land.
Henry was not his favourite.

26

The glories of the world struck me, made me aria, once.
—What happen then, Mr Bones?
if be you cares to say.
—Henry. Henry became interested in women's bodies,
his loins were & were the   scene of stupendous achievement.
Stupor. Knees, dear. Pray.

All the knobs & softnesses of, my God,
the ducking & trouble it swarm on Henry,
at one time.
—What happen then, Mr Bones?
you seems excited-like.
—Fell Henry back into   the original crime: art, rime

besides a sense of others, my God, my God,
and a jealousy for the honour (alive) of his country,
what can get more odd?
and discontent with the thriving gangs & pride.
—What happen then, Mr Bones?
—I had a most marvellous   piece of luck. I died.

28   SNOW LINE

It was wet & white & swift and where I am
we don't know. It was dark and then
it isn't.
I wish the barker would come. There seems to be to eat
nothing. I am unusually tired.
I'm alone too.

If only the strange one with so few legs would come,
I'd say my prayers out of my mouth, as usual.
Where are his notes I loved?
There may be horribles; it's hard to tell.
The barker nips me but somehow I feel
he too is on my side.

I'm too alone. I see no end. If we could all
run, even that would be better. I am hungry.
The sun is not hot.
It's not a good position I am in.
If I had to do the whole thing over again
I wouldn't.

44

Tell it to the forest fire, tell it to the moon,
mention it in general to the moon
on the way down,
he's about to have his lady, permanent;
and this is the worst of all came ever sent
writhing Henry's way.

Ha ha, fifth column, quisling, genocide,
he held his hands & laught from side to side
a loverly time.
The berries & the rods left him alone less.
Thro' a race of water once I went: happiness.
I'll walk into the sky.

There the great flare & stench, O flying creatures,
surely will dim-dim? Bars will be closed.
No girl will again
conceive above your throes. A fine thunder peals
will with its friends and soon, from agony
put the fire out.

46

I am, outside. Incredible panic rules.
People are blowing and beating each other without mercy.
Drinks are boiling. Iced

drinks are boiling. The worse anyone feels, the worse
treated he is. Fools elect fools.
A harmless man at an intersection said, under his breath:
"Christ!"

That word, so spoken, affected the vision
of, when they trod to work next day, shopkeepers
who went & were fitted for glasses.
Enjoyed they then an appearance of love & law.
Millenia whift & waft—one, one—er, er . . .
Their glasses were taken from them, & they saw.

Man has undertaken the top job of all,
son fin. Good luck.
I myself walked at the funeral of tenderness.
Followed other deaths. Among the last,
like the memory of a lovely fuck,
was: *Do, ut des.*

47   APRIL FOOL'S DAY, OR, ST MARY OF EGYPT

—Thass a funny title, Mr Bones.
—When down she saw her feet, sweet fish, on the threshold,
she considered her fair shoulders
and all them hundreds who have held them, all
the more who to her mime thickened & maled
from the supple stage,

and seeing her feet, in a visit, side by side
paused on the sill of The Tomb, she shrank: 'No.
They are not worthy,
fondled by many' and rushed from The Crucified
back through her followers out of the city ho
across the suburbs, plucky

to dare my desert in her late daylight
of animals and sands. She fall prone.
Only wind whistled.
And forty-seven years went by like Einstein.
We celebrate her feast with our caps on,
whom God has not visited.

67

I don't operate often. When I do,
persons take note.
Nurses look amazed. They pale.
The patient is brought back to life, or so.
The reason I don't do this more (I quote)
is: I have a living to fail—

because of my wife & son—to keep from earning
—Mr Bones, I sees that.
They for these operations thanks you, what?
not pays you. —Right.
You have seldom been so understanding.
Now there is further a difficulty with the light:

I am obliged to perform in complete darkness
operations of great delicacy
on my self.
—Mr Bones, you terrifies me.
No wonder they don't pay you. Will you die?
—My
                    friend, I succeeded. Later.

74

Henry hates the world. What the world to Henry
did will not bear thought.
Feeling no pain,
Henry stabbed his arm and wrote a letter
explaining how bad it had been
in this world.

Old yellow, in a gown
might have made a difference, 'these lower beauties',
and chartreuse could have mattered

"Kyoto, Toledo,
Benares—the holy cities—
and Cambridge shimmering do not make up

for, well, the horror of unlove,
nor south from Paris driving in the Spring
to Siena and on . . .''

Pulling together Henry, somber Henry
woofed at things.
Spry disappointments of men
and vicing adorable children
miserable women, Henry mastered, Henry
tasting all the secret bits of life.

75

Turning it over, considering, like a madman
Henry put forth a book.
No harm resulted from this.
Neither the menstruating   stars (nor man) was moved
at once.
Bare dogs drew closer for a second look

and performed their friendly operations there.
Refreshed, the bark rejoiced.
Seasons went and came.
Leaves fell, but only a few.
Something remarkable about this
unshedding bulky bole-proud blue-green moist

thing made by savage & thoughtful
surviving Henry
began to strike the passers from despair
so that sore on their shoulders old men hoisted
six-foot sons and polished women called
small girls to dream awhile toward the flashing & bursting tree!

76 HENRY'S CONFESSION

Nothin very bad happen to me lately.
How you explain that? ——I explain that, Mr Bones,
terms o' your bafflin odd sobriety.

Sober as man can get, no girls, no telephones,
what could happen bad to Mr Bones?
—*If* life is a handkerchief sandwich,

in a modesty of death I join my father
who dared so long agone leave me.
A bullet on a concrete stoop
close by a smothering southern sea
spreadeagled on an island, by my knee.
—You is from hunger, Mr Bones,

I offers you this handkerchief, now set
your left foot by my right foot,
shoulder to shoulder, all that jazz,
arm in arm, by the beautiful sea,
hum a little, Mr Bones.
—I saw nobody coming, so I went instead.

77

Seedy Henry rose up shy in de world
& shaved & swung his barbells, duded Henry up
and p.a.'d poor thousands of persons on topics of grand
moment to Henry, ah to those less & none.
Wif a book of his in either hand
he is stript down to move on.

—Come away, Mr Bones.

—Henry is tired of the winter,
& haircuts, & a squeamish comfy   ruin-prone proud national
     mind,   & Spring (in the city so called).
Henry likes Fall.
Hé would be prepared to líve in a world of Fáll
for ever, impenitent Henry.
But the snows and summers grieve & dream;

thése fierce & airy occupations, and love,
raved away so many of Henry's years
it is a wonder that, with in each hand
one of his own mad books and all,
ancient fires for eyes, his head full
& his heart full, he's making ready to move on.

ROBERT LOWELL

Robert Lowell was born in 1917 in Boston, Massachusetts. He was educated at Kenyon and Harvard, and has taught at various universities. He was a conscientious objector during World War II and spent a year in prison. He lives with his wife and daughter in New York City. His books of verse are Land of Unlikeness, Lord Weary's Castle, The Mills of the Kavanaughs, Life Studies, Imitations, For the Union Dead, *and* Near the Ocean. *He has translated* Phaedra *and is the author of a play,* The Old Glory.

MEMORIES OF WEST STREET AND LEPKE

Only teaching on Tuesdays, book-worming
in pajamas fresh from the washer each morning,
I hog a whole house on Boston's
"hardly passionate Marlborough Street,"
where even the man
scavenging filth in the back alley trash cans,
has two children, a beach wagon, a helpmate,
and is a "young Republican."
I have a nine months' daughter,
young enough to be my granddaughter.
Like the sun she rises in her flame-flamingo infants' wear.

These are the tranquilized *Fifties,*
and I am forty. Ought I to regret my seedtime?
I was a fire-breathing Catholic C.O.,
and made my manic statement,
telling off the state and president, and then
sat waiting sentence in the bull pen
beside a Negro boy with curlicues
of marijuana in his hair.

Given a year,
I walked on the roof of the West Street Jail, a short
enclosure like my school soccer court,
and saw the Hudson River once a day
through sooty clothesline entanglements
and bleaching khaki tenements.
Strolling, I yammered metaphysics with Abramowitz,
a jaundice-yellow ("it's really tan")
and fly-weight pacifist,
so vegetarian,
he wore rope shoes and preferred fallen fruit.
He tried to convert Bioff and Brown,
the Hollywood pimps, to his diet.
Hairy, muscular, suburban,
wearing chocolate double-breasted suits,
they blew their tops and beat him black and blue.

I was so out of things, I'd never heard
of the Jehovah's Witnesses.
"Are you a C.O.?" I asked a fellow jailbird.

"No," he answered, "I'm a J.W."
He taught me the "hospital tuck,"
and pointed out the T shirted back
of *Murder Incorporated's* Czar Lepke,
there piling towels on a rack,
or dawdling off to his little segregated cell full
of things forbidden the common man:
a portable radio, a dresser, two toy American
flags tied together with a ribbon of Easter palm.
Flabby, bald, lobotomized,
he drifted in a sheepish calm,
where no agonizing reappraisal
jarred his concentration on the electric chair—
hanging like an oasis in his air
of lost connections. . . .

FOR THE UNION DEAD

   "Relinquunt Omnia Servare Rem Publicam."

The old South Boston Aquarium stands
in a Sahara of snow now. Its broken windows are boarded.
The bronze weathervane cod has lost half its scales.
The airy tanks are dry.

Once my nose crawled like a snail on the glass;
my hand tingled
to burst the bubbles
drifting from the noses of the cowed, compliant fish.

My hand draws back. I often sigh still
for the dark downward and vegetating kingdom
of the fish and reptile. One morning last March,
I pressed against the new barbed and galvanized

fence on the Boston Common. Behind their cage,
yellow dinosaur steamshovels were grunting
as they cropped up tons of mush and grass
to gouge their underworld garage.

Parking spaces luxuriate like civic
sandpiles in the heart of Boston.

A girdle of orange, Puritan-pumpkin colored girders
braces the tingling Statehouse,

shaking over the excavations, as it faces Colonel Shaw
and his bell-cheeked Negro infantry
on St. Gauden's shaking Civil War relief,
propped by a plank splint against the garage's earthquake.

Two months after marching through Boston,
half the regiment was dead;
at the dedication,
William James could almost hear the bronze Negroes breathe.

Their monument sticks like a fishbone
in the city's throat.
Its Colonel is as lean
as a compass-needle.

He has an angry wrenlike vigilance,
a greyhound's gentle tautness;
he seems to wince at pleasure,
and suffocate for privacy.

He is out of bounds now. He rejoices in man's lovely,
peculiar power to choose life and die—
when he leads his black soldiers to death,
he cannot bend his back.

On a thousand small town New England greens,
the old white churches hold their air
of sparse, sincere rebellion; frayed flags
quilt the graveyards of the Grand Army of the Republic.

The stone statues of the abstract Union Soldier
grow slimmer and younger each year—
wasp-wasted, they doze over muskets
and muse through their sideburns . . .

Shaw's father wanted no monument
except the ditch,
where his son's body was thrown
and lost with his "niggers."

The ditch is nearer.
There are no statues for the last war here;
on Boyleston Street, a commercial photograph
shows Hiroshima boiling

over a Mosler Safe, the "Rock of Ages"
that survived the blast. Space is nearer.
When I crouch to my television set,
the drained faces of Negro school-children rise like balloons.

Colonel Shaw
is riding on his bubble,
he waits
for the blessèd break.

The Aquarium is gone. Everywhere,
giant finned cars nose forward like fish;
a savage servility
slides by on grease.

THE MOUTH OF THE HUDSON

(For Esther Brooks)

A single man stands like a bird-watcher,
and scuffles the pepper and salt snow
from a discarded, gray
Westinghouse Electric cable drum.
He cannot discover America by counting
the chains of condemned freight-trains
from thirty states. They jolt and jar
and junk in the siding below him.
He has trouble with his balance.
His eyes drop,
and he drifts with the wild ice
ticking seaward down the Hudson,
like the blank sides of a jig-saw puzzle.

The ice ticks seaward like a clock.
A Negro toasts
wheat-seeds over the coke-fumes

of a punctured barrel.
Chemical air
sweeps in from New Jersey,
and smells of coffee.

Across the river,
ledges of suburban factories tan
in the sulphur-yellow sun
of the unforgivable landscape.

JULY IN WASHINGTON

The stiff spokes of this wheel
touch the sore spots of the earth.

On the Potomac, swan-white
power launches keep breasting the sulphurous wave.

Otters slide and dive and slick back their hair,
raccoons clean their meat in the creek.

On the circles, green statues ride like South American
liberators above the breeding vegetation—

prongs and spearheads of some equatorial
backland that will inherit the globe.

The elect, the elected . . . they come here bright as dimes,
and die dishevelled and soft.

We cannot name their names, or number their dates—
circle on circle, like rings on a tree—

but we wish the river had another shore,
some further range of delectable mountains,

distant hills powdered blue as a girl's eyelid.
It seems the least little shove would land us there,

that only the slightest repugnance of our bodies
we no longer control could drag us back.

BLACK SPRING

A half-holiday for the burial. Of course, they punish
the provincial copper bells for hours;
terribly the nose tilts up like a tallow candle
from the coffin. Does it wish to draw breath
from its torso in a mourning suit? The last snow
fell somberly—white, then the roads were bread-crumbed with
        pebbles.
Poor winter, honeycombed with debts,
poured to corruption. Now the dumb, black springtime
must look into the chilly eye . . . from under the mould
on the roof-shingles, the liquid oatmeal
of the roads, the green stubble of life
on our faces! High in the splinter elm,
shrill the annual fledglings with their spikey necks.
They say to man that his road is mud,
his luck is rutted—there is nothing
sorrier than the marriage of two deaths.

Annensky

SPARROW HILLS

Like water pouring from a pitcher, my mouth on your nipples!
Not always. The summer well runs dry.
Not for long the dust of our stamping feet, encore on encore
from the saxes in the casino's midnight gazebo.

I've heard of age—its obese warbling!
When no wave will clap hands to the stars.
If they speak, you doubt it. No face in the meadows,
no heart in the pools, no god among the pines.

Split your soul like wood. Let today froth from your mouth.
It's the world's noontide. Have you no eyes for it?
Look, conception bubbles from the bleached fallows;
fir-cones, woodpeckers, clouds, pine-needles, heat.

Here the city's trolley tracks give out.
Further, you must put up with peeled pine. The trolley poles are
        detached.

Further, it's Sunday. Boughs screwed loose for the picnic bonfire,
playing tag in your bra.

"The world is always like this," say the woods,
as they mix the midday glare, Whitsunday and walking.
All's planned with checkerberry couches, inspired with clearings—
the piebald clouds spill down on us like a country woman's house-dress.

Pasternak

SEPTEMBER

The much-hugged rag-doll is oozing cotton from her ruined figure.
Unforgetting September cannot hide its peroxide curls of leaf.
Isn't it time to board up the summer house?
The carpenter's gavel pounds for new and naked roof-ribs.

The moment the sun rises, it disappears.
Last night the marsh by the swimming pool shivered with fever;
the last bell-flowers waste under the rheumatic dewdrop,
a dirty lilac stain souses the birches.

The woods are discomforted. The animals
head for the snow-stopped bear holes in the fairy tales;
behind the black park fences, tree trunks and pillars
form columns like a newspaper's death column.

The thinning birchwood has not ceased to water its color—
more and more watery, its once regal shade.
Summer keeps mumbling, "I am only a few months old.
A lifetime of looking back, what shall I do with it?

"I've so many mind-bruises, I should give up playing.
They are like birds in the bushes, mushrooms on the lawn.
Now we have begun to paper our horizon with them
to fog out each other's distance."

Stricken with polio, Summer, *le roi soleil,*
hears the gods' Homeric laughter from the dignitaries' box—
with the same agony, the country house
stares forward, hallucinated, at the road to the metropolis.

Pasternak

SYLVIA

Sylvia, do you remember the minutes
in this life overhung by death,
when beauty flamed
through your shy, serious meditations,
and you leapt beyond the limits
of girlhood?

Wild,
lightning-eyed child,
your incessant singing
shook the mirror-bright cobbles,
and even the parlor,
shuttered from summer,
where you sat at your sewing
and such girlish things—
happy enough to catch
at the future's blurred offer.
It was the great May,
and this is how you spent your day.

I could forget
the fascinating studies in my bolted room,
where my life was burning out,
and the heat
of my writings made the letters wriggle and melt
under drops of sweat.
Sometimes, I lolled on the railing of my father's house,
and pricked up my ears, and heard the noise
of your voice
and your hand run
to the hum of the monotonous loom.

I marvelled at the composed sky,
the little sun-gilded dust-paths,
and the gardens, running high
and half out of sight,
with the mountains on one side and the Adriatic
far off to the right.
How can human tongue
say what I felt?

What tremendous meaning, supposing,
and light-heartedness, my Sylvia!
What a Marie-Antoinette
stage-set
for life and its limits!
When I think of that great puff of pride,
sour constrictions choke me,
I turn aside to deride
my chances wrenched into misadventure.
Nature, harsh Nature,
why will you not pay
your promise today?
Why have you set
your children a bird-net?

Even before the Sirocco had sucked
the sap from the grass,
some undiagnosable disease
struck you and broke you—
you died, child,
and never saw your life flower,
or your flower plucked
by young men courting you
and arguing love
on the long Sunday walk—
their heads turned and lost
in your quick, shy talk.

Thus hope subsided
little by little;
fate decided
I was never to flower.
Hope, dear comrade of my shrinking summer,
how little you could keep
your color! You make me weep.
Is this your world?
These, its diversions, its infatuations,
its accomplishments, its sensations,
we used to unravel together?
You broke before the first
advance of truth;
the grave
was the final, shining milestone

you had always been pointing to
with such insistence
in the undistinguishable distance.

Leopardi: A Silvia

NEWS FROM MOUNT AMIATA

I

Come night,
the ugly weather's fire-cracker simmer
will deepen to the gruff buzz of beehives.
Termites tunnel the public room's rafters to sawdust,
an odor of bruised melons oozes from the floor.
A sick smoke lifts from the elf-huts and funghi of the valley—
like an eagle it climbs our mountain's bald cone,
and soils the windows.
I drag my table to the window,
and write to you—
here on this mountain, in this beehive cell
on the globe rocketed through space.
My letter is a paper hoop.
When I break through it, you will be imprisoned.

Here mildew sprouts like grass from the floor,
the canary cage is hooded with dirty green serge,
chestnuts explode on the grate.
Outside, it's raining.
There you are legendary.
Any legend falls short, if it confine you,
your gold-gated icon unfolding on gold.

II

Magnesium flares light up the hidden summits;
but the narrow feudal streets below are too dark
for the caravan of black donkeys kicking up sparks.

You are devoted to precarious
sentiments and sediment—blackened architecture;
rectangular courtyards centered
on bottomless wells. You are led
by the sinister wings of nightbirds,

the infinite pit, the luminous gape of the galaxies—
all their sleight of hand and torture.
But the step that carries out into darkness
comes from a man going alone,
who sees nothing but the nearest light-chinked shutter.
The stars' pattern is too deep for him,
atmospheric ivy only chokes his darkness,
his campanile shuts its eye at two o'clock.

III

Here on this mountain,
the world has no custom-barriers.
Let tomorrow be colder, let the north wind
shatter the stringy ribbons of old Missals,
the sandstone bastion of the barbarians.
When our sensations have no self-assurance,
everything must be a lens.
Then the polar winds will return clearer,
and convert us to our chains, the chains of the possible.

IV

Today, the monotonous oratory of the dead,
ashes, lethargic winds—
a reluctant trickle drips
from the thatched huts.
Time is water.
The rain rains down black letters—
a *contemptu mundi!* What part of me does it bring you?

Now at this late hour
of my watch and your endless, prodigal sleep,
my tiny straw city is breaking up.
The porcupine sips a quill of mercy.

Montale: Notizie dall' Amiata

THE MAGNOLIA'S SHADOW

The shadow of the dwarf magnolia
is a scarecrow now that the turkey-wattle
blossoms are blown. Like something wired,
the cicada vibrates at timed intervals.

It is no longer the Easter of voices in unison,
Clizia, the season of the infinite deity,
who devours his faithful, then revives them in blood.
It was more facile to expend one's self,
and die at the first wing-flutter, at the first
hectic rumbling from the adversary—a nursery game.
The hard way begins now; but not for you,
eaten by sunlight, rooted—yet a fragile thrush,
flying high over those frogskin mudbanks,
not for you to whom zenith, nadir, capricorn
and cancer rush together, so that the war may be
inside you, and in your adorer, who sees on you
the stigmata of the Bridegroom—the shiver
of snowfall doesn't jar you. Others
shy backwards and hold back. The artisan's
subtle file shall be silent; the hollow husk
of the singer shall be powdered glass
under your feet; the shadow is neutral.
It's autumn, it's winter, it's the other
side of the sky, that leads you—there
I break water, a fish left high and dry
under the new moon.
                    Goodbye.

                    Montale: L'ombra della magnolia

THE COASTGUARD HOUSE

A death-cell? The shack of the coastguards
is a box over the drop to the breakers;
it waits for you without an owner,
ever since the mob of your thoughts
bullied a welcome,
and stayed on there, unrequited.
You didn't take it to heart.

For years the sirocco gunned the dead stucco with sand;
the sound of your laugh is a jagged coughing;
the compass, a pin-head, spins at random;
the dizzy dice screw up the odds.

You haven't taken my possession to heart;
another time has thinned your nostalgia;
a thread peels from the spool.

I hold an end of it,
but the house balks backward;
its sea-green weathercock
creaks and caws without pity.
I keep one end of the thread,
but you house alone
and hold your hollow breath there in the dark.

Oh the derelict horizon,
sunless except for the
orange hull of a lonely, drudging tanker!
The breakers bubble on the dead-drop.
You haven't taken my one night's possession to heart;
I have no way of knowing
who forces an entrance.

Montale: La Casa dei doganieri

THE EEL

I

The eel, the North Sea siren,
who leaves dead-pan Icelandic gods
and the Baltic for our Mediterranean,
our estuaries, our rivers—
who lances through their profound places,
and flinty portages, from branch to branch,
twig to twig, thinning down now,
ever snaking inward, worming
for the granite's heartland, threading
delicate capillaries of slime—
and in the Romagna one morning
the blaze of the chestnut blossoms
ignites its smudge in the dead water
pooled from chiselings
of the Apennines . . .

the eel, a whipstock, a Roman candle,
love's arrow on earth, which only
reaches the paradise of fecundity
through our gullies and fiery, charred streams;
a green spirit, potent only
where desolation and arson burn;
a spark that says everything
begins where everything is clinker;
this buried rainbow, this iris, twin sister
of the one you set in your eye's target center
to shine on the sons of men,
on us, up to our gills in your life-giving mud—
can you call her *Sister?*

II

If they called you a fox,
it will be for your monstrous hurtle,
your sprint that parts and unites,
that kicks up and freshens the gravel,
(your black lace balcony, overlooking
the home for deformed children, a meadow,
and a tree, where my carved name quivers,
happy, humble, defeated)—
or perhaps only for the phosphorescent wake
of your almond eyes,
for the craft of your alert panic,
for the annihilation of dishevelled feathers
in your child's hand's python hug;
if they have likened you to the blond lioness,
to the avaricious demon of the undergrowth
(and why not to the filthy fish
that electrocutes, the torpedo fish?)
it is perhaps because the blind
have not seen the wings
on your delectable shoulder-blades,
because the blind haven't shot for
your forehead's luminous target,
the furrow I pricked there in blood,
cross, chrism, incantation, —and
prayer—damnation, salvation;
if they can only think of you
as a weasel or a woman,

with whom can I share my discovery,
where bury the gold I carry,
the red-hot, pot-bellied furnace raging
inside me, when, leaving me,
you turn up stairs?

Montale: L'anguilla: Se t'hanno assomigliato

THE POET AT SEVEN

When the timeless, daily, tedious affair
was over, his Mother shut
her Bible; her nose was in the air;
from her summit
of righteousness, she could not see the boy:
his lumpy forehead knotted
with turmoil, his soul returned to its vomit.

All day he would sweat obedience.
He was very intelligent, but wrung,
and every now and then a sudden jerk
showed dark hypocrisies at work.
He would clap his hands on his rump,
and strut where the gloom of the hallway rotted
the hot curtains. He stuck out his tongue,
clenched his eyes shut, and saw dots.
A terrace gave on the twilight;
one used to see him up there in the lamplight,
sulking on the railing
under an abyss of air
which hung from the roof. His worst block
was the stultifying slump
of mid-summer—he would lock
himself up in the toilet and inhale
its freshness; there he could breathe.

When winter snowed under the breath of flowers,
and the moon blanched the little bower
behind the house, he would crawl
to the foot of the wall

and lie with his eyeballs squeezed to his arm,
dreaming of some dark revelation,
or listening to the legions of termites swarm
in the horny espaliers. As for compassion,
the only children he could speak to
were creepy, abstracted boys, who hid
match-stick thin fingers yellow and black with mud
under rags stuck with diarrhea.
Their dull eyes drooled on their dull cheeks,
they spoke with the selflessness of morons.
His Mother was terrified,
she thought they were losing caste. This was good—
she had the true blue look that lied.

At seven he was making novels
about life in the Sahara,
where ravished Liberty had fled—
sunrises, buffaloes, jungle, savannahs!
For his facts, he used illustrated weeklies,
and blushed at the rotogravures of naked, red
Hawaiian girls dancing.
A little eight year old tomboy,
the daughter of the next door workers,
came, brown-eyed, terrible,
in a print dress. Brutal and in the know,
she would jump on his back,
and ride him like a buffalo,
and shake out her hair.

Wallowing below
her once, he bit her crotch—
she never wore bloomers—
kicked and scratched, he carried back
the taste of her buttocks to his bedroom.

What he feared most
were the sticky, lost December Sundays,
when he used to stand with his hair gummed back
at a little mahogony stand, and hold
a Bible pocked with cabbage-green mould.
Each night in his alcove, he had dreams.
He despised God, the National Guard,
and the triple drum-beat

of the town-crier calling up the conscripts.
He loved the swearing
workers, when they crowded back, black
in the theatrical twilight to their wards.
He felt clean
when he filled his lungs with the smell—
half hay fever, half iodine—
of the wheat,
he watched its public golden tassels swell
and steam in the heat,
then sink back calm.

What he liked best were dark things:
the acrid, dank rings
on the ceiling, and the high,
bluish plaster, as bald as the sky
in his bare bedroom, where he could close
the shutters and lose
his world for hundreds of hours,
mooning doggedly
over his novel, endlessly
expanding with jaundiced skies,
drowned vegetation, and carnations
that flashed like raw flesh
in the underwater green
of the jungle starred with flowers—
dizziness, mania, revulsions, pity!
Often the town playground
below him grew loud with children;
the wind brought him their voices,
and he lay alone on pieces of unbleached canvas,
violently breaking into sail.

Rimbaud: Les poètes de sept ans

ON FREEDOM IN POETRY

My two rules in writing free verse are that I don't ever scan a line while I am composing it, and that the words must fall into lines. In the back of my head somewhere I am conscious that rhythm is usually made up of iambics, trochees, anapests and spondees. I think I feel the presence of these four feet when I write them, but the law and opportunity is that I am completely free. Complete freedom though is something I've used in very few poems. Usually even in more or less free verse I set down restrictions: stanzas with the same number of lines (most often quatrains), rhymes or off-rhymes sometimes at random, sometimes with a fixed place in the stanza, lines of a more or less uniform length on the page, sometimes the lines are accentual and *will* scan, though this is a meter that allows great license, and the accenting of a syllable is often arbitrary. The joy and strength of unscanned verse is that it can be as natural as conversation or prose, or can follow the rhythm of the ear that knows no measure. Yet often a poem only becomes a poem and worth writing because it has struggled with fixed meters and rhymes. I can't understand how any poet, who has written both metered and unmetered poems, would be willing to settle for one and give up the other.

I have never worked my intuitions on this subject into a theory. When I drop one style of writing, it's usually a surprise to me.

An afterthought—the glory of free verse is in those poems that would be thoroughly marred and would indeed be inconceivable in meter—first the translations of the Bible: Job, the Song of Solomon, the best psalms, David's Lament, supreme poems, written when their translators merely intended prose and were forced by the structure of their originals to write poetry; then Whitman, whose Song of Myself is the only important long nineteenth century American poem, then Lawrence's bird and animal poems, Pound's Cantos, and most of William Carlos Williams. These works would have lost all their greatness and possibility in meter.

Robert Lowell
Castine, Maine
June 25, 1967

DENISE LEVERTOV

Denise Levertov was born in 1923, in Ilford, Essex, England, and was educated at home. She is married to the novelist Mitchell Goodman, and they live with their son in New York City and Maine. Her books of verse are Here and Now, Overland to the Islands, With Eyes at the Back of Our Heads, The Jacob's Ladder, O Taste and See, *and* The Sorrow Dance.

LOSING TRACK

Long after you have swung back
away from me
I think you are still with me:

you come in close to the shore
on the tide
and nudge me awake the way

a boat adrift nudges the pier:
am I a pier
half-in half-out of the water?

and in the pleasure of that communion
I lose track,
the moon I watch goes down, the

tide swings you away before
I know I'm
alone again long since,

mud sucking at gray and black
timbers of me,
a light growth of green dreams drying.

THE DEPTHS

When the white fog burns off,
the abyss of everlasting light
is revealed. The last cobwebs
of fog in the
black firtrees are flakes
of white ash in the world's hearth.

Cold of the sea is counterpart
to this great fire. Plunging
out of the burning cold of ocean
we enter an ocean of intense
noon. Sacred salt
sparkles on our bodies.

After mist has wrapped us again
in fine wool, may the taste of salt
recall to us the great depths about us.

THE BREATHING

An absolute
patience.
Trees stand
up to their knees in
fog. The fog
slowly flows
uphill.
      White
cobwebs, the grass
leaning where deer
have looked for apples.
The woods
from brook to where
the top of the hill looks
over the fog, send up
not one bird.
So absolute, it is
no other than
happiness itself, a breathing
too quiet to hear.

COME INTO ANIMAL PRESENCE

Come into animal presence.
No man is so guileless as
the serpent. The lonely white
rabbit on the roof is a star
twitching its ears at the rain.
The llama intricately
folding its hind legs to be seated
not disdains but mildly
disregards human approval.

What joy when the insouciant
armadillo glances at us and doesn't
quicken his trotting
across the track into the palm brush.

What is this joy? That no animal
falters, but knows what it must do?
That the snake has no blemish,
that the rabbit inspects his strange surroundings
in white star-silence? The llama
rests in dignity, the armadillo
has some intention to pursue in the palm-forest.
Those who were sacred have remained so,
holiness does not dissolve, it is a presence
of bronze, only the sight that saw it
faltered and turned from it.
An old joy returns in holy presence.

'...ELSE A GREAT PRINCE IN PRISON LIES'

All that blesses the step of the antelope
all the grace a giraffe lifts to the highest leaves
all steadfastness and pleasant gazing, alien to ennui,
dwell secretly behind man's misery.

Animal face, when the lines
of human fear, knots of a net, become transparent
and your brilliant eyes and velvet muzzle
are revealed, who shall say you are not the face of a man?

In the dense light of wakened flesh
animal man is a prince. As from alabaster
a lucency animates him from heel to forehead.
Then his shadows are deep and not gray.

THE PRESENCE

To the house on the grassy hill
where rams rub their horns against the porch

and your bare feet on the floors of silence
speak in rhymed stanzas to the furniture,

solemn chests of drawers and heavy chairs
blinking in the sun you have let in!

Before I enter the rooms of your solitude
in my living form, trailing my shadow,

I shall have come unseen. Upstairs and down with you
and out across road and rocks to the river

to drink the cold spray. You will believe
a bird flew by the window, a wandering bee

buzzed in the hallway, a wind
rippled the bronze grasses. Or will you

know who it is?

THE SECRET

Two girls discover
the secret of life
in a sudden line of
poetry.

I who don't know the
secret wrote
the line. They
told me

(through a third person)
they had found it
but not what it was
not even

what line it was. No doubt
by now, more than a week
later, they have forgotten
the secret,

the line, the name of
the poem. I love them
for finding what
I can't find,

and for loving me
for the line I wrote,
and for forgetting it
so that

a thousand times, till death
finds them, they may
discover it again, in other
lines

in other
happenings. And for
wanting to know it,
for

assuming there is
such a secret, yes,
for that
most of all.

THE NOVICES

They enter the bare wood, drawn
by a clear-obscure summons they fear
and have no choice but to heed.

A rustling underfoot, a
long trail to go, the thornbushes grow
across the dwindling paths.

Until the small clearing, where they
anticipate violence, knowing some rite
to be performed, and compelled to it.

The man moves forward, the boy
sees what he means to do: from an oaktree
a chain runs at an angle into earth

and they pit themselves to uproot it,
dogged and frightened, to pull the iron
out of the earth's heart.

But from the further depths of the wood
as they strain and weigh on the great chain
appears the spirit,

the wood-demon who summoned them.
And he is not bestial, not fierce
but an old woodsman,

gnarled, shabby, smelling of smoke and sweat,
of a bear's height and shambling like a bear.
Yet his presence is a spirit's presence

and awe takes their breath.
Gentle and rough, laughing a little,
he makes his will known:

not for an act of force he called them,
for no rite of obscure violence
but that they might look about them

and see intricate branch and bark,
stars of moss and the old scars
left by dead men's saws,

and not ask what that chain was.
To leave the open fields
and enter the forest,

that was the rite.
Knowing there was mystery, they could go.
Go back now! And he receded

among the multitude of forms,
the twists and shadows they saw now, listening
to the hum of the world's wood.

OUR BODIES

Our bodies, still young under
the engraved anxiety of our
faces, and innocently

more expressive than faces:
nipples, navel, and pubic hair
make anyway a

sort of face: or taking
the rounded shadows at
breast, buttock, balls,

the plump of my belly, the
hollow of your
groin, as a constellation,

how it leans from earth to
dawn in a gesture of
play and

wise compassion—
nothing like this
comes to pass
in eyes or wistful
mouths.
      I have

a line or groove I love
runs down
my body from breastbone
to waist. It speaks of
eagerness, of
distance.

      Your long back,
the sand color and
how the bones show, say

what sky after sunset
almost white
over a deep woods to which

rooks are homing, says.

THE ABSENCE

Here I lie asleep
or maybe I'm awake yet—

not alone—and yet
it seems by moonlight

I'm alone, hardly hearing
a breath beside me. And those shadows

on the wall indeed are
not shadows but the
featherweight dancing echoes
of headlights sliding by.

Here I lie and wonder
what it is has left me, what element.
I can't remember my dreams
by morning.
            Maybe, as Frazer tells,

my soul flew out in that moment
of almost-sleep.   If it should go
back to the scenes and times
of its wars and losses

how would I ever lure it
back? It would

be looking for something, it would be
too concentrated to hear me.

O moon, watching everything,
delay it in the garden among the white flowers

until the cold air before sunrise
makes it glad to come back to me through the screens.

SONG FOR ISHTAR

The moon is a sow
and grunts in my throat
Her great shining shines through me
so the mud of my hollow gleams
and breaks in silver bubbles

She is a sow
and I a pig and a poet

When she opens her white
lips to devour me I bite back
and laughter rocks the moon

In the black of desire
we rock and grunt, grunt and
shine

THE OLD ADAM

A photo of someone else's childhood,
a garden in another country—world
he had no part in and has no power to imagine:

yet the old man who has failed his memory
keens over the picture—'Them happy days—
gone—gone for ever!'—glad for a moment to suppose

a focus for unspent grieving, his floating
sense of loss.
He wanders

asking the day of the week, the time,
over and over the wrong questions.
Missing his way in the streets

he acts out
the bent of his life,
the lost way

never looked for, life
unlived, of which he is dying
very slowly.

'A man,'
says his son, 'who never
made a right move in all his life.' A man

who thought **the dollar was sweet** and
couldn't make a buck, riding the subway
year after year to untasted sweetness,

loving his sons obscurely, incurious
who they were, these men, his sons—
a shadow of love, for love longs

to know the beloved, and a light goes with it
into the dark mineshafts of feeling . . . A man
who now, without knowing,

in endless concern for the smallest certainties,
looking again and again at a paid bill,
inquiring again and again, 'When was I here last?'

asks what it's too late to ask:
'Where is my life? Where is my life?
What have I done with my life?'

PARTIAL RESEMBLANCE

A doll's hair concealing
an eggshell skull delicately
throbbing, within which
maggots in voluptuous unrest

jostle and shrug. Oh, Eileen, my
big doll, your gold hair was
not more sunny than this
human fur, but
your head was
radiant in its emptiness,
a small clean room.

Her warm and rosy mouth
is telling lies—she would
believe them if she could believe:
her pretty eyes
search out corruption. Oh, Eileen,
how kindly your silence was, and
what virtue
shone in the opening and shutting of your
ingenious blindness.

THE MUTES

Those groans men use
passing a woman on the street
or on the steps of the subway

to tell her she is a female
and their flesh knows it,

are they a sort of tune,
an ugly enough song, sung
by a bird with a slit tongue

but meant for music?

Or are they the muffled roaring
of deafmutes trapped in a building that is
slowly filling with smoke?

Perhaps both.

Such men most often
look as if groan were all they could do,
yet a woman, in spite of herself,

knows it's a tribute:
if she were lacking all grace
they'd pass her in silence:

so it's not only to say she's
a warm hole. It's a word

in grief-language, nothing to do with
primitive, not an ur-language;
language stricken, sickened, cast down

in decrepitude. She wants to
throw the tribute away, dis-
gusted, and can't,

it goes on buzzing in her ear,
it changes the pace of her walk,
the torn posters in echoing corridors

spell it out, it
quakes and gnashes as the train comes in.
Her pulse sullenly

had picked up speed,
but the cars slow down and
jar to a stop while her understanding

keeps on translating:
'Life after life after life goes by

without poetry,
without seemliness,
without love.'

BEDTIME

We are a meadow where the bees hum,
mind and body are almost one

as the fire snaps in the stove
and our eyes close,

and mouth to mouth, the covers
pulled over our shoulders,

we drowse as horses drowse afield,
in accord; though the fall cold

surrounds our warm bed, and though
by day we are singular and often lonely.

TWO VARIATIONS

i   Enquiry

You who go out on schedule
to kill, do you know
there are eyes that watch you,
eyes whose lids you burned off,
that see you eat your steak
and buy your girlflesh
and sell your PX goods
and sleep?
She is not old,
she whose eyes
know you.
She will outlast you.
She saw
her five young children
writhe and die;
in that hour
she began to watch you,
she whose eyes are open forever.

ii   The Seeing

Hands over my eyes I see
blood and the little bones;
or when a blanket covers
the sockets I see the
weave; at night the glare softens
but I have power now
to see there is only gray
on gray, the sleepers, the

altar. I see the living
and the dead; the dead are
as if alive, the mouth of
my youngest son pulls my
breast, but there is no milk, he
is a ghost; through his flesh
I see the dying of those
said to be alive, they
eat rice and speak to me but
I see dull death in them
and while they speak I see
myself on my mat, body
and eyes, eyes that see a
hand in the unclouded sky,
a human hand, release
wet fire, the rain that gave
my eyes their vigilance.

A DAY BEGINS

A headless squirrel, some blood
oozing from the unevenly
chewed-off neck

lies in rainsweet grass
near the woodshed door.
Down the driveway

the first irises
have opened since dawn,
ethereal, their mauve

almost a transparent gray,
their dark veins
bruise-blue.

SOME NOTES ON ORGANIC FORM

For me, back of the idea of organic form is the concept that there is a form in all things (and in our experience) which the poet can discover and reveal. There are no doubt temperamental differences between poets who use prescribed forms and those who look for new ones—people who need a tight schedule to get anything done, and people who have to have a free hand—but the difference in their conception of "content" or "reality" is functionally more important. On the one hand is the idea that content, reality, experience, is essentially fluid and must be given form; on the other, this sense of seeking out inherent, though not immediately apparent, form. Gerard Manley Hopkins invented the word inscape to denote intrinsic form, the pattern of essential characteristics both in single objects and (what is more interesting) in objects in a state of relation to each other; and the word instress to denote the experiencing of the perception of inscape, the apperception of inscape. In thinking of the process of poetry as I know it, I extend the use of these words, which he seems to have used mainly in reference to sensory phenomena, to include intellectual and emotional experience as well; I would speak of the inscape of an experience (which might be composed of any and all of these elements, including the sensory) or of the inscape of a sequence or constellation of experiences.

A partial definition, then, of organic poetry might be that it is a method of apperception, i.e., of recognizing what we perceive, and is based on an intuition of an order, a form beyond forms, in which forms partake, and of which man's creative works are analogies, resemblances, natural allegories. Such poetry is exploratory.

How does one go about such a poetry? I think it's like this: First there must be an experience, a sequence or constellation of perceptions of sufficient interest, felt by the poet intensely enough to demand of him their equivalence in words: he is brought to speech. Suppose there's the sight of the sky through a dusty window, birds and clouds and bits of paper flying through the sky, the sound of music from his radio, feelings of anger and love and amusement roused by a letter just received, the memory of some long thought or event associated with what's seen or heard or felt, and an idea, a concept, he has been pondering, each qualifying the other; together with what he knows about history; and what he has been dreaming—whether or not he remembers it—working in him. This is only a rough outline of a possible moment in a life. But the condition of being a poet is that periodically such a cross-section, or constellation, of experiences (in which one or another element may predominate) demands, or wakes in him this demand, the poem. The beginning of the fulfillment of this demand is to contemplate, to meditate; words which connote a state in which the heat of feeling warms the intellect. To contemplate comes from "templum, temple, a place, a space for observation, marked out by the augur." It means, not simply to observe, to regard, but to do these things in the presence of a god. And to meditate is "to keep the mind in a state of contemplation"; its synonym is "to muse," and to muse comes from a word meaning "to stand with open mouth"—not so comical if we think of "inspiration"—to breathe in.

So—as the poet stands open-mouthed in the temple of life, contemplating his experience, there come to him the first words of the poem: the words which are to be his way in to the poem, if there is to be a poem. The pressure of demand and the meditation on its elements culminate in a moment of vision, of crystallization, in which some inkling of the correspondence between those elements occurs; and it occurs as words. If he forces a beginning before this point, it won't work. These words sometimes remain the first, sometimes in the completed poem their eventual place may be elsewhere, or they may turn out to have been only forerunners, which fulfilled their function in bringing him to the words which are the actual beginning of the poem. It is faithful attention to the experience from the first moment of crystallization that allows those first or those forerunning words to rise to the surface: and with that same fidelity of attention the poet, from that moment of being let in to the possibility of the poem, must follow through, letting the experience lead him through the world of the poem, its unique inscape revealing itself as he goes.

During the writing of a poem the various elements of the poet's being are in communion with each other, and heightened. Ear and eye, intellect and passion, interrelate more subtly than at other times; and the "checking for accuracy," for precision of language, that must take place throughout the writing is not a matter of one element supervising the others but of intuitive interaction between all the elements involved.

In the same way, content and form are in a state of dynamic interaction; the understanding of whether an experience is a linear sequence or a constellation raying out from and in to a central focus or axis, for instance, is discoverable only in the work, not before it.

Rhyme, chime, echo, reiteration: they not only serve to knit the elements of an experience but often are the very means, the sole means, by which the density of texture and the returning or circling of perception can be transmuted into language, apperceived. A may lead to E directly through B, C, and D: but if then there is the sharp remembrance or revisioning of A, this return must find its metric counterpart. It could do so by actual repetition of the words that spoke of A the first time (and if this return occurs more than once, one finds oneself with a refrain—not put there because one decided to write something with a refrain at the end of each stanza but directly because of the demand of the content). Or it may be that since the return to A is now conditioned by the journey through B, C, and D, its words will not be a simple repetition but a variation. . . . Again, if B and D are of a complementary nature, then their thought- or feeling-rhyme may find its corresponding word-rhyme. Corresponding images are a kind of non-aural rhyme. It usually happens that within the whole, that is between the point of crystallization that marks the beginning or onset of a poem and the point at which the intensity of contemplation has ceased, there are distinct units of awareness; and it is—for me anyway—these that indicate the duration of stanzas. Sometimes these units are of such equal duration that one gets a whole poem of, say, three-line stanzas, a regularity of pattern that looks like, but is not, predetermined.

When my son was eight or nine I watched him make a crayon drawing of a tournament. He was not interested in the forms as such but was grappling with the need to speak in graphic terms, to say, "And a great crowd of people were watching the jousting knights." There was a need to show the tiers of seats, all those people sitting in them. And out of the need arose a formal design that was beautiful— composed of the rows of shoulders and heads. It is in very much the same way that there can arise, out of fidelity to instress, a design that is the form of the poem—both its total form, its length and pace and tone, and the form of its parts (e.g., the rhythmic relationships of syllables within the line, and of line to line; the sonic relationships of vowels and consonants; the recurrence of images, the play of associations, etc.). "Form follows function" (Louis Sullivan).

Frank Lloyd Wright wrote that the idea of organic architecture is that "the reality of the building lies in the space within it, to be lived in." And he quotes Coleridge: "Such as the life is, such is the form." (Emerson says, "Ask the fact for the form.") The Oxford Dictionary quotes Huxley (Thomas, presumably) as stating that he used the word organic "almost as an equivalent for the word 'living.' "

In organic poetry the metric movement, the measure, is the direct expression of the movement of perception. And the sounds, acting together with the measure, are a kind of extended onomatopoeia— i.e., they imitate, not the sounds of an experience (which may well be soundless, or to which sounds contribute only incidentally)—but the feeling of an experience, its emotional tone, its texture. The varying speed and gait of different strands of perception within an experience (I think of strands of seaweed moving within a wave) result in counterpointed measures.

Thinking about how organic poetry differs from free verse, I wrote that "most free verse is failed organic poetry, that is, organic poetry from which the attention of the writer had been switched off too soon, before the intrinsic form of the experience had been revealed." But Robert Duncan pointed out to me that there is a "free verse" of which this is not true, because it is written not with any desire to seek a form, indeed perhaps with the longing to avoid form (if that were possible) and to express inchoate emotion as purely as possible.* There is a contradiction here, however, because if, as I suppose, there is an inscape of emotion, of feeling, it is impossible to avoid presenting something of it if the rhythm or tone of the feeling is given voice in the poem. But perhaps the difference is this: that free verse isolates the "rightness" of each line or cadence—if it seems expressive, O.K., never mind the relation of it to the next; while in organic poetry the peculiar rhythms of the parts are in some degree modified, if necessary, in order to discover the rhythm of the whole.

But doesn't the character of the whole depend on, arise out of, the character of the parts? It does; but it is like painting from nature: suppose you absolutely imitate, on the palette, the separate colors of the various objects you are going to paint; yet when they are closely juxtaposed in the actual painting, you may have to lighten, darken, cloud, or sharpen each color in order to produce an effect equivalent to what you see in nature. Air, light, dust, shadow, and distance have to be taken into account.

Or one could put it this way: in organic poetry the form sense or "traffic sense," as Stepan Wolpe speaks of it, is ever present along with (yes, paradoxically) fidelity to the revelations of meditation. The form sense is a sort of Stanislavsky of the imagination: putting a chair two feet downstage there, thickening a knot of bystanders upstage left, getting this actor to raise his voice a little and that actress to enter more slowly; all in the interest of a total form he intuits. Or it is a sort of helicopter scout flying over the field of the poem, taking aerial photos and reporting on the state of the forest and its creatures—or over the sea to watch for the schools of herring and direct the fishing fleet towards them.

A manifestation of form sense is the sense the poet's ear has of some

---

*See for instance some of the forgotten poets of the early 20's—also, some of Amy Lowell—Sandburg—John Gould Fletcher. Some Imagist poems were written in 'free verse' in this sense; but by no means all.

rhythmic norm peculiar to a particular poem, from which the individual lines depart and to which they return. I heard Henry Cowell tell that the drone in Indian music is known as the horizon note. Al Kresch, the painter, sent me a quotation from Emerson: "The health of the eye demands a horizon." This sense of the beat or pulse underlying the whole I think of as the horizon note of the poem. It interacts with the nuances or forces of feeling which determine emphasis on one word or another, and decides to a great extent what belongs to a given line. It relates the needs of that feeling-force which dominates the cadence to the needs of the surrounding parts and so to the whole.

Duncan also pointed to what is perhaps a variety of organic poetry: the poetry of linguistic impulse. It seems to me that the absorption in language itself, the awareness of the world of multiple meaning revealed in sound, word, syntax, and the entering into this world in the poem, is as much an experience or constellation of perceptions as the instress of nonverbal sensuous and psychic events. What might make the poet of linguistic impetus appear to be on another tack entirely is that the demands of his realization may seem in opposition to truth as we think of it; that is, in terms of sensual logic. But the apparent distortion of experience in such a poem for the sake of verbal effects is actually a precise adherence to truth since the experience itself was a verbal one.

Form is never more than a revelation of content.

"The law—one perception must immediately and directly lead to a further perception." I've always taken this to mean, no loading of the rifts with ore, because there are to be no rifts. Yet alongside of this truth is another truth (that I've learned from Duncan more than from anyone else)—that there must be a place in the poem for rifts too—(never to be stuffed with imported ore). Great gaps between perception and perception which must be leapt across if they are to be crossed at all.

The X factor, the magic, is when we come to those rifts and make those leaps. A religious devotion to the truth, to the splendor of the authentic, involves the writer in a process rewarding in itself; but when that devotion brings us to undreamed abysses and we find ourselves sailing slowly over them and landing on the other side—that's ecstasy.

Denise Levertov
September 1965

ROBERT BLY

Michael Corrigan

Robert Bly was born in 1926 in western Minnesota, and educated at St. Olaf, Harvard, and Iowa. He is the editor of the influential magazine The Sixties *(formerly* The Fifties*), and of* The Sixties Press, *which has issued several valuable books, including selections from the work of Neruda and Vallejo. He lives with his wife and children on a farm near Madison, Minnesota. His books of verse are* Silence in the Snowy Fields *and* The Light Around the Body.

AFTER DRINKING ALL NIGHT WITH A FRIEND,
WE GO OUT IN A BOAT AT DAWN
TO SEE WHO CAN WRITE THE BEST POEM

These pines, these fall oaks, these rocks,
This water dark and touched by wind—
I am like you, you dark boat,
Drifting over water fed by cool springs.

Beneath the waters, since I was a boy,
I have dreamt of strange and dark treasures,
Not of gold, or strange stones, but the true
Gift, beneath the pale lakes of Minnesota.

This morning also, drifting in the dawn wind,
I sense my hands, and my shoes, and this ink—
Drifting, as all of this body drifts,
Above the clouds of the flesh and the stone.

A few friendships, a few dawns, a few glimpses of grass,
A few oars weathered by the snow and the heat,
So we drift toward shore, over cold waters,
No longer caring if we drift or go straight.

SURPRISED BY EVENING

There is unknown dust that is near us,
Waves breaking on shores just over the hill,
Trees full of birds that we have never seen,
Nets drawn down with dark fish.

The evening arrives; we look up and it is there,
It has come through the nets of the stars,
Through the tissues of the grass,
Walking quietly over the asylums of the waters.

The day shall never end, we think:
We have hair that seems born for the daylight;
But, at last, the quiet waters of the night will rise,
And our skin shall see far off, as it does under water.

DRIVING TOWARD THE LAC QUI PARLE RIVER

I

I am driving; it is dusk; Minnesota.
The stubble field catches the last growth of sun.
The soybeans are breathing on all sides.
Old men are sitting before their houses on carseats
In the small towns. I am happy,
The moon rising above the turkey sheds.

II

The small world of the car
Plunges through the deep fields of the night,
On the road from Willmar to Milan.
This solitude covered with iron
Moves through the fields of night
Penetrated by the noise of crickets.

III

Nearly to Milan, suddenly a small bridge,
And water kneeling in the moonlight.
In small towns the houses are built right on the ground;
The lamplight falls on all fours in the grass.
When I reach the river, the full moon covers it;
A few people are talking low in a boat.

POEM IN THREE PARTS

I

Oh, on an early morning I think I shall live forever!
I am wrapped in my joyful flesh,
As the grass is wrapped in its clouds of green.

II

Rising from a bed, where I dreamt
Of long rides past castles and hot coals,
The sun lies happily on my knees;
I have suffered and survived the night
Bathed in dark water, like any blade of grass.

III

The strong leaves of the box-elder tree,
Plunging in the wind, call us to disappear
Into the wilds of the universe,
Where we shall sit at the foot of a plant,
And live forever, like the dust.

AWAKENING

We are approaching sleep: the chestnut blossoms in the
      mind
Mingle with thoughts of pain
And the long roots of barley, bitterness
As of the oak roots staining the waters dark
In Louisiana, the wet streets soaked with rain
And sodden blossoms, out of this
We have come, a tunnel softly hurtling into darkness.

The storm is coming. The small farmhouse in Minnesota
Is hardly strong enough for the storm.
Darkness, darkness in grass, darkness in trees.
Even the water in wells trembles.
Bodies give off darkness, and chrysanthemums
Are dark, and horses, who are bearing great loads of hay
To the deep barns where the dark air is moving from
      corners.

Lincoln's statue and the traffic. From the long past
Into the long present
A bird, forgotten in these pressures, warbling,
As the great wheel turns around, grinding
The living in water.
Washing, continual washing, in water now stained
With blossoms and rotting logs,
Cries, half-muffled, from beneath the earth, the living
      awakened at last like the dead.

DRIVING TO TOWN LATE TO MAIL A LETTER

It is a cold and snowy night. The main street is deserted.
The only things moving are swirls of snow.
As I lift the mailbox door, I feel its cold iron.
There is a privacy I love in this snowy night.
Driving around, I will waste more time.

GETTING UP EARLY

I am up early. The box-elder leaves have fallen.
The eastern sky is the color of March.
The sky has spread out over the world like water.
The bootlegger and his wife are still asleep.

I saw the light first from the barn well.
The cold water fell into the night-chilled buckets,
Deepening to the somber blue of the southern sky.
Over the new trees, there was a strange light in the east.

The light was dawn. Like a man who has come home
After seeing many dark rivers, and will soon go again,
The dawn stood there with a quiet gaze;
Our eyes met through the top leaves of the young ash.

Dawn has come. The clouds floating in the east have turned
        white.
The fence posts have stopped being a part of the darkness.
The depth has disappeared from the puddles on the ground.
I look up angrily at the light.

AFTERNOON SLEEP

I

I was descending from the mountains of sleep.
Asleep I had gazed east over a sunny field,
And sat on the running board of an old Model A.
I awoke happy, for I had dreamt of my wife,

And the loneliness hiding in grass and weeds
That lies near a man over thirty, and suddenly enters.

II

When Joe Sjolie grew tired, he sold his farm,
Even his bachelor rocker, and did not come back.
He left his dog behind in the cob shed.
The dog refused to take food from strangers.

III

I drove out to that farm when I awoke;
Alone on a hill, sheltered by trees.
The matted grass lay around the house.
When I climbed the porch, the door was open.
Inside were old abandoned books,
And instructions to Norwegian immigrants.

WATERING THE HORSE

How strange to think of giving up all ambition!
Suddenly I see with such clear eyes
The white flake of snow
That has just fallen in the horse's mane!

IN A TRAIN

There has been a light snow.
Dark car tracks move in out of the darkness.
I stare at the train window marked with soft dust.
I have awakened at Missoula, Montana, utterly happy.

AFTER WORKING

I

After many strange thoughts,
Thoughts of distant harbors, and new life,
I came in and found the moonlight lying in the room.

II

Outside it covers the trees like pure sound,
The sound of tower bells, or of water moving under the ice,
The sound of the deaf hearing through the bones
       of their heads.

III

We know the road; as the moonlight
Lifts everything, so in a night like this
The road goes on ahead, it is all clear.

NIGHT

I

If I think of a horse wandering about sleeplessly
All night on this short grass covered with moonlight,
I feel a joy, as if I had thought
Of a pirate ship ploughing through dark flowers.

II

The box elders around us are full of joy,
Obeying what is beneath them.
The lilacs are sleeping, and the plants are sleeping,
Even the wood made into a casket is asleep.

III

The butterfly is carrying loam on his wings;
The toad is bearing tiny bits of granite in his skin;
The leaves at the crown of the tree are asleep
Like the dark bits of earth at its root.

IV

Alive, we are like a sleek black water beetle,
Skating across still water in any direction
We choose, and soon to be swallowed
Suddenly from beneath.

OLD BOARDS

I

I love to see boards lying on the ground in early spring:
The ground beneath them is wet, and muddy—
Perhaps covered with chicken tracks—
And they are dry and eternal.

II

This is the wood one sees on the decks of ocean ships,
Wood that carries us far from land,
With a dryness of something used for simple tasks,
Like a horse's tail.

III

This wood is like a man who has a simple life,
Living through the spring and winter on the ship of his own
        desire.
He sits on dry wood surrounded by half-melted snow
As the rooster walks away springily over the dampened hay.

THE CLEAR AIR OF OCTOBER

I can see outside the gold wings without birds
Flying around, and the wells of cold water
Without walls standing eighty feet up in the air,
I can feel the crickets' singing carrying them into the sky.

I know these cold shadows are falling for hundreds of miles,
Crossing lawns in tiny towns, and the doors of Catholic
        churches;
I know the horse of darkness is riding fast to the east,
Carrying a thin man with no coat.

And I know the sun is sinking down great stairs,
Like an executioner with a great blade walking into a cellar,
And the gold animals, the lions, and the zebras, and the
        pheasants,
Are waiting at the head of the stairs with robbers' eyes.

DEPRESSION

I felt my heart beat like an engine high in the air,
Like those scaffolding engines standing only on planks;
My body hung about me like an old grain elevator,
Useless, clogged, full of blackened wheat.
My body was sour, my life dishonest, and I fell asleep.

I dreamt that men came toward me, carrying thin wires;
I felt the wires pass in, like fire; they were old Tibetans,
Dressed in padded clothes, to keep out cold;
Then three work gloves, lying fingers to fingers,
In a circle, came toward me, and I awoke.

Now I want to go back among the dark roots;
Now I want to see the day pulling its long wing;
I want to see nothing more than two feet high;
I want to see no one, I want to say nothing,
I want to go down and rest in the black earth of silence.

SILENCE

The fall has come, clear as the eyes of chickens.
Strange muffled sounds come from the sea,
Sounds of muffled oarlocks,
And swampings in lonely bays,
Surf crashing on unchristened shores,
And the wash of tiny snail shells in the wandering gravel.

My body also wanders among these doorposts and cars,
Cradling a pen, or walking down a stair
Holding a cup in my hand,
And not breaking into the pastures that lie in the sunlight.
This is the sloth of the man inside the body,
The sloth of the body lost among the wandering stones of
        kindness.

Something homeless is looking on the long roads—
A dog lost since midnight, a small duck
Among the odorous reeds,
Or a tiny box-elder bug searching for the window pane.

Even the young sunlight is lost on the window pane,
Moving at night like a diver among the bare branches
    silently lying on the floor.

LOOKING AT NEW-FALLEN SNOW FROM A TRAIN

Snow has covered the next line of tracks,
And filled the empty cupboards in the milkweed pods;
It has stretched out on the branches of weeds,
And softened the frost-hills, and the barbed-wire rolls
Left leaning against a fencepost—
It has drifted onto the window ledges high in the peaks of barns.

    A man throws back his head, gasps
    And dies. His ankles twitch, his hands open and close,
    And the fragment of time that he has eaten is exhaled from his
        pale mouth to nourish the snow.
    A salesman falls, striking his head on the edge of the counter.

Snow has filled out the peaks on the tops of rotted fence posts.
It has walked down to meet the slough water,
And fills all the steps of the ladder leaning against the eaves.
It rests on the doorsills of collapsing children's houses,
And on transformer boxes held from the ground forever in the
    center of cornfields.

    A man lies down to sleep.
    Hawks and crows gather around his bed.
    Grass shoots up between the hawks' toes.
    Each blade of grass is a voice.
    The sword by his side breaks into flame.

HURRYING AWAY FROM THE EARTH

The poor, and the dazed, and the idiots
Are with us, they live in the casket of the sun
And the moon's coffin, as I walk out tonight
Seeing the night wheeling their dark wheelbarrow

All about the plains of heaven,
And the stars inexorably rising.
Dark moon! Sinister tears!
Shadow of slums and of the conquering dead!

Some men have pierced the chest with a long needle
To stop their heart from beating any more;
 ⋅ Another put blocks of ice in his bed
So he would die, women
Have washed their hair, and hanged themselves
In the long braids, one woman climbed
A high elm above her lawn,
Opened a box, and swallowed poisonous spiders. . . .

The time for exhortation is past. I have heard
The iron chairs scraping in asylums,
As the cold bird hunches into the winter
In the windy night of November.
The coal miners rise from their pits
Like a flash flood,
Like a rice field disintegrating.
Men cry when they hear stories of someone rising from the dead.

THOSE BEING EATEN BY AMERICA

The cry of those being eaten by America,
Others pale and soft being stored for later eating

And Jefferson
Who saw hope in new oats

The wild houses go on
With long hair growing from between their toes
The feet at night get up
And run down the long white roads by themselves

The dams reverse themselves and want to go stand alone in the desert

Ministers who dive headfirst into the earth
The pale flesh
Spreading guiltily into new literatures

That is why these poems are so sad
The long dead running over the fields

The mass sinking down
The light in children's faces fading at six or seven

The world will soon break up into small colonies of the saved

THE EXECUTIVE'S DEATH

Merchants have multiplied more than the stars of heaven.
Half the population are like the long grasshoppers
That sleep in the bushes in the cool of the day:
The sound of their wings is heard at noon, muffled, near the earth.
The crane handler dies, the taxi driver dies, slumped over
In his taxi. Meanwhile, high in the air, executives
Walk on cool floors, and suddenly fall:
Dying, they dream they are lost in a snowstorm in mountains,
On which they crashed, carried at night by great machines.
As he lies on the wintry slope, cut off and dying,
A pine stump talks to him of Goethe and Jesus.
Commuters arrive in Hartford at dusk like moles
Or hares flying from a fire behind them,
And the dusk in Hartford is full of their sighs;
Their trains come through the air like a dark music,
Like the sound of horns, the sound of thousands of small wings.

COUNTING SMALL-BONED BODIES

Let's count the bodies over again.

If we could only make the bodies smaller,
The size of skulls,
We could make a whole plain white with skulls in the moonlight!

If we could only make the bodies smaller,
Maybe we could get
A whole year's kill in front of us on a desk!

If we could only make the bodies smaller,
We could fit
A body into a finger-ring, for a keepsake forever.

ASIAN PEACE OFFERS REJECTED
WITHOUT PUBLICATION

These suggestions by Asians are not taken seriously.
We know Rusk smiles as he passes them to someone.
Men like Rusk are not men:
They are bombs waiting to be loaded in a darkened hangar.
Rusk's assistants eat hurriedly,
Talking of Teilhard de Chardin,
Longing to get back to their offices
So they can cling to the underside of the steel wings shuddering
        faintly in the high altitudes.
They land first, and hand the coffee cup to the drawn pilot.
They start the projector, and show the movie about the mad
        professor.

Lost angels huddled on a night branch!
The waves crossing
And recrossing beneath,
The sound of the rampaging Missouri,
Bending the reeds again and again—something inside us
Like a ghost train in the Rockies
About to be buried in snow!
Its long hoot
Making the owl in the Douglas fir turn his head . . .

HATRED OF MEN WITH BLACK HAIR

I hear voices praising Tshombe, and the Portuguese
In Angola, these are the men who skinned Little Crow!
We are all their sons, skulking
In back rooms, selling nails with trembling hands!

We distrust every person on earth with black hair;
We send teams to overthrow Chief Joseph's government;

We train natives to kill Presidents with blowdarts;
We have men loosening the nails on Noah's ark.

The State Department floats in the heavy jellies near the bottom
Like exhausted crustaceans, like squids who are confused,
Sending out beams of black light to the open sea,
Fighting their fraternal feeling for the great landlords.

We have violet rays that light up the jungles at night, showing
The friendly populations; we are teaching the children of ritual
To overcome their longing for life, and we send
Sparks of black light that fit the holes in the generals' eyes.

Underneath all the cement of the Pentagon
There is a drop of Indian blood preserved in snow:
Preserved from a trail of blood that once led away
From the stockade, over the snow, the trail now lost.

A DREAM OF SUFFOCATION

Accountants hover over the earth like helicopters,
Dropping bits of paper engraved with Hegel's name.
Badgers carry the papers on their fur
To their den, where the entire family dies in the night.

A chorus girl stands for hours behind her curtains
Looking out at the street.
In a window of a trucking service
There is a branch painted white.
A stuffed baby alligator grips that branch tightly
To keep away from the dry leaves on the floor.

The honeycomb at night has strange dreams:
Small black trains going round and round—
Old warships drowning in the raindrop.

WRITTEN IN DEJECTION NEAR ROME

What if these long races go on repeating themselves
century after century, living in houses painted light colors
on the beach,
black spiders,
having turned pale and fat,
men walking thoughtfully with their families,
vibrations
of exhausted violin-bodies,
horrible eternities of sea pines!
Some men cannot help but feel it,
they will abandon their homes
to live on rafts tied together on the ocean;
those on shore will go inside tree trunks,
surrounded by bankers whose fingers have grown long and slender,
piercing through rotting bark for their food.

LOOKING AT SOME FLOWERS

Light is around the petals, and behind them:
Some petals are living on the other side of the light.
Like sunlight drifting onto the carpet
Where the casket stands, not knowing which world it is in.
And fuzzy leaves, hair growing from some animal
Buried in the green trenches of the plant.
Or the ground this house is on,
Only free of the sea for five or six thousand years.

LOOKING FOR DRAGON SMOKE

1

In ancient times, in the "time of inspiration," the poet flew from one world to another, "riding on dragons," as the Chinese said. Isaiah rode on these dragons; so did Li Po, and Pindar. They dragged behind them long tails of dragon smoke. The verse of Beowulf still retains some of that ancient freedom. The poet holds fast to Danish soil, or leaps after Grendel into the sea. That leaping—really a leaping about the psyche— is what disappeared. The corridors to the unconscious, which were open in ancient poetry, for example in the Greek plays drawn from the mystery initiations, gradually became blocked off in Europe.

By the 18th century, association had become drastically curtailed. Content in the rhymed couplets proceeded through the poem, line to line, like a prisoner through a series of jail cells. A sepulchral rationalism charted the pauses, and jollied the prisoner along. A form developed, full of closing and opening doors. It became apparent how much some free verse was needed.

Blake took the first step: he abducted the thought of poetry, and took it off to some obscure psychic woods. His woods were real woods. Occult ceremonies took place in them, just as ceremonies had taken place in ancient poems. In Germany Novalis and Hölderlin abducted a child and raised it deep in the forest. All over Europe, thought in poetry began to flow more and more from deep in the unconscious. Later, Freud pointed out that the images of dreams had something significant to say which European rationalism had failed to grasp. By the end of the 19th century, after long and hard work, the poem and the dream had been set free: the rationalists had lost control of them. The movement to deepen association in poetry, and return to it the freedom of ancient poetry, had begun.

2

Poets like Blake and Novalis have tried first to widen their range of association; only later did they turn to experiments with form. But in the United States we have tended to reverse this order. While European poets have struggled primarily for freedom of association, American poets have struggled primarily for freedom from old technique.

3

In the United States poets rarely talk about association, and it's clear the idea of association has never really taken root in our poetry.

When news of the new thought penetrated to the United States, very few understood what happened. Whitman understood it very well. He said goodbye to the libraries, invited animals into his poems, and let his form out of school. He belonged to what we could call the second generation of modern poets, along with Baudelaire and Mallarmé, and he was the bravest.

Our 1917 poets came at the tail end of this great series of infant abductions. We may take Eliot, Pound and Williams as American examples of the powerful third generation of free verse poets, to which Trakl also belonged. Europeans had done most of the work, however, and taken the risks in trusting the unconscious—Hölderlin, Gerard de Nerval and Nietzsche had all gone insane. The American 1917 poets had their free verse without having gone through much agony themselves to free it. Eliot, like Pound, was more an inheritor than an innovator. Being distant from the fight, neither ever really understood why Blake and Novalis were so passionate, so rebellious, why they had no irony, why they hated objectivity so much. In short, American twentieth century poetry had not fought for its freedom, and it soon showed an irresistible desire to leave the forest and be locked up again. In the very next generation after Eliot and Pound, American poetry voluntarily turned itself in. Tate and Ransom went through town after town asking, "Does anyone know of a good jail near here?"

We see now a fourth generation of poets active in Europe and America. A vast effort is being made once more to open the doors of association. When the poet is in the middle of the poem, about to set down a word, how many worlds is he free to visit? How swiftly does he leap from one part of the psyche to another?

American poetry now is about half-free. This generalization is true of all contemporary American poetry I know, including my own. Creeley and Simpson are both excellent poets, opposite in temperament, and we might take their work as instances of the best recent poetry. Poems of Creeley or Simpson often have a magnificent human depth, but we will find in their work little or none of the occult association that deepens the work of Blake or Trakl. The forms of their poems are original, and cannot be deciphered by the old codes; on the other hand it is not very adventurous either. Their poetry tends to restrict itself to certain mapped out sections of the psyche. The reason is that this fourth generation, instead of going to the sources of "free verse" in Europe, have modeled themselves basically on Eliot, Pound, and Williams. Passionate association is not to be found in the work of Eliot, Pound, or Williams. The excitement of The Waste Land springs partly from the presence of association, but more from the elision of it. Pound in the Cantos leaps from the Chinese world to the Boston world, but he does not go by secret paths of the imagination—he does it primarily by juxtaposition of texts; he simply abuts one anecdote to another or one fact to another. Yeats said that rhetoric was the *will* trying to do the work of the imagination, but juxtaposition, when it becomes a device, is the *history textbook* and the *typewriter* trying to do the work of the imagination. We have not yet regained in American poetry that swift movement all over the psyche, from conscious to unconscious, from a pine table to mad inward desires, that the ancient poets had, or that Lorca and others gained back for poetry in Spanish. Why not? Every time we get started, we get sidetracked into technique.

4

Let me take the Black Mountain poetry as an example of the American love of technique. When poets talk of technique, they are usually headed for jail. Charles Olson says in *Projective Verse:*

> It is now only a matter of the recognition of the conventions of composition by field for us to bring into being an open verse as formal as the closed, with all its traditional advantages.

There we go again! The Olsonite poets are always approaching poetry through technique; Creeley is a perfect example. All their talk about technique is academic, and a repetition, in a different decade and different terms, of the Tate-Ransom nostalgia for jails. All technical essays are attempts to construct poetry machines, so that even people with no imagination can write it. I like Olson's gambling with ideas in his cultural essays, but I think that what is blocking the further development of American poetry is the formalist obsession which Olson embodies—the middle-class worship of technique which he represents and which he feeds. If we use the Russian experience as an image for the poetic revolution, we can say that Charles Olson is not a czar—he is no enemy of freedom—nor is he Lenin or Trotsky; he is Kerensky. When the Russian revolution was still going on, Kerensky attempted to control the energies with his ideas of order—an order that would be open and yet have all the traditional advantages. The Russians tossed him out. Voznesensky recently said:

> In literature, as in architecture, technique is changing and becoming astonishing. You can balance a building on a needle's point. Rhyme has become boring. In poetry, the future lies with the ability to associate. Form must be transparent, infinitely disturbing, and have its own subtle meaning, like a sky in which only radar can sense the presence of an airplane.

It should be possible to put a great deal of attention on technique, and also on imaginative association, but in fact, among Americans at least, absorption in the first eventually rules out the second. The threat of throttling poetry by technique-talk is particularly strong now, when universities are sheltering so many poets. The universities have always supported the study of poetry as technique.

Blake and Whitman left behind no technical essays about how to write poetry because they knew that obsession with technique is destructive to the growth of the imagination. Our task is not to invent and encourage jargon about "open form" and breath patterns, but to continue to open new corridors into the psyche by association.

5

What we need is some way to talk about poetry that doesn't descend to technique and technical terms. The term "free verse" seems better to me than the term "open form" because it implies not a technique, but a longing.

I refuse to say anything at all about prosody. What an ugly word it is! In the true poem, both the form and the content rise from the same place; they have the same swiftness and darkness. Both are expressions of a certain rebellious energy rising in the psyche: they are what Boehme calls "the shooting up of life from nature to spirit." What is important is this rebellious energy, not technique. If I write a bad poem it is because I have somehow taken the thought from someone else—I haven't really lived it: it isn't my energy. Technique is beside the point in this matter.

I know that in drawing such a flat contrast between absorption in technique and absorption in association, I have exaggerated. But every drawer who draws a clean line outlining a shape is exaggerating, since no clean lines appear in nature.

Study of technique cannot help us to write an intense poem—and for some poets, emphasis on technique is positively harmful. When I have fought against what was weak in my own poems, I have often found myself fighting the American longing to lie down in technique and rest. The truth is that no one knows what a poem as intense as the twentieth century would look like, or how to write it, but I think that poem would be full of dragon smoke. I think Gary Snyder is right when he says that wherever we are is not where we're heading: we're going somewhere else. Talk of technique "throws light" on poetry, but the last thing we need is light. St. John of the Cross said, "If a man wants to be sure of his road, he must close his eyes and walk in the dark."

Robert Bly
Madison, Minnesota
1967

ROBERT CREELEY

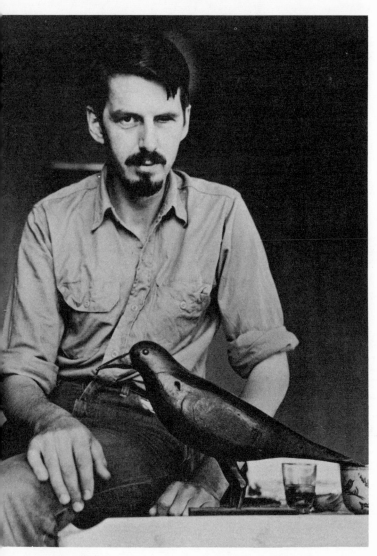

Harry Redl

Robert Creeley was born in 1926, in Massachusetts, and was educated at Harvard. He has taught at Black Mountain College, and worked with the American Field Service in India and Burma. His books of verse include For Love, A Form of Women, The Whip, Words, *and* All That is Lovely in Men; *he is also the author of a novel,* The Island.

OH NO

If you wander far enough
you will come to it
and when you get there
they will give you a place to sit

for yourself only, in a nice chair,
and all your friends will be there
with smiles on their faces
and they will likewise all have places.

AFTER LORCA

for M. Marti

The church is a business, and the rich
are the business men.
                       When they pull on the bells, the
poor come piling in and when a poor man dies, he has a wooden
cross, and they rush through the ceremony.

But when a rich man dies, they
drag out the Sacrament
and a golden Cross, and go *doucement, doucement*
to the cemetery.

And the poor love it
and think its crazy.

THE OPERATION

By Saturday I said you would be better on Sunday.
The insistence was a part of a reconciliation.

Your eyes bulged, the grey
light hung on you, you were hideous.

My involvement is just an old
habitual relationship.

Cruel, cruel to describe
what there is no reason to describe.

THE WHIP

I spent a night turning in bed,
my love was a feather, a flat

sleeping thing. She was
very white

and quiet, and above us on
the roof, there was another woman I

also loved, had
addressed myself to in

a fit she
returned. That

encompasses it. But now I was
lonely, I yelled,

but what is that? Ugh,
she said, beside me, she put

her hand on
my back, for which act

I think to say this
wrongly.

ALL THAT IS LOVELY IN MEN

Nothing for a dirty man
but soap in his bathtub, a

greasy hand, lover's
nuts

perhaps. Or else

something like sand
with which to scour him

for all
that is lovely in women.

A FORM OF WOMEN

I have come far enough
from where I was not before
to have seen the things
looking in at me through the open door

and have walked tonight
by myself
to see the moonlight
and see it as trees

and shapes more fearful
because I feared
what I did not know
but have wanted to know.

My face is my own, I thought.
But you have seen it
turn into a thousand years.
I watched you cry.

I could not touch you.
I wanted very much to
touch you
but could not.

If it is dark
when this is given to you,
have care for its content
when the moon shines.

My face is my own.
My hands are my own.

My mouth is my own
but I am not.

Moon, moon,
when you leave me alone
all the darkness is
an utter blackness,

a pit of fear,
a stench,
hands unreasonable
never to touch.

But I love you.
Do you love me.
What to say
when you see me.

A GIFT OF GREAT VALUE

Oh that horse I see so high
when the world shrinks into its
relationships, my mother
sees as well as I.

She was born, but I bore with her.
This horse was a mighty occasion!
The intensity of its feet! The height
of its immense body!

Now then in wonder at evening, at
the last small entrance of the night,
my mother calls it, and I
call it *my father*.

With angry face, with no
rights, with impetuosity and
sterile vision—and a great
wind we ride.

THE MECHANIC

Were we now to fall
to our stubborn knees
and sink to rest, my-
self sunk in yours, then

what would hold us
together but uninteresting
weight. Do you believe
love, and how much.

THE WORLD

I wanted so ably
to reassure you, I wanted
the man you took to be me,

to comfort you, and got
up, and went to the window,
pushed back, as you asked me to,

the curtain, to see
the outline of the trees
in the night outside.

The light, love,
the light we felt then,
greyly, was it, that

came in, on us, not
merely my hands or yours,
or a wetness so comfortable,

but in the dark then
as you slept, the grey
figure came so close

and leaned over,
between us, as you
slept, restless, and

my own face had to
see it, and be seen by it,
the man it was, your

grey lost tired bewildered
brother, unused, untaken—
hated by love, and dead,

but not dead, for an
instant, saw me, myself
the intruder, as he was not.

I tried to say, it is
all right, she is
happy, you are no longer

needed. I said,
he is dead, and he
went as you shifted

and woke, at first afraid,
then knew by my own knowing
what had happened—

and the light then
of the sun coming
for another morning
in the world.

A REASON

Each gesture
is a common one, a
black dog, crying, a
man, crying.

All alike, people
or things grow
fixed with what
happens to them.

I throw a stone.
It hits the wall,
it hits a dog,
it hits a child—

my sentimental
names for years
and years ago, from
something I've not become.

If I look
in the mirror,
the wall, I
see myself.

If I try
to do better
and better, I
do the same thing.

Let me hit you.
Will it hurt.
Your face is hurt
all the same.

A SIGHT

Quicker
than that, can't
get off "the
dead center of"

myself. *He/I*
were walking. Then
the place *is/was*
not ever enough. But

the house, if
admitted, were
a curiously wrought
complexity of flesh.

The eyes
windows, the head
roof form with
stubbornly placed

bricks of chimney.
I can remember, I
can. Then when
she first touched me,

when we were
lying in that bed,
was the feeling of
falling into no

matter we both lay
quiet, where
was it. I
felt her flesh

enclose mine. *Cock,*
they say, *prick, dick,*
I put it in her,
I lay there.

Come back, breasts,
come. Back. The sudden
thing of being
no one. I

never felt guilty,
I was confused but
could not feel
wrong, about it.

I wanted to kill her.
I tried it, tentatively,
just a little
hurt. Hurt me.

So immense she was.
All the day
lying flat, lying it seemed
upon a salty sea, the houses

bobbing
around her, under
her, I hung on
for dear life to her.

But when
now I walk, when
the day comes
to trees and a road,

where
is she. Oh, on my
hands and knees, crawl-
ing forward.

SOMETHING

I approach with such
a careful tremor, always
I feel the finally foolish

question of how it is,
then, supposed to be felt,
and by whom. I remember

once in a rented room on
27th street, the woman I loved
then, literally, after we

had made love on the large
bed sitting across from
a basin with two faucets, she

had to pee but was nervous,
embarrassed I suppose I
would watch her who had but

a moment ago been completely
open to me, naked, on
the same bed. Squatting, her

head reflected in the mirror,
the hair dark there, the
full of her face, the shoulders,

sat spread-legged, turned on
one faucet and shyly pissed. What
love might learn from such a sight.

FOR THE NEW YEAR

From something in the trees
looking down at me

or else an inexact sign
of a remote and artificial tenderness—

a woman who passes me
and who will not consider me—

things I have tried to take
with which to make something

like a toy for my children
and a story to be quietly forgotten.

Oh God, send me an omen
that I may remember more often.

Keep me, see to me,
let me look.

Being unsure, there is the fate
of doing nothing right.

THE DOOR

for Robert Duncan

It is hard going to the door
cut so small in the wall where
the vision which echoes loneliness
brings a scent of wild flowers in a wood.

What I understood, I understand.
My mind is sometime torment,
sometimes good and filled with livelihood,
and feels the ground.

But I see the door,
and knew the wall, and wanted the wood,
and would get there if I could
with my feet and hands and mind.

Lady, do not banish me
for digressions. My nature
is a quagmire of unresolved
confessions. Lady, I follow.

I walked away from myself,
I left the room, I found the garden,
I knew the woman
in it, together we lay down.

Dead night remembers. In December
we change, not multiplied but dispersed,
sneaked out of childhood,
the ritual of dismemberment.

Mighty magic is a mother,
in her there is another issue
of fixture, repeated form, the race renewal,
the charge of the command.

The garden echoes across the room.
It is fixed in the wall like a mirror
that faces a window behind you
and reflects the shadows.

May I go now?
Am I allowed to bow myself down
in the ridiculous posture of renewal,
of the insistence of which I am the virtue?

Nothing for You is untoward.
Inside You would also be tall,
more tall, more beautiful.
Come toward me from the wall, I want to be with You.

So I screamed to You,
who hears as the wind, and changes
multiply, invariably,
changes in the mind.

Running to the door, I ran down
as a clock runs down. Walked backwards,
stumbled, sat down
hard on the floor near the wall.

Where were You.
How absurd, how vicious.
There is nothing to do but get up.
My knees were iron, I rusted in worship, of You.

For that one sings, one
writes the spring poem, one goes on walking.
The Lady has always moved to the next town
and you stumble on after Her.

The door in the wall leads to the garden
where in the sunlight sit
the Graces in long Victorian dresses,
of which my grandmother had spoken.

History sings in their faces.
They are young, they are obtainable,
and you follow after them also
in the service of God and Truth.

But the Lady is indefinable,
she will be the door in the wall
to the garden in sunlight.
I will go on talking forever.

I will never get there.
Oh Lady, remember me
who in Your service grows older
not wiser, no more than before.

How can I die alone.
Where will I be then who am now alone,
what groans so pathetically
in this room where I am alone?

I will go to the garden.
I will be a romantic, I will sell
myself in hell,
in heaven also I will be.

In my mind I see the door,
I see the sunlight before me across the floor
beckon to me, as the Lady's skirt
moves small beyond it.

ANGER

1

The time is.
The air seems a cover,
the room is quiet.

She moves, she
had moved. He
heard her.

The children
sleep, the dog fed,
the house around them

is open, descriptive,
a truck through the walls,
lights bright there,

glaring, the sudden
roar of its motor, all
familiar impact

as it passed
so close. He
hated it.

But what does she answer.
She moves
away from it.

In all they save,
in the way of his saving
the clutter, the accumulation

of the expected disorder—
as if each dirtiness,
each blot, blurred

happily, gave
purpose, happily—
she is not enough there.

He is angry. His
face grows—as if
a moon rose

of black light,
convulsively darkening,
as if life were black.

It is black.
It is an open
hole of horror, of

nothing as if not
enough there is
nothing. A pit—

which he recognizes,
familiar, sees
the use in, a hole

for anger and
fills it
with himself,

yet watches on
the edge of it,
as if she were

not to be pulled in,
a hand could
stop him. Then

as the shouting
grows and grows
louder and louder

with spaces
of the same open
silence, the darkness,

in and out, him-
self between them,
stands empty and

holding out his
hands to both,
now screaming

it cannot be
the same, she
waits in the one

while the other
moans in the hole
in the floor, in the wall.

    2
Is there some odor
which is anger,

a face
which is rage.

I think I think
but find myself in it.

The pattern
is only resemblance.

I cannot see myself
but as what I see, an

object but a man,
with lust for forgiveness,

raging, from that vantage,
secure in the purpose,

double, split.
Is it merely intention,

a sign quickly adapted,
shifted to make

a horrible place
for self-satisfaction.

I rage.
I rage, I rage.

3

You did it,
and didn't want to,

and it was simple.
You were not involved,

even if your head was cut off,
or each finger

twisted
from its shape until it broke,

and you screamed too
with the other, in pleasure.

4 .

Face me,
in the dark,
my face. See me.

It is the cry
I hear all
my life, my own

voice, my
eye locked in
self sight, not

the world what
ever it is
but the close

breathing beside
me I reach out
for, feel as

warmth in
my hands then
returned. The rage

is what I
want, what
I cannot give

to myself, of
myself, in
the world.

    5
After, what
is it—as if
the sun had

been wrong to return,
again. It was
another life, a

day, some
time gone, it
was done.

But also
the pleasure, the
opening

relief
even in what
was so hated.

6

All you say you want
to do to yourself you do
to someone else as yourself

and we sit between you
waiting for whatever will
be at last the real end of you.

NOTES APROPOS "FREE VERSE"

I think the term "free verse" proves awkward just now in that it seems anchored in an opposition to a sense of traditional verse patterns, which are, because of their situation as history, more trusted. "Free" has such a width of associations—"free man," "free fall," "free prizes," etc. Too, it seems relevant that this sense of verse comes largely from American practice and that its primary figure is Whitman.

It nonetheless provokes a real situation. For example, Yvor Winters' tracking of "impulse" as informing principle in Emerson's discussions of poetry, as equally in Whitman's, and then in Crane's, cites the significance of this way of stating oneself in poetry as well as the historical range of its occasion. If one thinks of the literal root of the word *verse*, "a line, furrow, turning—*vertere,* to turn . . . ," he will come to a sense of "free verse" as that instance of writing in poetry which "turns" upon an occasion intimate with, in fact, the issue of, its own nature rather than to an abstract decision of "form" taken from a prior instance.

The point is, simply enough, why does the "line" thus "turn" and what does inform it in that movement? Clearly to say that it is "free" or equally that it is "unfree" is to say nothing of much interest. I was impressed a few years ago, reading Joshua Whatmough's *Language,* to find him saying, as a linguist, that there was no explicit understanding as to why poetry "turns" in any instance at the precise moment it does—that is, no device of measure then defined could anticipate the precise articulations of this shifting in verse, no matter the verse be "traditional" or "free." Linguistics has, in other respects, qualified usefully the assumptions of traditional metrical systems in making evident the varying "weights" observable in "stress" (at least four in number) which had previously been dealt with in patterns which qualified syllables as "stressed" or "unstressed"—in short, a very imprecise and clumsy approximation of the activity.

I am myself hopeful that linguistic studies will bring to contemporary criticism a vocabulary and method more sensitive to the basic *activity* of poetry and less dependent upon assumed senses of literary style. Jacobsen's note of "contiguity" and "parallelism" as two primary modes of linguistic coherence interests me. Too, I would like to see a more viable attention paid to syntactical environment, to what I can call crudely "grammartology."

However, these are senses of things still far from my own experience in writing. So, briefly, as to that—I feel, as Robert Duncan put it, "a kind of readiness," much like that makes one feel like taking a walk, some imminence of occasion that has not as yet become literal. I have never, to my own recollection, anticipated the situation of my own writing in the sense of what I was about to say. It is certain enough that preoccupations recur—"themes," as Duncan has called them—but how these might gain statement as writing could not be proposed except as the literal writing then found means. I was struck by a comment Franz Kline once made: "If I paint what I know, I bore myself. If I paint what you know, I bore you. So I paint what I don't know . . ." I write what I don't know. I feel the situation parallel to what Pollock suggests by his statement, "when I am in my painting. . . ." This, I feel, to be the condition Charles Olson defines in the key essay, "Projective Verse":

> From the moment (a poet) ventures into FIELD COMPOSITION—
> puts himself in the open—he can go by no track other than
> the one the poem under hand declares, for itself. Thus
> he has to behave, and be, instant by instant, aware of
> some several forces just now beginning to be examined . . .

Pound notes Yeats' dependence upon "a chune in his head"—and it is that equally, an ordering that is taking place as one writes, which one follows much as he might that melodic line of some song.

The simplest way I have found to make clear my own sense of writing in this respect is to use the analogy of driving. The road, as it were, is creating itself momently in one's attention to it, there, visibly, in front of the car. There is no reason it should go on forever, and if one does so assume it, it very often disappears all too actually. When Pound says, "we must understand what is happening," one sense suggested, following. In that way there is nothing mindless about the procedure. It is, rather, a respect for the possibilities of such attention that brings Allen Ginsberg to say, "Mind is shapely." Mind, thus engaged, permits experience of "order" far more various and intensive than habituated and programmed limits of its subtleties can recognize.

I think each man writing will have some way, so to speak, intimate with his own condition. That is, I feel there will be an inherent condition for an ordering intimate to the fact of himself as organism. Again, one of the several virtues of Olson's "Projective Verse" was that of returning to poetry its relation with the *physiological* condition.

For my own part I feel a rhythmic possibility, an inherent periodicity in the weights and durations of words, to occur in the first few words, or first line, or lines, of what it is I am writing. Because I am the man I am, and think in the patterns I do, I tend to posit intuitively a balance of *four*, a four-square circumstance, be it walls of a room or legs of a table, that reassures me in the movement otherwise to be dealt with. I have, at times, made reference to my own interest when younger (and continuingly) in the music of Charlie Parker—an intensive variation on "foursquare" patterns such as "I've Got Rhythm." Listening to him play, I found he lengthened the experience of time, or shortened it, gained a very subtle experience of "weight," all some decision made within the context of what was called "improvisation"—but what I should rather call the experience of possibility within the limits of his materials (sounds and durations) and their environment (all that they had as what Pound calls "increment of association" but equally all they had as literal condition, their phenomenological fact). There is an interview with Dizzy Gillespie (in the *Paris Review* #35) in which he speaks of rhythm particularly in a way I very much respect. If *time* is measure of *change,* our sense of it becomes what we can apprehend as significant condition of *change*—in poetry as well as in music.

Finally, there was and is the fact of, what it was one had to say—in Louis Zukofsky's sense, "Out of deep need. . . ." I never spoke easily and had to write, for the most part, just as adamantly. There is a section of Williams' "The Desert Music" which might be my own:

> You seem quite normal. Can you tell me? Why
> does one want to write a poem?
> > Because it's there to be written.
> Oh. A matter of inspiration then?
> > Of necessity.
> Oh. But what sets it off?
> > I am that he whose brains
> > are scattered
> > > aimlessly . . .

Why after all say any of this—but for some fear one is not "doing it right" and isn't that, even, the occasion for such argument as still can exist on the subject of "free verse," which is at best some "historical" label. Williams, at the end of "The Desert Music," says all that anyone can:

> > I *am* a poet! I
> am. I am. I am a poet, I reaffirmed, ashamed
>
> Now the music volleys through as in
> a lonely moment I hear it. Now it is all
> about me. The dance! The verb detaches itself
> seeking to become articulate.
>
> > And I could not help thinking
> > of the wonders of the brain that
> > hears that music and of our
> > skill sometimes to record it.

Robert Creeley
Buffalo, N.Y., 1966

ALLEN GINSBERG

Allen Ginsberg was born in 1926, in Paterson, New Jersey; his father is the poet Louis Ginsberg. He was educated at Columbia and Berkeley, and has traveled widely in Europe, Latin America, and India. He lives with the poet Peter Orlovsky, mainly in New York and San Francisco. His books include The Empty Mirror, Howl, Kaddish, Reality Sandwiches, Wichita Vortex Sutra, *and* Planet News.

from HOWL, PART I

for Carl Solomon

I

I saw the best minds of my generation destroyed by madness,
    starving hysterical naked,
dragging themselves through the negro streets at dawn looking for
    an angry fix,
angelheaded hipsters burning for the ancient heavenly connection
    to the starry dynamo in the machinery of night,
who poverty and tatters and hollow-eyed and high sat up smoking
    in the supernatural darkness of cold-water flats floating
    across the tops of cities contemplating jazz,
who bared their brains to Heaven under the El and saw
    Mohammedan angels staggering on tenement roofs
    illuminated,
who passed through universities with radiant cool eyes hallucinating
    Arkansas and Blake-light tragedy among the scholars of war,
who were expelled from the academies for crazy & publishing
    obscene odes on the windows of the skull,
who cowered in unshaven rooms in underwear, burning their money
    in wastebaskets and listening to the Terror through the wall,
who got busted in their pubic beards returning through Laredo
    with a belt of marijuana for New York,
who ate fire in paint hotels or drank turpentine in Paradise Alley,
    death, or purgatoried their torsos night after night
with dreams, with drugs, with waking nightmares, alcohol and
    cock and endless balls,
incomparable blind streets of shuddering cloud and lightning in the
    mind leaping toward poles of Canada & Paterson,
    illuminating all the motionless world of Time between,
Peyote solidities of halls, backyard green tree cemetery dawns,
    wine drunkenness over the rooftops, storefront boroughs of
    teahead joyride neon blinking traffic light, sun and moon
    and tree vibrations in the roaring winter dusks of Brooklyn,
    ashcan rantings and kind king light of mind,
who chained themselves to subways for the endless ride from Battery
    to holy Bronx on benzedrine until the noise of wheels and
    children brought them down shuddering mouth-wracked
    and battered bleak of brain all drained of brilliance in the
    drear light of Zoo,

who sank all night in submarine light of Bickford's floated out and
        sat through the stale beer afternoon in desolate Fugazzi's,
        listening to the crack of doom on the hydrogen jukebox,
who talked continuously seventy hours from park to pad to bar to
        Bellevue to museum to the Brooklyn Bridge,
a lost battalion of platonic conversationalists jumping down the
        stoops off fire escapes off windowsills off Empire State out
        of the moon,
yacketayakking screaming vomiting whispering facts and memories
        and anecdotes and eyeball kicks and shocks of hospitals and
        jails and wars,
whole intellects disgorged in total recall for seven days and nights
        with brilliant eyes, meat for the Synagogue cast on the
        pavement,
who vanished into nowhere Zen New Jersey leaving a trail of
        ambiguous picture postcards of Atlantic City Hall,
suffering Eastern sweats and Tangerian bone-grindings and
        migraines of China under junk-withdrawal in Newark's
        bleak furnished room,
who wandered around and around at midnight in the railroad yard
        wondering where to go, and went, leaving no broken hearts,
who lit cigarettes in boxcars boxcars boxcars racketing through snow
        toward lonesome farms in grandfather night,
who studied Plotinus Poe St. John of the Cross telepathy and bop
        kaballa because the cosmos instinctively vibrated at their
        feet in Kansas,
who loned it through the streets of Idaho seeking visionary indian
        angels who were visionary indian angels,
who thought they were only mad when Baltimore gleamed in
        supernatural ecstasy,
who jumped in limousines with the Chinaman of Oklahoma on the
        impulse of winter midnight streetlight smalltown rain,
who lounged hungry and lonesome through Houston seeking jazz
        or sex or soup, and followed the brilliant Spaniard to
        converse about America and Eternity, a hopeless task, and so
        took ship to Africa,
who disappeared into the volcanoes of Mexico leaving behind
        nothing but the shadow of dungarees and the lava and ash
        of poetry scattered in fireplace Chicago,
who reappeared on the West Coast investigating the F.B.I. in
        beards and shorts with big pacifist eyes sexy in their dark
        skin passing out incomprehensible leaflets,

who burned cigarette holes in their arms protesting the narcotic
        tobacco haze of Capitalism,
who distributed Supercommunist pamphlets in Union Square
        weeping and undressing while the sirens of Los Alamos
        wailed them down, and wailed down Wall, and the Staten
        Island Ferry also wailed,
who broke down crying in white gymnasiums naked and
        trembling before the machinery of other skeletons,
who bit detectives in the neck and shrieked with delight in
        policecars for committing no crime but their own wild
        cooking pederasty and intoxication,
who howled on their knees in the subway and were dragged off
        the roof waving genitals and manuscripts,
who let themselves be fucked in the ass by saintly motorcyclists,
        and screamed with joy,
who blew and were blown by those human seraphim, the sailors,
        caresses of Atlantic and Caribbean love,
who balled in the morning in the evenings in rosegardens and the
        grass of public parks and cemeteries scattering their semen
        freely to whomever come who may,
who hiccupped endlessly trying to giggle but wound up with a sob
        behind a partition in a Turkish Bath when the blonde &
        naked angel came to pierce them with a sword,
who lost their loveboys to the three old shrews of fate the one eyed
        shrew of the heterosexual dollar the one eyed shrew that
        winks out of the womb and the one eyed shrew that does
        nothing but sit on her ass and snip the intellectual golden
        threads of the craftsman's loom,
who copulated ecstatic and insatiate with a bottle of beer a
        sweetheart a package of cigarettes a candle and fell off the
        bed, and continued along the floor and down the hall and
        ended fainting on the wall with a vision of ultimate cunt
        and come eluding the last gyzym of consciousness,
who sweetened the snatches of a million girls trembling in the
        sunset, and were red eyed in the morning but prepared to
        sweeten the snatch of the sunrise, flashing buttocks under
        barns and naked in the lake,
who went out whoring through Colorado in myriad stolen
        night-cars, N.C., secret hero of these poems, cocksman and
        Adonis of Denver—joy to the memory of his innumerable
        lays of girls in empty lots & diner backyards, moviehouses'
        rickety rows, on mountaintops in caves or with gaunt
        waitresses in familiar roadside lonely petticoat upliftings

& especially secret gas-station solipsisms of johns, &
hometown alleys too,

who faded out in vast sordid movies, were shifted in dreams, woke
on a sudden Manhattan, and picked themselves up out of
basements hungover with heartless Tokay and horrors of
Third Avenue iron dreams & stumbled to unemployment
offices,

who walked all night with their shoes full of blood on the
snowbank docks waiting for a door in the East River to
open to a room full of steamheat and opium,

who created great suicidal dramas on the apartment cliff-banks of
the Hudson under the wartime blue floodlight of the moon
& their heads shall be crowned with laurel in oblivion,

who ate the lamb stew of the imagination or digested the crab at
the muddy bottom of the rivers of Bowery,

who wept at the romance of the streets with their pushcarts full of
onions and bad music,

who sat in boxes breathing in the darkness under the bridge, and
rose up to build harpsichords in their lofts,

who coughed on the sixth floor of Harlem crowned with flame
under the tubercular sky surrounded by orange crates of
theology,

who scribbled all night rocking and rolling over lofty incantations
which in the yellow morning were stanzas of gibberish,

who cooked rotten animals lung heart feet tail borsht & tortillas
dreaming of the pure vegetable kingdom,

who plunged themselves under meat trucks looking for an egg,

who threw their watches off the roof to cast their ballot for
Eternity outside of Time, & alarm clocks fell on their heads
every day for the next decade,

who cut their wrists three times successively unsuccessfully, gave up
and were forced to open antique stores where they thought
they were growing old and cried,

who were burned alive in their innocent flannel suits on Madison
Avenue amid blasts of leaden verse & the tanked-up clatter
of the iron regiments of fashion & the nitroglycerine shrieks
of the fairies of advertising & the mustard gas of sinister
intelligent editors, or were run down by the drunken taxicabs
of Absolute Reality,

who jumped off the Brooklyn Bridge this actually happened and
walked away unknown and forgotten into the ghostly daze
of Chinatown soup alleyways & firetrucks, not even one
free beer,

who sang out of their windows in despair, fell out of the subway
        window, jumped in the filthy Passaic, leaped on negroes,
        cried all over the street, danced on broken wineglasses
        barefoot smashed phonograph records of nostalgic European
        1930's German jazz finished the whiskey and threw up
        groaning into the bloody toilet, moans in their ears and the
        blast of colossal steamwhistles,
who barreled down the highways of the past journeying to each
        other's hotrod-Golgotha jail-solitude watch or Birmingham
        jazz incarnation,
who drove crosscountry seventytwo hours to find out if I had a
        vision or you had a vision or he had a vision to find out
        Eternity,
who journeyed to Denver, who died in Denver, who came back to
        Denver & waited in vain, who watched over Denver &
        brooded & loned in Denver and finally went away to find
        out the Time, & now Denver is lonesome for her heroes,
who fell on their knees in hopeless cathedrals praying for each
        other's salvation and light and breasts, until the soul
        illuminated its hair for a second,
who crashed through their minds in jail waiting for impossible
        criminals with golden heads and the charm of reality in
        their hearts who sang sweet blues to Alcatraz,
who retired to Mexico to cultivate a habit, or Rocky Mount to
        tender Buddha or Tangiers to boys or Southern Pacific to
        the black locomotive or Harvard to Narcissus to Woodlawn
        to the daisychain or grave,
who demanded sanity trials accusing the radio of hypnotism &
        were left with their insanity & their hands & a hung jury,
who threw potato salad at CCNY lecturers on Dadaism and
        subsequently presented themselves on the granite steps of
        the madhouse with shaven heads and harlequin speech of
        suicide, demanding instantaneous lobotomy,
and who were given instead the concrete void of insulin metrasol
        electricity hydrotherapy psychotherapy occupational therapy
        pingpong & amnesia,
who in humorless protest overturned only one symbolic pingpong
        table, resting briefly in catatonia,
returning years later truly bald except for a wig of blood, and tears
        and fingers, to the visible madman doom of the wards of
        the madtowns of the East,
Pilgrim State's Rockland's and Greystone's foetid halls, bickering
        with the echoes of the soul, rocking and rolling in the

midnight solitude-bench dolmen-realms of love, dream of
life a nightmare, bodies turned to stone as heavy as the moon,
with mother finally ******, and the last fantastic book flung out
of the tenement window, and the last door closed at 4 AM
and the last telephone slammed at the wall in reply and the
last furnished room emptied down to the last piece of
mental furniture, a yellow paper rose twisted on a wire
hanger in the closet, and even that imaginary, nothing but
a hopeful little bit of hallucination—
ah, Carl, while you are not safe I am not safe, and now you're
really in the total animal soup of time—
and who therefore ran through the icy streets obsessed with a
sudden flash of the alchemy of the use of the ellipse the
catalog the meter & the vibrating plane,
who dreamt and made incarnate gaps in Time & Space through
images juxtaposed, and trapped the archangel of the soul
between 2 visual images and joined the elemental verbs
and set the noun and dash of consciousness together jumping
with sensation of Pater Omnipotens Aeterna Deus
to recreate the syntax and measure of poor human prose and stand
before you speechless and intelligent and shaking with
shame, rejected yet confessing out the soul to conform to
the rhythm of thought in his naked and endless head,
the madman bum and angel beat in Time, unknown, yet putting
down here what might be left to say in time come after
death,
and rose reincarnate in the ghostly clothes of jazz in the goldhorn
shadow of the band and blew the suffering of America's
naked mind for love into an eli eli lamma lamma sabacthani
saxophone cry that shivered the cities down to the last radio
with the absolute heart of the poem of life butchered out of their
own bodies good to eat a thousand years.

IN THE BAGGAGE ROOM AT GREYHOUND

I

In the depths of the Greyhound Terminal
sitting dumbly on a baggage truck looking at the sky waiting for
the Los Angeles Express to depart
worrying about eternity over the Post Office roof in the night-time
red downtown heaven,

staring through my eyeglasses I realized shuddering these thoughts
        were not eternity, nor the poverty of our lives, irritable
        baggage clerks,
nor the millions of weeping relatives surrounding the buses waving
        goodbye,
nor other millions of the poor rushing around from city to city to
        see their loved ones,
nor an indian dead with fright talking to a huge cop by the Coke
        machine,
nor this trembling old lady with a cane taking the last trip of her
        life,
nor the red capped cynical porter collecting his quarters and
        smiling over the smashed baggage,
nor me looking around at the horrible dream,
nor mustached negro Operating Clerk named Spade, dealing out
        with his marvelous long hand the fate of thousands of
        express packages,
nor fairy Sam in the basement limping from leaden trunk to trunk,
nor Joe at the counter with his nervous breakdown smiling cowardly
        at the customers,
nor the grayish-green whale's stomach interior loft where we keep
        the baggage in hideous racks,
hundreds of suitcases full of tragedy rocking back and forth waiting
        to be opened,
nor the baggage that's lost, nor damaged handles, nameplates
        vanished, busted wires & broken ropes, whole trunks
        exploding on the concrete floor,
nor seabags emptied into the night in the final warehouse.

    II

Yet Spade reminded me of Angel, unloading a bus,
dressed in blue overalls black face official Angel's workman cap,
pushing with his belly a huge tin horse piled high with black
        baggage,
looking up as he passed the yellow light bulb of the loft
and holding high on his arm an iron shepherd's crook.

    III

It was the racks, I realized, sitting myself on top of them now as is
        my wont at lunchtime to rest my tired foot,
it was the racks, great wooden shelves and stanchions posts and
        beams assembled floor to roof jumbled with baggage,

—the Japanese white metal postwar trunk gaudily flowered &
    headed for Fort Bragg,
one Mexican green paper package in purple rope adorned with
    names for Nogales,
hundreds of radiators all at once for Eureka,
crates of Hawaiian underwear,
rolls of posters scattered over the Peninsula, nuts to Sacramento,
one human eye for Napa,
an aluminum box of human blood for Stockton
and a little red package of teeth for Calistoga—
it was the racks and these on the racks I saw naked in electric
    light the night before I quit,
the racks were created to hang our possessions, to keep us together,
    a temporary shift in space,
God's only way of building the rickety structure of Time,
to hold the bags to send on the roads, to carry our luggage from
    place to place
looking for a bus to ride us back home to Eternity where the heart
    was left and farewell tears began.

  IV

A swarm of baggage sitting by the counter as the transcontinental
    bus pulls in.
The clock registering 12.15 A.M., May 9, 1956, the second hand
    moving forward, red.
Getting ready to load my last bus. —Farewell, Walnut Creek
    Richmond Vallejo Portland Pacific Highway
Fleet-footed Quicksilver, God of transience.
One last package sits lone at midnight sticking up out of the Coast
    rack high as the dusty fluorescent light.

The wage they pay us is too low to live on. Tragedy reduced to
    numbers.
This for the poor shepherds. I am a communist.

Farewell ye Greyhound where I suffered so much,
hurt my knee and scraped my hand and built my pectoral muscles
    big as vagina.

A SUPERMARKET IN CALIFORNIA

    What thoughts I have of you tonight, Walt Whitman, for
I walked down the sidestreets under the trees with a headache
self-conscious looking at the full moon.

In my hungry fatigue, and shopping for images, I went
into the neon fruit supermarket, dreaming of your enumerations!

What peaches and what penumbras! Whole families
shopping at night! Aisles full of husbands! Wives in the
avocados, babies in the tomatoes!—and you, Garcia Lorca,
what were you doing down by the watermelons?

I saw you, Walt Whitman, childless, lonely old grubber,
poking among the meats in the refrigerator and eyeing the
grocery boys.

I heard you asking questions of each: Who killed the
pork chops? What price bananas? Are you my Angel?

I wandered in and out of the brilliant stacks of cans
following you, and followed in my imagination by the store
detective.

We strode down the open corridors together in our
solitary fancy tasting artichokes, possessing every frozen
delicacy, and never passing the cashier.

Where are we going, Walt Whitman? The doors close in
an hour. Which way does your beard point tonight?

(I touch your book and dream of our odyssey in the
supermarket and feel absurd.)

Will we walk all night through solitary streets? The trees
add shade to shade, lights out in the houses, we'll both be
lonely.

Will we stroll dreaming of the lost America of love past
blue automobiles in driveways, home to our silent cottage?

Ah, dear father, graybeard, lonely old courage-teacher,
what America did you have when Charon quit poling his ferry
and you got out on a smoking bank and stood watching the
boat disappear on the black waters of Lethe?

Berkeley 1955

DEATH TO VAN GOGH'S EAR!

POET is Priest
Money has reckoned the soul of America
Congress broken thru to the precipice of Eternity
the President built a War machine which will vomit and rear up
      Russia out of Kansas

The American Century betrayed by a mad Senate which no
          longer sleeps with its wife
Franco has murdered Lorca the fairy son of Whitman
just as Mayakovsky committed suicide to avoid Russia
Hart Crane distinguished Platonist committed suicide to cave in
          the wrong America
just as millions of tons of human wheat were burned in secret
          caverns under the White House
while India starved and screamed and ate mad dogs full of rain
and mountains of eggs were reduced to white powder in the halls
          of Congress
no godfearing man will walk there again because of the stink of
          the rotten eggs of America
and the Indians of Chiapas continue to gnaw their vitaminless
          tortillas
aborigines of Australia perhaps gibber in the eggless wilderness
and I rarely have an egg for breakfast tho my work requires
          infinite eggs to come to birth in Eternity
eggs should be eaten or given to their mothers
and the grief of the countless chickens of America is expressed
          in the screaming of her comedians over the radio
Detroit has built a million automobiles of rubber trees and
          phantoms
but I walk, I walk, and the Orient walks with me, and all Africa
          walks
and sooner or later North America will walk
for as we have driven the Chinese Angel from our door he will
          drive us from the Golden Door of the future
we have not cherished pity on Tanganyika
Einstein alive was mocked for his heavenly politics
Bertrand Russell driven from New York for getting laid
and the immortal Chaplin has been driven from our shores with
          the rose in his teeth
a secret conspiracy by Catholic Church in the lavatories of
          Congress has denied contraceptives to the unceasing
          masses of India.
Nobody publishes a word that is not the cowardly robot ravings
          of a depraved mentality
the day of the publication of the true literature of the American
          body will be day of Revolution
the revolution of the sexy lamb
the only bloodless revolution that gives away corn
poor Genet will illuminate the harvesters of Ohio

Marijuana is a benevolent narcotic but J. Edgar Hoover prefers
       his deathly scotch
And the heroin of Lao-Tze & the Sixth Patriarch is punished
       by the electric chair
but the poor sick junkies have nowhere to lay their heads
fiends in our government have invented a cold-turkey cure for
       addiction as obsolete as the Defense Early Warning Radar
       System
I am the defense early warning radar system
I see nothing but bombs
I am not interested in preventing Asia from being Asia
and the governments of Russia and Asia will rise and fall but
       Asia and Russia will not fall
the government of America also will fall but how can America
       fall
I doubt if anyone will ever fall anymore except governments
fortunately all the governments will fall
the only ones which won't fall are the good ones
and the good ones don't yet exist
But they have to begin existing they exist in my poems
they exist in the death of the Russian and American governments
they exist in the death of Hart Crane & Mayakovsky
Now is the time for prophecy without death as a consequence
the universe will ultimately disappear
Hollywood will rot on the windmills of Eternity
Hollywood whose movies stick in the throat of God
Yes Hollywood will get what it deserves
Time
Seepage or nerve-gas over the radio
History will make this poem prophetic and its awful silliness a
       hideous spiritual music
I have the moan of doves and the feather of ecstasy
Man cannot long endure the hunger of the cannibal abstract
War is abstract
the world will be destroyed
but I will die only for poetry, that will save the world
Monument to Sacco & Vanzetti not yet financed to ennoble
       Boston
natives of Kenya tormented by idiot con-men from England
South Africa in the grip of the white fool
Vachel Lindsay Secretary of the Interior
Poe Secretary of Imagination
Pound Secty. Economics

and Kra belongs to Kra, and Pukti to Pukti
crossfertilization of Blok and Artaud
Van Gogh's Ear on the currency
no more propaganda for monsters
and poets should stay out of politics or become monsters
I have become monsterous with politics
the Russian poet undoubtedly monsterous in his secret notebook
Tibet should be left alone
These are obvious prophecies
America will be destroyed
Russian poets will struggle with Russia
Whitman warned against this 'fabled Damned of nations'
Where was Theodore Roosevelt when he sent out ultimatums
       from his castle in Camden
Where was the House of Representatives when Crane read aloud
       from his prophetic books
What was Wall Street scheming when Lindsay announced the
       doom of Money
Were they listening to my ravings in the locker rooms of Bick-
       fords Employment Offices?
Did they bend their ears to the moans of my soul when I
       struggled with market research statistics in the Forum at
       Rome?
No they were fighting in fiery offices, on carpets of heartfailure,
       screaming and bargaining with Destiny
fighting the Skeleton with sabres, muskets, buck teeth, indigestion,
       bombs of larceny, whoredom, rockets, pederasty,
back to the wall to build up their wives and apartments, lawns,
       suburbs, fairydoms,
Puerto Ricans crowded for massacre on 114th St. for the sake
       of an imitation Chinese-Moderne refrigerator
Elephants of mercy murdered for the sake of an Elizabethan
       birdcage
millions of agitated fanatics in the bughouse for the sake of the
       screaming soprano of industry
Money-chant of soapers—toothpaste apes in television sets—
       deodorizers on hypnotic chairs—
petroleum mongers in Texas—jet plane streaks among the
       clouds—
sky writers liars in the face of Divinity—fanged butchers of
       hats and shoes, all Owners! Owners! Owners! with
       obsession on property and vanishing Selfhood!

and their long editorials on the fence of the screaming negro
        attacked by ants crawled out of the front page!
Machinery of a mass electrical dream! A war-creating Whore of
        Babylon bellowing over Capitols and Academies!
Money! Money! Money! shrieking mad celestial money of
        illusion! Money made of nothing, starvation, suicide!
        Money of failure! Money of death!
Money against Eternity! and eternity's strong mills grind out
        vast paper of Illusion!

Paris 1958

IGNU

On top of that if you know me I pronounce you an ignu
Ignu knows nothing of the world
a great ignoramus in factories though he may own or inspire
        them or even be production manager
Ignu has knowledge of the angel indeed ignu is angel in comical
        form
W. C. Fields Harpo Marx ignus Whitman an ignu
Rimbaud a natural ignu in his boy pants
The ignu may be queer though like not kind ignu blows arch-
        angels for the strange thrill
agnostic women love him Christ overflowed with trembling
        semen for many a dead aunt
He's a great cocksman most beautiful girls are worshipped by
        ignu
Hollywood dolls or lone Marys of Idaho long-legged publicity
        women and secret housewives
have known ignu in another lifetime and remember their lover
Husbands also are secretly tender to ignu their buddy
oldtime friendship can do anything cuckold bugger drunk
        trembling and happy
Ignu lives only once and eternally and knows it
he sleeps in everybody's bed everyone's lonesome for ignu ignu
        knew solitude early
So ignu's a primitive of cock and mind
equally the ignu has written liverish tomes personal metaphysics
        abstract

images that scratch the moon 'lightningflash-flintspark' naked
          lunch fried shoes adios king
The shadow of the angel is waving in the opposite direction
dawn of intelligence turns the telephones into strange animals
he attacks the rose garden with his mystical shears snip snip snip
Ignu has painted Park Avenue with his own long melancholy
and ignu giggles in a hard chair over tea in Paris bald in his
          decaying room a black hotel
Ignu with his wild mop walks by Colosseum weeping
he plucks a clover from Keats' grave & Shelley's a blade of grass
knew Coleridge they had slow hung-up talks at midnight over
          tables of mahogany in London
sidestreet rooms in wintertime rain outside fog the cabman
          blows his hand
Charles Dickens is born ignu hears the wail of the babe
Ignu goofs nights under bridges and laughs at battleships
ignu is a battleship without guns in the North Sea lost O the
          flowerness of the moment
he knows geography he was there before he'll get out and die
          already
reborn a bearded humming Jew of Arabian mournful jokes
man with a star on his forehead and halo over his cranium
listening to music musing happy at the fall of a leaf the moon-
          light of immortality in his hair
table-hopping most elegant comrade of all most delicate man-
          nered in the Sufi court
he wasn't even there at all
wearing zodiacal blue sleeves and the long peaked conehat of a
          magician
harkening to the silence of a well at midnight under a red star
in the lobby of Rockefeller Center attentive courteous bare-eyed
          enthusiastic with or without pants
he listens to jazz as if he were a negro afflicted with jewish
          melancholy and white divinity
Ignu's a natural you can see it when he pays the cabfare
          abstracted
pulling off the money from an impossible saintly roll
or counting his disappearing pennies to give to the strange bus-
          driver whom he admires
Ignu has sought you out he's the seeker of God
and God breaks down the world for him every ten years
he sees lightning flash in empty daylight when the sky is blue

he hears Blake's disembodied Voice recite the Sunflower in a
       room in Harlem
No woe on him surrounded by 700 thousand mad scholars moths
       fly out of his sleeve
He wants to die give up go mad break through into Eternity
live on and teach an aged saint or break down to an eyebrow
       clown
All ignus know each other in a moment's talk and measure each
       other up at once
as lifetime friends romantic winks and giggles across continents
sad moment paying the cab goodby and speeding away uptown
One or two grim ignus in the pack
one laughing monk in dungarees
one delighted by cracking his eggs in an egg cup
one chews gum to music all night long rock and roll
one anthropologist cookoo in the Petén Rainforest
one sits in jail all year and bets karmaic racetrack
one chases girls down East Broadway into the horror movie
one pulls out withered grapes and rotten onions from his pants
one has a nannygoat under his bed to amuse visitors plasters the
       wall with his crap
collects scorpions whiskies skies etc. would steal the moon if he
       could find it
That would set fire to America but none of these make ignu
it's the soul that makes the style the tender firecracker of his
       thought
the amity of letters from strange cities to old friends
and the new radiance of morning on a foreign bed
A comedy of personal being his grubby divinity
Eliot probably an ignu one of the few who's funny when he eats
Williams of Paterson a dying American ignu
Burroughs a purest ignu his haircut is a cream his left finger
pinkey chopped off for early ignu reasons metaphysical spells love
       spells with psychoanalysts
his very junkhood an accomplishment beyond a million dollars
Celine himself an old ignu over prose
I saw him in Paris dirty old gentleman of ratty talk
with longhaired cough three wormy sweaters round his neck
brown mould under historic fingernails
pure genius his giving morphine all night to 1400 passengers on
       a sinking ship
'because they were all getting emotional'

Who's amazing you is ignu communicate with me
by mail post telegraph phone street accusation or scratching at
       my window
and send me a true sign I'll reply special delivery
DEATH IS A LETTER THAT WAS NEVER SENT
Knowledge born of stamps words coins pricks jails seasons sweet
       ambition laughing gas
history with a gold halo photographs of the sea painting a
       celestial din in the bright window
one eye in a black cloud
and the lone vulture on a sand plain seen from the window of a
       Turkish bus
It must be a trick. Two diamonds in the hand one Poetry one
       Charity
proves we have dreamed and the long sword of intelligence
over which I constantly stumble like my pants at the age six—
       embarrassed.

NY 1958

AMERICA

America I've given you all and now I'm nothing.
America two dollars and twentyseven cents January 17, 1956.
I can't stand my own mind.
America when will we end the human war?
Go fuck yourself with your atom bomb.
I don't feel good don't bother me.
I won't write my poem till I'm in my right mind.
America when will you be angelic?
When will you take off your clothes?
When will you look at yourself through the grave?
When will you be worthy of your million Trotskyites?
America why are your libraries full of tears?
America when will you send your eggs to India?
I'm sick of your insane demands.
When can I go into the supermarket and buy what I need with my
       good looks?
America after all it is you and I who are perfect not the next world.
Your machinery is too much for me.
You made me want to be a saint.

There must be some other way to settle this argument.
Burroughs is in Tangiers I don't think he'll come back it's sinister.
Are you being sinister or is this some form of practical joke?
I'm trying to come to the point.
I refuse to give up my obsession.
America stop pushing I know what I'm doing.
America the plum blossoms are falling.
I haven't read the newspapers for months, everyday somebody goes
        on trial for murder.
America I feel sentimental about the Wobblies.
America I used to be a communist when I was a kid I'm not sorry.
I smoke marijuana every chance I get.
I sit in my house for days on end and stare at the roses in the closet.
When I go to Chinatown I get drunk and never get laid.
My mind is made up there's going to be trouble.
You should have seen me reading Marx.
My psychoanalyst thinks I'm perfectly right.
I won't say the Lord's Prayer.
I have mystical visions and cosmic vibrations.
America I still haven't told you what you did to Uncle Max after
        he came over from Russia.

I'm addressing you.
Are you going to let your emotional life be run by Time Magazine?
I'm obsessed by Time Magazine.
I read it every week.
Its cover stares at me every time I slink past the corner candystore.
I read it in the basement of the Berkeley Public Library.
It's always telling me about responsibility. Businessmen are serious.
        Movie producers are serious. Everybody's serious but me.
It occurs to me that I am America.
I am talking to myself again.

Asia is rising against me.
I haven't got a chinaman's chance.
I'd better consider my national resources.
My national resources consist of two joints of marijuana millions of
        genitals an unpublishable private literature that goes 1400
        miles an hour and twentyfive-thousand mental institutions.
I say nothing about my prisons nor the millions of underprivileged
        who live in my flowerpots under the light of five hundred
        suns.

I have abolished the whorehouses of France, Tangiers is the next
    to go.
My ambition is to be President despite the fact that I'm a Catholic.

America how can I write a holy litany in your silly mood?
I will continue like Henry Ford my strophes are as individual as
    his automobiles more so they're all different sexes.
America I will sell you strophes $2500 apiece $500 down on your
    old strophe
America free Tom Mooney
America save the Spanish Loyalists
America Sacco & Vanzetti must not die
America I am the Scottsboro boys.
America when I was seven momma took me to Communist Cell
    meetings they sold us garbanzos a handful per ticket
    a ticket costs a nickel and the speeches were free
    everybody was angelic and sentimental about the workers
    it was all so sincere you have no idea what a good thing
    the party was in 1835 Scott Nearing was a grand old man
    a real mensch Mother Bloor made me cry I once saw
    Israel Amter plain. Everybody must have been a spy.
America you don't really want to go to war.
America it's them bad Russians.
Them Russians them Russians and them Chinamen. And them
    Russians.
The Russia wants to eat us alive. The Russia's power mad. She
    wants to take our cars from out our garages.
Her wants to grab Chicago. Her needs a Red Readers' Digest.
    Her wants our auto plants in Siberia. Him big bureaucracy
    running our fillingstations.
That no good. Ugh. Him make Indians learn read. Him need
    big black niggers. Hah. Her make us all work sixteen hours
    a day. Help.
America this is quite serious.
America this is the impression I get from looking in the television
    set.
America is this correct?
I'd better get right down to the job.
It's true I don't want to join the Army or turn lathes in precision
    parts factories, I'm nearsighted and psychopathic anyway.
America I'm putting my queer shoulder to the wheel.

LOVE POEM ON THEME BY WHITMAN

I'll go into the bedroom silently and lie down between the bridegroom
    and the bride,
those bodies fallen from heaven stretched out waiting naked and
    restless,
arms resting over their eyes in the darkness,
bury my face in their shoulders and breasts, breathing their skin,
and stroke and kiss neck and mouth and make back be open and
    known,
legs raised up crook'd to receive, cock in the darkness driven
    tormented and attacking
roused up from hole to itching head,
bodies locked shuddering naked, hot lips and buttocks screwed into
    each other
and eyes, eyes glinting and charming, widening into looks and
    abandon,
and moans of movement, voices, hands in hair, hands between thighs,
hands in moisture on softened lips, throbbing contraction of bellies
till the white come flow in the swirling sheets,
and the bride cry for forgiveness, and the groom be covered with tears
    of passion and compassion,
and I rise up from the bed replenished with last intimate gestures and
    kisses of farewell—
all before the mind wakes, behind shades and closed doors in a
    darkened house
where the inhabitants roam unsatisfied in the night,
nude ghosts seeking each other out in the silence.

from WICHITA VORTEX SUTRA

II

Face the Nation
Thru Hickman's rolling earth hills
        icy winter
            grey sky   bare trees lining the road
    South to Wichita
        you're in the Pepsi Generation   Signum enroute
Aiken Republican on the radio   60,000
    Northvietnamese troops now infiltrated but over 250,000

South Vietnamese   armed men
                    our Enemy—
                         Not Hanoi our enemy
                         Not China our enemy
                              The Viet Cong!
                    McNamara made a "bad guess"
"Bad Guess" chorused the Reporters?
          Yes, no more than a Bad Guess, in 1962
                         "8000 American Troops handle the
                              Situation"
                                   Bad Guess

     in 1956, 80% of the
          Vietnamese people would've voted for Ho Chi Minh
               wrote Ike   years later   *Mandate for Change*
                         A bad guess in the Pentagon
And the Hawks were guessing all along
                         Bomb China's 200,000,000
                         cried Stennis from Mississippi
                         I guess it was 3 weeks ago
          Holmes Alexander in Albuquerque Journal
               Provincial newsman
                    said I guess we better begin to do that Now.
               his typewriter clacking in his aged office
               on a side street   under Sandia Mountain?
                    Half the world away from China
Johnson got some bad advice   Republican Aiken sang
to the Newsmen over the radio
          The General guessed they'd stop infiltrating the South
               if they bombed the North—
                    So I guess they bombed!
          Pale Indochinese boys came thronging thru the jungle
                    in increased numbers
               to the scene of TERROR!
While the triangle-roofed Farmer's Grain Elevator
     sat quietly by the side of the road
          along the railroad track
American Eagle beating its wings over Asia
     million dollar helicopters
     a billion dollars worth of Marines
               who loved *Aunt Betty*
          Drawn from the shores and farms shaking
     from the high schools to the landing barge

blowing the air thru their cheeks with fear
in *Life* on Television
Put it this way on the radio
Put it this way in television language

                       Use the words
                           language, language:
                                 "A bad guess"

Put it this way in headlines
      Omaha World Herald—   *Rusk says Toughness*
                                Essential For Peace

Put it this way
      Lincoln Nebraska morning Star—

                         Vietnam War Brings Prosperity

Put it *this* way
        Declared McNamara,   speaking language
            Asserted Maxwell Taylor
            General, Consultant to White House
    Vietcong losses leveling up three five zero zero
                             per month
        Front page testimony February '66
    Here in Nebraska same as Kansas same known in Saigon
           in Peking, in Moscow, same known
        by the youths of Liverpool three five zero zero
        the latest quotation in the human meat market—
                  Father I cannot tell a lie!

A black horse bends its head to the stubble
        beside the silver stream winding thru the woods
        by an antique red barn on the outskirts of Beatrice—
                Quietness, quietness
      over this countryside
           except for unmistakable signals on radio
             followed by the honkytonk tinkle
                   of a city piano
to calm the nerves of taxpaying housewives of a Sunday morn.
        Has anyone looked in the eyes of the dead?
U.S. Army recruiting service sign *Careers With A Future*
    Is anyone living to look for future forgiveness?
Water hoses frozen on the street, the
        Crowd gathered to see a strange happening garage—
        Red flames on Sunday morning
           in a quiet town!

ALLEN GINSBERG 209

Has anyone looked in the eyes of the wounded?
Have we seen but paper faces, Life Magazine?
Are screaming faces made of dots,
electric dots on Television—
fuzzy decibels registering
the mammal voiced howl
from the outskirts of Saigon to console model picture tubes
in Beatrice, in Hutchinson, in El Dorado
in historic Abilene
O inconsolable!

Stop, and eat more flesh.
"We will negotiate anywhere anytime"
said the giant President
Kansas City Times 2/14/66: "Word reached U.S. authorities
that Thailand's leaders feared that in Honolulu Johnson might have
tried to persuade South Vietnam's rulers to ease their stand against
negotiating with the Viet Cong.
American officials said these fears were groundless and
Humphrey was telling the Thais so."
A.P. dispatch
The last week's paper is Amnesia.
Three five zero zero is numerals
Headline language poetry, nine decades after Democratic Vistas
and the Prophecy of the Good Grey Poet
Our nation "of the fabled damned"
or else . . .
Language, language
Ezra Pound the Chinese Written Character for truth
defined as man standing by his word
Word picture: forked creature
Man
standing by a box, birds flying out
representing mouth speech
Ham Steak please waitress, in the warm cafe.
Different from a bad guess.
The war is language,
language abused
for Advertisement,
language used
like magic for power on the planet:
Black Magic language,
formulas for reality—

Communism is a 9 letter word
used by inferior magicians with
the wrong alchemical formula for transforming earth into gold
—funky warlocks operating on guesswork,
handmedown   mandrake   terminology
that never worked in 1956
for grey-domed Dulles,
brooding over at State,
that never worked for Ike who knelt to take
the magic wafer in his mouth
from Dulles' hand
inside the church in Washington:
Communion of bum magicians
congress of failures from Kansas & Missouri
working with the wrong equations
Sorcerer's Apprentices who lost control
of the simplest broomstick in the world:
Language
O longhaired magician come home take care of your dumb helper
before the radiation deluge floods your livingroom,
your magic errandboy's
just made a bad guess again
that's lasted a whole decade.

N B C B S U P A P I N S L I F E
Time Mutual presents
World's Largest Camp Comedy:
Magic In Vietnam—
reality turned inside out
changing its sex in the Mass Media
for 30 days, TV den and bedroom farce
Flashing pictures Senate Foreign Relations Committee room
Generals faces flashing on and off screen
mouthing language
State Secretary speaking nothing but language
McNamara declining to speak public language
The President talking language,
Senators reinterpreting language
General Taylor *Limited Objectives*
Owls from Pennsylvania
Clark's Face *Open Ended*
Dove's *Apocalypse*
Morse's hairy ears

ALLEN GINSBERG   211

Stennis orating in Mississippi
                        half billion chinamen crowding into the
                                        polling booth,
                Clean shaven Gen. Gavin's image
                                        imagining *Enclaves*
                        Tactical Bombing the magic formula for
                        a silver haired Symington:
                Ancient Chinese apothegm:
                                        Old in vain.
                Hawks swooping thru the newspapers
                        talons visible
                wings outspread in the giant updraft of hot air
                                loosing their dry screech in the skies
                                                over the Capitol
Napalm and black clouds emerging in newsprint
        Flesh soft as a Kansas girl's
                        ripped open by metal explosion—
        three five zero zero   on the other side of the planet
                caught in barbed wire, fire ball
                bullet shock, bayonet electricity
        bomb blast terrific in skull & belly, shrapnelled
                                        throbbing meat
While this American nation argues war:
                conflicting language, language
                                proliferating in airwaves
        filling the farmhouse ear, filling
                the City Manager's head in his oaken office
                the professor's head in his bed at midnight
                the pupil's head at the movies
                        blond haired, his heart throbbing with desire
                        for the girlish image bodied on the screen:
                                or smoking cigarettes
                                and watching Captain Kangaroo
                                that fabled damned of nations
                                prophecy come true—
Though the highway's straight,
        dipping downward through low hills,
        rising narrow on the far horizon
                black cows browse in caked fields
                        ponds in the hollows lie frozen,
                                        quietness.
Is this the land that started war on China?
        This be the soil that thought Cold War for decades?

Are these nervous naked trees & farmhouses
                              the vortex
                        of oriental anxiety molecules
that've imagined   American Foreign Policy
      and magick'd up paranoia in Peking
                        and curtains of living blood
                              surrounding far Saigon?
Are these the towns where the language emerged
      from the mouths here
                        that makes a Hell of riots in Dominica
sustains the aging tyranny of Chiang in silent Taipeh city
Paid for the lost French war in Algeria
            overthrew the Guatemalan polis in '54
maintaining United Fruit's banana greed
                        another thirteen years
      for the secret prestige of the Dulles family lawfirm?

Here's Marysville—
      a black railroad engine in the children's park,
                        at rest—
and the Track Crossing
      with Cotton Belt flatcars
                  carrying autos west from Dallas
      Delaware & Hudson gondolas filled with power stuff—
a line of boxcars far east as the eye can see
                  carrying battle goods to cross the Rockies
            into the hands of rich longshoreman loading
                              ships on the Pacific—
            Oakland Army Terminal lights
                        blue illumined all night now—
Crash of couplings and the great American train
            moves on carrying its cushioned load of metal doom
      Union Pacific linked together with your Hoosier Line
                  followed by passive Wabash
                        rolling behind
                  all Erie carrying cargo in the rear,
            Central Georgia's rust colored truck proclaiming
                        The Right Way, concluding
      the awesome poem writ by the train
                  across northern Kansas,
            land which gave right of way
            to the massing of metal meant for explosion
                        in Indochina—

Passing thru Waterville,
      Electronic machinery in the bus humming prophecy—
         paper signs blowing in cold wind,
                mid-Sunday afternoon's silence
                    in town
        under frost-grey sky
                that covers the horizon—
That the rest of earth is unseen,
            an outer universe invisible,
         Unknown except thru
                language
                airprint
                    magic images
or prophecy of the secret
        heart the same
        in Waterville as Saigon one human form:
        When a woman's heart bursts in Waterville
          a woman screams equal in Hanoi—
On to Wichita to prophesy!   O frightful Bard!
   into the heart of the Vortex
      where anxiety rings
        the University with millionaire pressure,
      lonely crank telephone voices sighing in dread,
and students waken trembling in their beds
      with dreams of a new truth warm as meat,
      little girls suspecting their elders of murder
        committed by remote control machinery,
      boys with sexual bellies aroused
        chilled in the heart by the mailman
      with a letter from an aging white haired General
        Director of selection for service in
              Deathwar
      all this black language
        writ by machine!
        O hopeless Fathers and Teachers
      in Hué   do you know
          the same woe too?

I'm an old man now, and a lonesome man in Kansas
   but not afraid
      to speak my lonesomeness in a car,
      because not only my lonesomeness
        it's Ours, all over America,
          O tender fellows—

& spoken lonesomeness is Prophecy
in the moon 100 years ago or in
the middle of Kansas now.
It's not the vast plains mute our mouths
that fill at midnite with ecstatic language
when our trembling bodies hold each other
breast to breast on a mattress—
Not the empty sky that hides
the feeling from our faces
nor our skirts and trousers that conceal
the bodylove emanating in a glow of beloved skin,
white smooth abdomen down to the hair
between our legs,
It's not a God that bore us that forbid
our Being, like a sunny rose
all red with naked joy
between our eyes & bellies, yes
All we do is for this frightened thing
we call Love, want and lack—
fear that we aren't the one whose body could be
beloved of all the brides of Kansas City,
kissed all over by every boy of Wichita—
O but how many in their solitude weep aloud like me—
On the bridge over Republican River
almost in tears to know
how to speak the right language—
on the frosty broad road
uphill between highway embankments
I search for the language
that is also yours—
almost all our language has been taxed by war.
Radio antennae high tension
wires ranging from Junction City across the plains—
highway cloverleaf sunk in a vast meadow
lanes curving past Abilene
to Denver filled with old
heroes of love—
to Wichita where McClure's mind
burst into animal beauty
drunk, getting laid in a car
in a neon misted street
15 years ago—
to Independence where the old man's still alive
who loosed the bomb that's slaved all human consciousness

ALLEN GINSBERG   215

and made the body universe a place of fear—
Now, speeding along the empty plain,
                no giant demon machine
                    visible on the horizon
        but tiny human trees and wooden houses at the sky's edge
                I claim my birthright!
                    reborn forever as long as Man
                        in Kansas or other universe—Joy
                reborn after the vast sadness of War Gods!
A lone man talking to myself, no house in the brown vastness to hear,
                imagining the throng of Selves
                    that make this nation one body of Prophecy
                        languaged by Declaration as
                            Happiness!
I call all Powers of imagination
        to my side in this auto to make Prophecy,
                            all Lords
                of human kingdoms to come
Shambu Bharti Baba naked covered with ash
                Khaki Baba fat-bellied mad with the dogs
Dehorahava Baba who moans Oh how wounded, How wounded
            Citaram Onkar Das Thakur who commands
                            give up your desire
Satyananda who raises two thumbs in tranquillity
            Kali Pada Guha Roy whose yoga drops before the void
                Shivananda who touches the breast and says OM
Srimata Krishnaji of Brindaban who says take for your guru
        William Blake the invisible father of English visions
        Sri Ramakrishna master of ecstasy eyes
            half closed who only cries for his mother
Chaitanya arms upraised singing & dancing his own praise
        merciful Chango judging our bodies
                Durga-Ma covered with blood
                    destroyer of battlefield illusions
                million-faced Tathagata gone past suffering
        Preserver Harekrishna returning in the age of pain
Sacred Heart my Christ acceptable
                Allah the Compassionate One
                    Jaweh Righteous One
                all Knowledge-Princes of Earth-man, all
        ancient Seraphim of heavenly Desire, Devas, yogis
                & holymen I chant to—
                    Come to my lone presence
                        into this Vortex named Kansas,

I lift my voice aloud,
            make Mantra of American language now,
                    pronounce the words beginning my own millennium,
                            I here declare the end of the War!
                    Ancient days' Illusion!—
Let the States tremble,
            let the Nation weep,
                    let Congress legislate its own delight
                            let the President execute his own desire—
this Act done by my own voice,
                            nameless Mystery—
published to my own senses,
                    blissfully received by my own form
            approved with pleasure by my sensations
            manifestation of my very thought
            accomplished in my own imagination
                    all realms within my consciousness fulfilled
            60 miles from Wichita
                    near El Dorado,
                            The Golden One,
in chill earthly mist
            houseless brown farmland plains rolling heavenward
                                    in every direction
one midwinter afternoon Sunday called the day of the Lord—
            Pure Spring Water gathered in one tower
                    where Florence is
                            set on a hill,
                    stop for tea & gas

            Cars passing their messages along country crossroads
                    to populaces cement-networked on flatness,
                            giant white mist on earth
            and a Wichita Eagle-Beacon headlines
            "Kennedy Urges Cong Get Chair in Negotiations"
The War is gone,
            Language emerging on the motel news stand,
                            the right magic
            Formula, the language known
            in the back of the mind before, now in black print
                            daily consciousness
Eagle News Services Saigon—
            Headline Surrounded Vietcong Charge Into Fire Fight
                    the suffering not yet ended
                            for others

The last spasms of the dragon of pain
                    shoot thru the muscles
            a crackling around the eyeballs
            of a sensitive yellow boy by a muddy wall
Continued from page one   area
            after the Marines killed 256 Vietcong captured 31
            ten day operation Harvest Moon last December
                            Language language
            U.S. Military Spokesmen
                        Language language
                                Cong death toll
                has soared to 100 in First Air Cavalry
                Division's Sector of
                            Language language
                        Operation White Wing near Bong Son
Some of the
            Language language
                        Communist
                            Language language soldiers
charged so desperately
            they were struck with six or seven bullets before they fell
        Language Language M 60 Machine Guns
                        Language language in La Drang Valley
        the terrain is rougher infested with leeches and scorpions
                        The war was over several hours ago!
Oh at last again the radio opens
            blue Invitations!
                    Angelic Dylan singing across the nation
                        "When all your children start to resent you
                        Won't you come see me, Queen Jane?"
            His youthful voice making glad
                            the brown endless meadows
            His tenderness penetrating aether,
                soft prayer on the airwaves,
                        Language language, and sweet music too
                        even unto thee,
                            hairy flatness!
                        even unto thee
                                despairing Burns!

Future speeding on swift wheels
                    straight to the heart of Wichita!
Now radio voices cry population hunger world
                        of unhappy people

                    waiting for Man to be born
                              O man in America!
        you certainly smell good
                              the radio says
        passing mysterious families of winking towers
        grouped round a quonset-hut on a hillock—
                    feed storage or military fear factory here?
Sensitive City, Ooh! Hamburger & Skelley's Gas
                        lights feed man and machine,
        Kansas Electric Substation aluminum robot
                signals thru thin antennae towers
                above the empty football field
                                                        at Sunday dusk
to a solitary derrick that pumps oil from the unconscious
                        working night & day
        & factory gas-flares edge a huge golf course
                where tired businessmen can come and play—
Cloverleaf, Merging Traffic East Wichita turnoff
                        McConnell Airforce Base
                                    nourishing the city—
        Lights rising in the suburbs
        Supermarket Texaco brilliance starred
                        over streetlamp vertebrae on Kellogg,
                green jewelled traffic lights
                        confronting the windshield,
Centertown ganglion entered!
                    Crowds of autos moving with their lightshine,
                    signbulbs winking in the driver's eyeball—
        The human nest collected, neon lit,
                                and sunburst signed
                for business as usual, except on the Lord's Day—
        Redeemer Lutheran's three crosses lit on the lawn
                                reminder of our sins
        and Titsworth offers insurance on Hydraulic
        by De Voors Guard's Mortuary for outmoded bodies
                                of the human vehicle
                which no Titsworth of insurance will customise
                                        for resale—
So home, traveller, past the newspaper language factory
        under Union Station railroad bridge on Douglas
        to the center of the Vortex, calmly returned
                to Hotel Eaton—
Carry Nation began the war on Vietnam here

                                        ALLEN GINSBERG   219

                    with an angry smashing axe
                              attacking Wine—
          Here fifty years ago, by her violence
began a vortex of hatred that defoliated the Mekong Delta—
          Proud Wichita!   vain Wichita
                    cast the first stone!—
                              That murdered my mother
               who died of the communist anticommunist psychosis
                    in the madhouse one decade long ago
          complaining about wires of masscommunication in her head
                    and phantom political voices in the air
                              besmirching her girlish character.
          Many another has suffered death and madness
               in the Vortex from Hydraulic
                         to the end of 17th—enough!
The war is over now—
          Except for the souls
                    held prisoner in Niggertown
still pining for love of your tender white bodies O children of Wichita!

SOME METAMORPHOSES OF PERSONAL PROSODY

Much earlier training in versification & time sense modeled after pages of Wyatt resulted in overwritten coy stanzas permutating abstract concepts derived secondhand from Silver Poets, which carefulness managed to suppress almost all traces of native sensibility diction concrete fact & personal breath on my own vers de collège. "In this mode perfection is basic," W. C. Williams reproved me correctly; simultaneously he responded with enthusiasm to short fragments of personal notation drawn from diaries & rearranged in lines emphasizing crude breath-stop syncopations. Later practice in this mode (Kerouac urging "speak now or ever hold thy peace") trained my sensibility to the eccentric modulations of long-line composition displayed by Smart, Blake, Whitman, Jeffers, Rimbaud, Artaud & other precursors including now Edward Carpenter (whose *Towards Democracy* read me this year by his later lover Gavin Arthur struck me as the combine of Blake-visionary & Whitmanic-direct-notation nearest my own intuition that I'd ever stumbled upon) (In fact I decided ruefully for 24 hours that I was like Carpenter just another fine minor Whitman necessary but forgettable.)

But young minstrels have now arisen on the airwaves whose poetic forms outwardly resemble antique verse including regular stanzas refrains and rhymes: Dylan and Donovan and some fragments of the Rolling Stones because they *think* not only in words but also in music simultaneously have out of the necessities of their own space-age media and electric machinery tunes evolved a natural use of—a personal realistic imaginative rhymed verse. Principle of composition here is, however, unlike antique literary form, primarily spontaneous & improvised (in the studio if need be at the last minute), and prophetic in character in that tune and language are invoked shamanistically on the spot from the unconscious. This new ear is not dead only for eye-page, it's connected with a voice improvising, with hesitancies aloud, a living musician's ear. The old library poets had lost their voices; natural voice was rediscovered; and now natural song for physical voice. Oddly this fits Pound's paradigm tracing the degeneration of Poesy from the Greek dance-foot chorus thru minstrel song thru 1900 abstract voiceless page. So now returned to song and song forms we may yet anticipate inspired Creators like Shiva Krishna Chaitanya Mirabai & Ramakrishna who not only composed verse in ecstatic fits, but also chanted their verse in melody, and lifted themselves off the floor raised their arms and danced in time to manifest Divine Presence. Mantra repetition—a form of prayer in which a short magic formula containing various God names is chanted hypnotically—has entered Western consciousness & a new Mantra-rock is formulated in the Byrds & Beatles.

Not being a musician from childhood my own Japa and Kirtan is home-made but not without influence on verbal composition practice. Introduction of tape recorder also catalyses changes in possibilities of composition via improvisation. *Wichita Vortex Sutra,* a short fragment of longer trans-american voyage poetries, is therefore composed directly on tape by voice, and then transcribed to page: page arrangement notates the thought-stops, breath-stops, runs of inspiration, changes of mind, startings and stoppings of the car.

Allen Ginsberg
Sept 10, 1966

GALWAY KINNELL

Galway Kinnell was born in 1927 in Rhode Island, and was educated at Rochester and Princeton. He has taught at Grenoble, Chicago, Teheran, Reed, and Irvine. When he is not teaching, he, his wife, and his children live on a farm near Sheffield, Vermont. His books of verse are What a Kingdom It Was, Flower Herding on Mount Monadnock, *and* Body Rags; *he has translated* The Poems of François Villon *and Yves Bonnefoy's* On the Motion and Immobility of Douve, *and is the author of a novel,* Black Light.

Jill Krementz

THE POEM

1

On this hill crossed
by the last birds, a sprinkling
of soil covers up the rocks
with green, as
the face
drifts on a skull scratched with glaciers.

The poem too
is a palimpsest, streaked
with erasures, smelling
of departure and burnt stone.

2

The full moon
slides from the clouds, the trees'
graves all lie out at their feet:

the leaf
shaped tongue
of the new born and the dying
quivers, and no one interprets it.

3

Where is "The Apocalypse of Lamech"?
Where is the "Iliupersis"?
Where is the "Khavadhaynamagh"?
Where is the "Rommant du Pet au Deable"?
Where is "The Book of the Lion"?
Where is the servantose of the sixty girls of Florence?
Where are the small poems Li Po folded into boats and pushed out
         on the river?
Where are the snows that fell in these graves?

4

On this hillside strewn with
fistbones unclasping for the first time from the pistol and club,
fatalist wishbones,
funnybones gone up in laughing gas,
astralagi from which the butterflies have flown,

innominate bones,
sacrums the eucharist-platters of kites,
and here and there a luz-bone dead of non-resurrection,

we hunt
the wild hummingbird
who once loved nesting in these
pokeweed-spouting, pismired
ribcages dumped down all over the place.

5

On a branch
in the morning light, at the tip
of an icicle, the letter C
comes into being—trembles,
to drop, or to cling?

Suddenly a roman
carapace glitters all over it. Look:

6

Here is a fern-leaf binding *utter* to the image of *illume,*
here is a lightning-split fir the lines down its good side
      becoming whitmanesque and free,
here is *unfulfilled* reflected as *mellifica* along the feather of a crow,
here is a hound chasing his bitch in trochaic dimeter brachycatalectic,
here are the pits where the tongue-bone is hurled at its desolate cry,
here are my own clothes composing *emptiness* in khaskura,
here is a fly convulsing down the poisoned labyrinth of this poem,
here is an armful of last-year's-snows.

7

The moment
in the late night, when baby birds
closed in dark wings almost stir, and objects
on the page grow suddenly
heavy, hugged
by a rush of strange gravity:

the surgery of the funeral
and of the funeral oration, the absence
in the speech I will have left in the world
of

8

Where are "The Onions"
that I saw swollen with tears on a grocery shelf
in 1948?

brong ding plang ching of a spike
driven crazy on a locust
post.

THE PORCUPINE

1

Fatted
on herbs, swollen on crabapples,
puffed up on bast and phloem, ballooned
on willow flowers, poplar catkins, first
leafs of aspen and larch,
the porcupine
drags and bounces his last meal through ice,
mud, roses and goldenrod, into the stubbly high fields.

2

In character
he resembles us in seven ways:
he puts his mark on outhouses,
he alchemizes by moonlight,
he shits on the run,
he uses his tail for climbing,
he chuckles softly to himself when scared,
he's overcrowded if there's more than one of him per five acres,
his eyes have their own inner redness.

3

Digger of
goings across floors, of hesitations
at thresholds, of
handprints of dread
at doorpost or window jamb, he would
gouge the world

empty of us, hack and crater
it
until it is nothing, if that
could rinse it of all our sweat and pathos.

Adorer of ax
handles aflow with grain, of arms
of Morris chairs, of hand
crafted objects
steeped in the juice of fingertips,
of surfaces wetted down
with fist grease and elbow oil,
of clothespins that have
grabbed our body-rags by underarm and crotch . . .

Unimpressed—bored—
by the whirl of the stars, by *these*
he's astonished, ultra-
Rilkean angel!

for whom the true
portion of the sweetness of earth
is one of those bottom-heavy, glittering, saccadic
bits
of salt water that splash down
the haunted ravines of a human face.

4

A farmer shot a porcupine three times
as it dozed on a tree limb. On
the way down it tore open its belly
on a broken
branch, hooked its gut,
and went on falling. On the ground
it sprang to its feet, and
paying out gut heaved
and spartled through a hundred feet of goldenrod
before
the abrupt emptiness.

5

The Avesta
puts porcupine killers

into hell for nine generations, sentencing them
to gnaw out
each other's hearts for the
salts of desire.

I roll
this way and that in the great bed, under
the quilt
that mimics this country of broken farms and woods,
the fatty sheath of the man
melting off,
the self-stabbing coil
of bristles reversing, blossoming outward—
a red-eyed, hard-toothed, arrow-stuck urchin
tossing up mattress feathers,
pricking the
woman beside me until she cries.

6

In my time I have
crouched, quills erected,
Saint
Sebastian of the
scared heart, and been
beat dead with a locust club
on the bare snout.
And fallen from high places
I have fled, have
jogged
over fields of goldenrod,
terrified, seeking home,
and among flowers
I have come to myself empty, the rope
strung out behind me
in the fall sun
suddenly glorified with all my blood.

7

And tonight I think I prowl broken
skulled or vacant as a
sucked egg in the wintry meadow, softly chuckling, blank
template of myself, dragging

a starved belly through the lichflowered acres,
where
burdock looses the arks of its seed
and thistle holds up its lost blooms
and rosebushes in the wind scrape their dead limbs
for the forced-fire
of roses.

SPINDRIFT

1

On this tree thrown up
From the sea, its tangle of roots
Letting the wind go through, I sit
Looking down the beach: old
Horseshoe crabs, broken skates,
Sand dollars, sea horses, as though
Only primeval creatures get destroyed,
At chunks of sea-mud still quivering,
At the light as it glints off the water
And the billion facets of the sand,
At the soft, mystical shine the wind
Blows over the dunes as they creep.

2

Sit down
By the clanking shore
Of this bitter, beloved sea,

Pluck sacred
Shells from the icy surf,
Fans of gold light, sunbursts,

Lift one to the sun
As a sign you accept to go,
As bid, to the shrine of the dead,

And as it blazes
See the lost life within
Alive again in the fate-shine.

3

This little bleached root
Drifted from some foreign shore,
Brittle, cold, practically weightless,

If anything is dead, it is,
This castout worn
To the lost grip it always essentially was.

If it has lost hold
It at least keeps the wild
Shape of what it held,

And it remains the hand
Of that gravel, one of the earth's
Wandering icons of "to have."

4

I sit listening
To the surf as it falls,
The power and inexhaustible freshness of the sea,
The suck and inner boom
As a wave tears free and crashes back
In overlapping thunders going away down the beach.

It is the most we know of time,
And it is our undermusic of eternity.

5

I think of how I
Sat by a dying woman,
Her shell of a hand,
Wet and cold in both of mine,
Light, nearly out, existing as smoke,
I sat in the glow of her wan, absorbed smile.

6

Under the high wind
That moans in the grass
And whistles through crabs' claws
I sit holding this little lamp,
This icy fan of the sun.

Across gull tracks
And wind ripples in the sand
The wind seethes. My footprints
Slogging for the absolute
Already begin vanishing.

7

What does he really love,
That old man,
His wrinkled eyes
Tortured by smoke,
Walking in the ungodly
Rasp and cackle of old flesh?

The swan dips her head
And peers at the mystic
In-life of the sea,
The gull drifts up
And eddies towards heaven,
The breeze in his arms . . .

Nobody likes to die
But an old man
Can know
A kind of gratefulness
Towards time that kills him,
Everything he loved was made of it.

In the end
What is he but the scallop shell
Shining with time like any pilgrim?

POEMS OF NIGHT

1

I touch your face,
I move my hand over
Slopes, falls, lumps of sight,
Lashes barely able to be touched,
Lips that give way so easily

It's a shock to feel underneath
The hard grin of the bones.

Muffled a little, barely cloaked,
Zygoma, maxillary, turbinate.

2

I put my hand
On the side of your face,
You lean your head a little
Into my hand—and so,
I know you're a dormouse
Taken up in winter sleep,
A lonely, stunned weight
Shut in the natural mystery.

3

A cheekbone,
A curved piece of brow,
A pale eyelid
Float in the dark,
And now I make out
An eye, dark,
Wormed with far-off, unaccountable lights.

4

Hardly touching, I hold
What I can only think of
As some deepest of memories in my arms,
Not mine, but as if the life in me
Were slowly remembering what it is.

You lie here now in your physicalness,
This beautiful degree of reality.

5

And now the day, raft that breaks up, comes on.

I think of a few bones
Floating on a river at night,
The starlight blowing in place on the water,
The river leaning like a wave towards the emptiness.

FREEDOM, NEW HAMPSHIRE

1

We came to visit the cow
Dying of fever,
Towle said it was already
Shovelled under, in a secret
Burial-place in the woods.
We prowled through the woods
Weeks, we never

Found where. Other
Kids other summers
Must have found the place
And asked, Why is it
Green here? The rich
Guess a grave, maybe,
The poor think a pit

For dung, like the one
We shovelled in in the fall
That came up green
The next year, that may as well
Have been the grave
Of a cow or something
For all that shows. A kid guesses
By whether his house has a bathroom.

2

We found a cowskull once; we thought it was
From one of the asses in the Bible, for the sun
Shone into the holes through which it had seen
Earth as an endless belt carrying gravel, had heard
Its truculence cursed, had learned how sweat
Stinks, and had brayed—shone into the holes
With solemn and majestic light, as if some
Skull somewhere could be Baalbek or the Parthenon.

That night passing Towle's Barn
We saw lights. Towle had lassoed a calf
By its hind legs, and he tugged against the grip
Of the darkness. The cow stood by chewing millet.

Derry and I took hold, too, and hauled.
It was sopping with darkness when it came free.
It was a bullcalf. The cow mopped it awhile,
And we walked around it with a lantern,

And it was sunburned, somehow, and beautiful.
It took a dug as the first business
And sneezed and drank at the milk of light.
When we got it balanced on its legs, it went wobbling
Towards the night. Walking home in darkness
We saw the July moon looking on Freedom New Hampshire,
We smelled the fall in the air, it was the summer,
We thought, Oh this is but the summer!

3

Once I saw the moon
Drift into the sky like a bright
Pregnancy pared
From a goddess who thought
To be beautiful she must keep slender—
Cut loose, and drifting up there
To happen by itself—
And waning, in lost labor;

As we lost our labor
Too—afternoons
When we sat on the gate
By the pasture, under the Ledge,
Buzzing and skirling on toilet-
papered combs tunes
To the rumble-seated cars
Taking the Ossipee Road

On Sundays; for
Though dusk would come upon us
Where we sat, and though we had
Skirled out our hearts in the music,
Yet the dandruffed
Harps we skirled it on
Had done not much better than
Flies, which buzzed, when quick

We trapped them in our hands,
Which went silent when we
Crushed them, which we bore
Downhill to the meadowlark's
Nest full of throats
Which Derry charmed and combed
With an Arabian air, while I
Chucked crushed flies into

Innards I could not see,
For the night had fallen
And the crickets shrilled on all sides
In waves, as if the grassleaves
Shrieked by hillsides
As they grew, and the stars
Made small flashes in the sky,
Like mica flashing in rocks

On the chokecherried Ledge
Where bees I stepped on once
Hit us from behind like a shotgun,
And where we could see
Windowpanes in Freedom flash
And Loon Lake and Winnipesaukee
Flash in the sun
And the blue world flashing.

4

The fingerprints of our eyeballs would zigzag
On the sky; the clouds that came drifting up
Our fingernails would drift into the thin air;
In bed at night there was music if you listened,
Of an old surf breaking far away in the blood.

Kids who come by chance on grass green for a man
Can guess cow, dung, man, anything they want,
To them it is the same. To us who knew him as he was
After the beginning and before the end, it is green
For a name called out of the confusions of the earth—

Winnipesaukee coined like a moon, a bullcalf
Dragged from the darkness where it breaks up again,
Larks which long since have crashed for good in the grass

To which we fed the flies, buzzing ourselves like flies,
While the crickets shrilled beyond us, in July . . .

The mind may sort it out and give it names—
When a man dies he dies trying to say without slurring
The abruptly decaying sounds. It is true
That only flesh dies, and spirit flowers without stop
For men, cows, dung, for all dead things; and it is good, yes—

But an incarnation is in particular flesh
And the dust that is swirled into a shape
And crumbles and is swirled again had but one shape
That was this man. When he is dead the grass
Heals what he suffered, but he remains dead,
And the few who loved him know this until they die.

For my brother, 1925–1957

FLOWER HERDING ON MOUNT MONADNOCK

1

I can support it no longer.
Laughing ruefully at myself
For all I claim to have suffered
I get up. Damned nightmarer!

It is New Hampshire out there,
It is nearly the dawn.
The song of the whippoorwill stops
And the dimension of depth seizes everything.

2

The song of a peabody bird goes overhead
Like a needle pushed five times through the air,
It enters the leaves, and comes out little changed.

The air is so still
That as they go off through the trees
The love songs of birds do not get any fainter.

3

The last memory I have
Is of a flower which cannot be touched,

Through the bloom of which, all day,
Fly crazed, missing bees.

4

As I climb sweat gets up my nostrils,
For an instant I think I am at the sea,

One summer off Cap Ferrat we watched a black seagull
Straining for the dawn, we stood in the surf,

Grasshoppers splash up where I step,
The mountain laurel crashes at my thighs.

5

There is something joyous in the elegies
Of birds. They seem
Caught up in a formal delight,
Though the mourning dove whistles of despair.

But at last in the thousand elegies
The dead rise in our hearts,
On the brink of our happiness we stop
Like someone on a drunk starting to weep.

6

I kneel at a pool,
I look through my face
At the bacteria I think
I see crawling through the moss.

My face sees me,
The water stirs, the face,
Looking preoccupied,
Gets knocked from its bones.

7

I weighed eleven pounds
At birth, having stayed on

Two extra weeks in the womb.
Tempted by room and fresh air
I came out big as a policeman
Blue-faced, with narrow red eyes.
It was eight days before the doctor
Would scare my mother with me.

Turning and craning in the vines
I can make out through the leaves
The old, shimmering nothingness, the sky.

8

Green, scaly moosewoods ascend,
Tenants of the shaken paradise,

At every wind last night's rain
Comes splattering from the leaves,

It drops in flurries and lies there,
The footsteps of some running start.

9

From a rock
A waterfall
A single trickle like a strand of wire
Breaks into beads halfway down.

I know
The birds fly off
But the hug of the earth wraps
With moss their graves and the giant boulders.

10

In the forest I discover a flower.

The invisible life of the thing
Goes up in flames that are invisible
Like cellophane burning in the sunlight.

It burns up. Its drift is to be nothing.

In its covertness it has a way
Of uttering itself in place of itself,
Its blossoms claim to float in the Empyrean,

A wrathful presence on the blur of the ground.

The appeal to heaven breaks off.
The petals begin to fall, in self-forgiveness.
It is a flower. On this mountainside it is dying.

CELLS BREATHE IN THE EMPTINESS

1

When the flowers turn to husks
And the great trees suddenly die
And rocks and old weasel bones lose
The little life they suddenly had
And the air quells and goes so still
It gives the ears something like the bends,
It is an eerie thing to keep vigil,
The senses racing in the emptiness.

2

From the compost heap
Now arises the sound of the teeth
Of one of those sloppy green cabbageworms
Eating his route through a cabbage,
Now snarling like a petite chainsaw, now droning on . . .

A butterfly blooms on a buttercup,
From the junkpile flames up a junco.

3

How many plants are really very quiet animals?
How many inert molecules are ready to break into life?

RUINS UNDER THE STARS

1

All day under acrobat
Swallows I have sat, beside ruins
Of a plank house sunk to its windows
In burdock and raspberry canes,
The roof dropped, the foundation broken in,
Nothing left perfect but axe-marks on the beams.

A paper in a cupboard talks about "Mugwumps,"
In a V-letter a farmboy in the Marines has "tasted battle . . ."
The apples are pure acid on the tangle of boughs,
The pasture has gone to popple and bush.
Here on this perch of ruins
I listen for the crunch of the porcupines.

2

Overhead the skull-hill rises
Crossed on top by the stunted apple,
Infinitely beyond it, older than love or guilt,
Lie the stars ready to jump and sprinkle out of space.

Every night under the millions of stars
An owl dies or a snake sloughs his skin,
But what if a man feels the dark
Homesickness for the inconceivable realm?

3

Sometimes I see them,
The south-going Canada geese,
At evening, coming down
In pink light, over the pond, in great,
Loose, always dissolving V's—
I go out into the field,
Amazed and moved, and listen
To the cold, lonely yelping
Of those tranced bodies in the sky,
Until I feel on the point
Of breaking to a sacred, bloodier speech.

4

This morning I watched
Milton Norway's sky-blue Ford
Dragging its ass down the dirt road
On the other side of the valley.

Later, off in the woods I heard
A chainsaw agonizing across the top of some stump.
A while ago the tracks of a little, snowy,
SAC bomber went crawling across heaven.

What of that little hairstreak
That was flopping and batting about
Deep in the goldenrod—
Did she not know, either, where she was going?

5

Just now I had a funny sensation,
As if some angel, or winged star,
Had been perched nearby watching, maybe speaking.
I turned, in the chokecherry bush
There was a twig just ceasing to tremble . . .

The bats come spelling the swallows.
In the smoking heap of old antiques
The porcupine-crackle starts up again,
The bone-saw, the pure music of this sphere,
And up there the old stars rustling and whispering.

HOW MANY NIGHTS

How many nights
have I lain in terror,
O Creator Spirit, Maker of night and day,

only to walk out
the next morning over the frozen world
hearing under the creaking of snow
faint, peaceful breaths . . .
snake,
bear, earthworm, ant . . .

and above me
a wild crow crying 'yaw yaw yaw'
from a branch nothing cried from ever in my life.

THE HOMECOMING OF EMMA LAZARUS

1

Having no father anymore, having got up
In England without hope, having sailed the strewn
Atlantic and been driven under Bedloe
In the night, where the Green Lady lifts
Over that slow, bleating, most tragic of harbors,

Her burning hand, Emma came floating home,
To the thick, empty whistling of the tugs.
Thoreau's pocket compass had been her keepsake,
She made her way in without it, through the fog,
It was hard for her, in fact, coming in to die,

A little unfair, her father having died already.
In the attic on Union Square? Thrown out? Ah,
Somewhere in the mess of things! From Governor's Island
A bugler's loneliest notes roll slowly in,
And birds rock in the fog on the slapping waves.

2

As a child she had chased a butterfly
Through Battery Park, the only one decorating
Manhattan that afternoon, its clumsy, wind-thin
Wings making cathedral windows in the sun,

While the despised grandmother
With the gleety lashes, cruddy with age,
Of the eyebeams, held on. Alas, the crone's
Doughy ears must also have been golden in the sun!

It was towards you, gilded in the day's going down,
Green Lady, that we crawled—but from what ground of nausea
Had we turned, what relinquished plot of earth
Had we spit at, which was, anyway, the earth?

3

Dark haired, ephebic Emma, you knew
The night you floated into New York Harbor
Atlantis had sunk while you were abroad,
You could see the rainbows of it shining queerly
The many thousand leagues of your life away—

Weekends on Union Square, from his shaving mug
You blew bubbles crawling with colors that buoyed
Into the sunshine, you made up little rhymes,
You skipped rope, at your father's knee he put
Lilacs in your hair. Everybody loved you!

And on the last ride across 14th,
Did the English success suddenly become nothing,
Did the American childhood, including the odd affliction,
Your neurotic longing to be English, turn out
To be the one paradise you died longing for?

4

Facing the Old World the Green Lady whispers, "Eden!"
Seeing her looking so trim in American verdigris
They thought she was saying how it was here,
Seeing her looking to sea we heard the pure nostalgia,
Vacuumed in the wind from the Dry Cleaning Store
She may, herself, have wondered what she meant.

She crouches on the floor. She read once,
In the paper, a poem she had composed herself.
Was it just poetry, all that? It was pretty,
There is nothing she can do about it, it really was.
Her arm lies along the bench, her hand
Hangs over the edge as if she has just let something drop.

She has wept a long time now, and now poetry
Can do no more to her. Her shoulder shrugs as though
To drive away birds which, anyway, weren't intending
To alight. In the Harbor the conscript bugler
Blows the old vow of acceptance into the night—
It fades, and the wounds of all we had accepted open.

4

First Sun Day of the year. Tonight,
When the sun will have turned from the earth,
She will appear outside Hy's Luncheonette,
The crone who sells the *News* and the *Mirror,*
The oldest living thing on Avenue C,
Outdating much of its brick and mortar.
If you ask for the *News* she gives you the *Mirror*
And squints long at the nickel in her hand
Despising it, perhaps, for being a nickel,
And stuffs it in her apron pocket
And sucks her lips. Rain or stars, every night
She is there, squatting on the orange crate,
Issuing out only in darkness, like the cucarachas
And strange nightmares in the chambers overhead.
She can't tell one newspaper from another,
She has forgotten how Nain her dead husband looked,
She has forgotten her children's whereabouts
Or how many there were, or what the *News*
And *Mirror* tell about that we buy them with nickels.
She is sure only of the look of a nickel
And that there is a Lord in the sky overhead.
She dwells in a flesh that is of the Lord
And drifts out, therefore, only in darkness
Like the streetlamp outside the Luncheonette
Or the lights in the secret chamber
In the firmament, where Yahweh himself dwells.
Like Magdelene in the Battistero of Saint John
On the carved-up continent, in the land of sun,
She lives shadowed, under a feeble bulb
That lights her face, her crab's hands, her small bulk on the crate.

She is Pulchería mother of murderers and madmen,
She is also Alyona whose neck was a chicken leg.

Mother was it the insufferable wind?
She sucks her lips a little further into the mousehole.
She stares among the stars, and among the streetlamps.

The mystery is hers.

In the pushcart market, on Sunday,
A crate of lemons discharges light like a battery.
Icicle-shaped carrots that through black soil
Wove away lie like flames in the sun.
Onions with their shirts ripped seek sunlight
On green skins. The sun beats
On beets dirty as boulders in cowfields,
On turnips pinched and gibbous
From budging rocks, on embery sweets,
Peanut-shaped Idahos, shore-pebble Long Islands and Maines,
On horseradishes still growing weeds on the flat ends,
Cabbages lying about like sea-green brains
The skulls have been shucked from,
On tomatoes, undented plum-tomatoes, alligator-skinned
Cucumbers, that float pickled
In the wooden tubs of green skim milk—

Sky-flowers, dirt-flowers, underdirt-flowers,
Those that climbed for the sun in their lives
And those that wormed away—equally uprooted,
Maimed, lopped, shucked, and misaimed.

In the market in Damascus a goat
Came to a stall where twelve goatheads
Were lined up for sale. It sniffed them
One by one. Finally thirteen goats started
Smiling in their faintly sardonic way.

A crone buys a pickle from a crone,
It is wrapped in the *Mirror,*
At home she will open the wrapping, stained,
And stare and stare and stare at it.
And the cucumbers, and the melons,
And the leeks, and the onions, and the garlic.

8

The promise was broken too freely
To them and to their fathers, for them to care.
They survive like cedars on a cliff, roots

Hooked in any crevice they can find.
They walk Avenue C in shadows
Neither conciliating its Baalim
Nor whoring after landscapes of the senses,
Tarig bab el Amoud being in the blood
Fumigated by Puerto Rican cooking.

Among women girthed like cedar trees
Other, slenderer ones appear:
One yellow haired, in August,
Under shooting stars on the lake, who
Believed in promises which broke by themselves—
In a German flower garden in the Bronx
The wedding of a child and a child, one flesh
Divided in the Adirondack spring—
One who found in the desert city of the West
The first happiness, and fled therefore—
And by a southern sea, in the pines, one loved
Until the mist rose blue in the trees
Around the spiderwebs that kept on shining,
Each day of the shortening summer.

And as rubbish burns
And the pushcarts are loaded
With fruit and vegetables and empty crates
And clank away on iron wheels over cobblestones,
And merchants infold their stores
And the carp ride motionlessly sleeplessly
In the dark tank in the fishmarket,
The figures withdraw into chambers overhead—
In the city of the mind, chambers built
Of care and necessity, where, hands lifted to the blinds,
They glimpse in mirrors backed with the blackness of the world
Awkward, cherished rooms containing the familiar selves.

9

Children set fires in ashbarrels,
Cats prowl the fires, scraps of fishes burn.

A child lay in the flames.
It was not the plan. Abraham

Stood in terror at the duplicity.
Isaac whom he loved lay in the flames.
The Lord turned away washing
His hands without soap and water
Like a common housefly.

The children laugh.
Isaac means *he laughs*.
Maybe the last instant,
The dying itself, *is* easier,
Easier anyway than the hike
From Pitt the blind gut
To the East River of Fishes,
Maybe it is as the poet said,
And the soul turns to thee
O vast and well-veiled Death
And the body gratefully nestles close to thee—

I think of Isaac reading Whitman in Chicago,
The week before he died, coming across
Such a passage and muttering, Oi!
What shit! And smiling, but not for you—I mean,

For *thee,* Sane and Sacred Death!

11

The fishmarket closed, the fishes gone into flesh.
The smelts draped on each other, fat with roe,
The marble cod hacked into chunks on the counter,
Butterfishes mouths still open, still trying to eat,
Porgies with receding jaws hinged apart
In a grimace of dejection, as if like cows
They had died under the sledgehammer, perches
In grass-green armor, spotted squeteagues
In the melting ice meek-faced and croaking no more,
Except in the plip plop plip plip in the bucket,
Mud-eating mullets buried in crushed ice,
Tilefishes with scales like chickenfat,
Spanish mackerels, buttercups on the flanks,
Pot-bellied pikes, two-tone flounders

After the long contortion of pushing both eyes
To the brown side that they might look up,
Brown side down, like a mass laying-on of hands,
Or the oath-taking of an army.

The only things alive are the carp
That drift in the black tank in the rear,
Kept living for the usual reason, that they have not died,
And perhaps because the last meal was garbage and they might
    begin stinking
On dying, before the customer was halfway home.
They nudge each other, to be netted,
The sweet flesh to be lifted thrashing in the air,
To be slugged, and then to keep on living
While they are opened on the counter.

Fishes do not die exactly, it is more
That they go out of themselves, the visible part
Remains the same, there is little pallor,
Only the cataracted eyes which have not shut ever
Must look through the mist which crazed Homer.

These are the vegetables of the deep,
The Sheol-flowers of darkness, swimmers
Of denser darknesses where the sun's rays bend for the last time
And in the sky there burns this shifty jellyfish
That degenerates and flashes and re-forms.

Motes in the eye land is the lid of,
They are plucked out of the green skim milk of the eye.

Fishes are nailed on the wood,
The big Jew stands like Christ, nailing them to the wood,
He scrapes the knife up the grain, the scales fly,
He unnails them, reverses them, nails them again,
Scrapes and the scales fly. He lops off the heads,
Shakes out the guts as if they did not belong in the first place,
And they are flesh for the first time in their lives.

Dear Frau _____:
    Your husband, _____, died in the Camp Hospital on
_____. May I express my sincere sympathy on your bereavement.
_____ was admitted to the Hospital on _____ with

severe symptoms of exhaustion, complaining of difficulties in
breathing and pains in the chest. Despite competent medication
and devoted medical attention, it proved impossible, unfortunately,
to keep the patient alive. The deceased voiced no final requests.

Camp Commandant, ―――――――――

On 5th Street Bunko Certified Embalmer Catholic
Leans in his doorway drawing on a Natural Bloom Cigar.
He looks up the street. Even the Puerto Ricans are Jews
And the Chinese Laundry closes on Saturday.

14

Behind the Power Station on 14th, the held breath
Of light, as God is a held breath, withheld,
Spreads the East River, into which fishes leak:
The brown sink or dissolve,
The white float out in shoals and armadas,
Even the gulls pass them up, pale
Bloated socks of riverwater and rotted seed,
That swirl on the tide, punched back
To the Hell Gate narrows, and on the ebb
Steam seaward, seeding the sea.

On the Avenue, through air tinted crimson
By neon over the bars, the rain is falling.
You stood once on Houston, among panhandlers and winos
Who weave the eastern ranges, learning to be free,
To not care, to be knocked flat and to get up clear-headed
Spitting the curses out. "Now be nice,"
The proprietor threatens; "Be nice," he cajoles.
"Fuck you," the bum shouts as he is hoisted again,
"God fuck your mother." (In the empty doorway,
Hunched on the empty crate, the crone gives no sign.)

That night a wildcat cab whined crosstown on 7th.
You knew even the traffic lights were made by God,
The red splashes growing dimmer the farther away
You looked, and away up at 14th, a few green stars;
And without sequence, and nearly all at once,

The red lights blinked into green,
And just before there was one complete Avenue of green,
The little green stars in the distance blinked.

It is night, and raining. You look down
Towards Houston in the rain, the living streets,
Where instants of transcendence
Drift in oceans of loathing and fear, like lanternfishes,
Or phosphorus flashings in the sea, or the feverish light
Skin is said to give off when the swimmer drowns at night.

For the blind gut Pitt to the East River of Fishes
The Avenue cobbles a swath through the discolored air,
A roadway of refuse from the teeming shores and ghettos
And the Caribbean Paradise, into the new ghetto and new paradise,
This God-forsaken Avenue bearing the initial of Christ
Through the haste and carelessness of the ages,
The sea standing in heaps, which keeps on collapsing,
Where the drowned suffer a C-change,
And remain the common poor.

Since Providence, for the realization of some unknown purpose, has
seen fit to leave this dangerous people on the face of the earth, and
did not destroy it . . .

Listen! the swish of the blood,
The sirens down the bloodpaths of the night,
Bone tapping on the bone, nerve-nets
Singing under the breath of sleep—

We scattered over the lonely seaways,
Over the lonely deserts did we run,
In dark lanes and alleys we did hide ourselves . . .

The heart beats without windows in its night,
The lungs put out the light of the world as they
Heave and collapse, the brain turns and rattles
In its own black axlegrease—

               In the nighttime
Of the blood they are laughing and saying,
Our little lane, what a kingdom it was!

         oi weih, oi weih

W. S. MERWIN

W. S. Merwin was born in 1927 in New York City. He was educated at Princeton and has lived with his wife in England, Spain and most recently France. His books of verse are A Mask for Janus, The Dancing Bears, Green with Beasts, The Drunk in the Furnace, The Moving Target, *and* The Lice. *In addition, he is a prolific translator of Spanish, French, Russian, and Latin poetry; his translations include* The Poem of The Cid, Spanish Ballads, *and* The Satires of Persius.

AIR

Naturally it is night.
Under the overturned lute with its
One string I am going my way
Which has a strange sound.

This way the dust, that way the dust.
I listen to both sides
But I keep right on.
I remember the leaves sitting in judgment
And then winter.

I remember the rain with its bundle of roads.
The rain taking all its roads.
Nowhere.

Young as I am, old as I am,

I forget tomorrow, the blind man.
I forget the life among the buried windows.
The eyes in the curtains.
The wall
Growing through the immortelles.
I forget silence
The owner of the smile.

This must be what I wanted to be doing,
Walking at night between the two deserts,
Singing.

AVOIDING NEWS BY THE RIVER

As the stars hide in the light before daybreak
Reed warblers hunt along the narrow stream
Trout rise to their shadows
Milky light flows through the branches
Fills with blood
Men will be waking

In an hour it will be summer
I dreamed that the heavens were eating the earth
Waking it is not so
Not the heavens
I am not ashamed of the wren's murders
Nor the badger's dinners
On which all worldly good depends
If I were not human I would not be ashamed of anything

THE ASIANS DYING

When the forests have been destroyed their darkness remains
The ash the great walker follows the possessors
Forever
Nothing they will come to is real
Nor for long
Over the watercourses
Like ducks in the time of the ducks
The ghosts of the villages trail in the sky
Making a new twilight

Rain falls into the open eyes of the dead
Again again with its pointless sound
When the moon finds them they are the color of everything

The nights disappear like bruises but nothing is healed
The dead go away like bruises
The blood vanishes into the poisoned farmlands
Pain the horizon
Remains
Overhead the seasons rock
They are paper bells
Calling to nothing living

The possessors move everywhere under Death their star
Like columns of smoke they advance into the shadows
Like thin flames with no light
They with no past
And fire their only future

THE ROOM

I think all this is somewhere in myself
The cold room unlit before dawn
Containing a stillness such as attends death
And from a corner the sounds of a small bird trying
From time to time to fly a few beats in the dark
You would say it was dying it is immortal

DUSK IN WINTER

The sun sets in the cold without friends
Without reproaches after all it has done for us
It goes down believing in nothing
When it has gone I hear the stream running after it
It has brought its flute it is a long way

THE GODS

If I have complained I hope I have done with it

I take no pride in circumstances but there are
Occupations
My blind neighbor has required of me
A description of darkness
And I begin I begin but

All day I keep hearing the fighting in the valley
The blows falling as rice and
With what cause
After these centuries gone and they had
Each their mourning for each of them grief
In hueless ribbons hung on walls
That fell
Their moment
Here in the future continues to find me
Till night wells up through the earth

I
Am all that became of them
Clearly all is lost

The gods are what has failed to become of us
Now it is over we do not speak

Now the moment has gone it is dark
What is man that he should be infinite
The music of a deaf planet
The one note
Continues clearly this is

The other world
These strewn rocks belong to the wind
If it could use them

WHENEVER I GO THERE

Whenever I go there everything is changed

The stamps on the bandages the titles
Of the professors of water

The portrait of Glare the reasons for
The white mourning

In new rocks new insects are sitting
With the lights off
And once more I remember that the beginning

Is broken

No wonder the addresses are torn

To which I make my way eating the silence of animals
Offering snow to the darkness

Today belongs to few and tomorrow to no one

SIRE

Here comes the shadow not looking where it is going,
And the whole night will fall; it is time.
Here comes the little wind which the hour
Drags with it everywhere like an empty wagon through leaves.
Here comes my ignorance shuffling after them
Asking them what they are doing.

Standing still, I can hear my footsteps
Come up behind me and go on
Ahead of me and come up behind me and
With different keys clinking in the pockets,
And still I do not move. Here comes
The white-haired thistle seed stumbling past through the branches
Like a paper lantern carried by a blind man.
I believe it is the lost wisdom of my grandfather
Whose ways were his own and who died before I could ask.

Forerunner, I would like to say, silent pilot,
Little dry death, future,
Your indirections are as strange to me
As my own. I know so little that anything
You might tell me would be a revelation.

Sir, I would like to say,
It is hard to think of the good woman
Presenting you with children, like cakes,
Granting you the eye of her needle,
Standing in doorways, flinging after you
Little endearments, like rocks, or her silence
Like a whole Sunday of bells. Instead, tell me:
Which of my many incomprehensions
Did you bequeath me, and where did they take you? Standing
In the shoes of indecision, I hear them
Come up behind me and go on ahead of me
Wearing boots, on crutches, barefoot; they could never
Get together on any doorsill or destination—
The one with the assortment of smiles, the one
Jailed in himself like a forest, the one who comes
Back at evening drunk with despair and turns
Into the wrong night as though he owned it—oh small
Deaf disappearance in the dusk, in which of their shoes
Will I find myself tomorrow?

THE INDIGESTION OF THE VAMPIRE

Look at this red pear
Hanging from a good family

Where the butcher hung the rag on the tree.

The bat's bloated again,
Hooked on his dark nimbus
Getting over it.
Here is the cure of pity
Upside down.

Elsewhere the laundry
Is buried,
The deer tracks left by his teeth
Look for the cross-roads,
The veins that are still good
Hold out their hands.

Here's his story.

His bridges are not burned only folded.
In a while the swollen life
He calls his own
Will shrink back till it fits the mirrors,
No worse for no wear;
The eyes will come
To conceal movement again;
He will find his voice to fly by.

That's how he does it: rock-a-bye,
Hanging there with his silence all wool
And others at heart,
Two pounds in his pound bag,

Shaped like a tear but
Not falling for anyone.

THE STUDENTS OF JUSTICE

All night I hear the hammers
Of the blind men in the next building
Repairing their broken doors

When it is silent it is
That they are gone
Before the sun lights the way for
The young thieves

All day the blind neighbors are at their lesson
Coloring a rough book
Oh a long story
And under their white hair they keep forgetting

It tells of gorges hung with high caves and
Little rotting flags
And through the passes caravans of bugs
Bearing away our blood in pieces

What can be done what can be done

They take their hammers to the lesson

The last words so they promise me
Will be thank you and they will know why

And that night they will be allowed to move

Every day
They leave me their keys which they never use

FOR NOW

The year a bird flies against the drum

I come to myself miles away with
Tickets dying in my hand

You are not here will the earth last till you come
I must say now what cannot
Be said later Goodbye
The name of the statues but who needs them
As for myself I

Look back at the rain
I grew up in the rooms of the rain
So that was home so let the grass grow
Goodbye faces in stains churches
In echoes dusters at windows
Schools without floors envelopes full of smoke
Goodbye hands of those days I keep the fossils
Goodbye iron Bible containing my name in rust
Cock Robin and
The date
Goodbye Cock Robin I never saw you

On plates upside down in token of mourning
I eat to your vanishing

I bearing messages

With all my words my silence being one

From childhood to childhood the
Message Goodbye from the shoulders of victory
To the followers
From the sea to the nearest of kin

From the roller skates to the death in the basement
From the lightning to
Its nest from myself to my name
Goodbye

I begin with what was always gone

Ancestors in graves of broken glass
In empty cameras

Mistakes in the mail Goodbye to the same name

Goodbye what you learned for me I have to learn anyway

You that forgot your rivers they are gone
Myself I would not know you

Goodbye as
The eyes of a whale say goodbye having never seen
Each other

And to you that vanished as I watched goodbye
Walter the First
Jacques the Clown
Marica the Good

Goodbye pain of the past that
Will never be made better goodbye
Pain of the innocent that will never
Not have existed
Goodbye you that are
Buried with the name of the florist in your hands
And a box from our
Box society your finger holding the place
Your jaws tied with a ribbon marked Justice
To help us

The dead say Look
The living in their distress sink upward weeping
But who could reach them in such a sea

Goodbye kites painted with open mouths over the
Scarlet road of the animals

Goodbye prophets sometimes we are
Here sometimes we remember it
Sometimes we walk in your
Eyes which sometimes you lost
Sometimes we walk in your old brains and are forgotten

Or this character gets on the bus with an open razor
Bends down to my face at once thinking he
Knows me goodbye
Yard where I was supposed
To be safe behind the fences of sand
Watched over by an empty parasol and the sound of
Pulleys I who
Had built the ark

Goodbye cement street address of cement tears
Grief of the wallpaper the witness
Cold banisters worn thin with fright
Photo of me wondering what it would be like
The girls at last the hips full of dice the names

In smoke for the lamps the
Calling Goodbye among the wishes
Among the horses

If I had known what to say there would be the same hands
Holding white crosses in front of the windows

Goodbye to the dew my master

And you masters with feathers on your key rings
Wardens of empty scales
When I find where I am goodbye

Goodbye sound of a voice spelling its name to a uniform
Spelling it
Again goodbye white
Truck that backs up to drugstores after dark
Arriving at
Apartment houses in the afternoon
And the neighbors calling can you come up for a minute

Goodbye anniversaries I pass without knowing
Days for which the chairs are wired
The law on the throne of ice above the salting floor
Its eyes full of falling snow
Friend Instead and the rest of the
Brothers Meaningless

Those who will drown next bow to their straw

Goodbye to the water a happy person
The longer its story the
Less it tells
Goodbye to the numbers starting with God

To the avenues
No one asked their permission so they had none

Goodbye hands wrapped in newspaper

And when the towers are finished the frameworks are
Thrown from the tops and descend slowly
Waving as they

Dissolve

Tell me what you see vanishing and I
Will tell you who you are
To whom I say Goodbye
You my neighbors in the windows in the registers you
The sizes of your clothes
You born with the faces of presidents on your eyelids

Tell me how your hands fall and I will tell you
What you will wave to next
Guests of yourselves expecting hosts
You in the cold of whose
Voices I can hear
The hanged man in the chimney turning
You with mouths full of pebbles
In the rising elevator in the falling building you
With your destinations written in your shoelaces
And your lies elected

They return in the same
Skins to the same seats by the flags of money
Goodbye to the Bibles hollowed for swearing on
A hole knocks on the panes but is not heard

Around them the crashes occur in silence
The darkness that flows from the sirens passes the windows
The blackness spreads from the headlines
Over their spectacles they light the ceilings

Goodbye what we may never see
Age would have kissed false teeth if any
Its caresses making a bed slowly
Even as a child I hoped it would spare me
I made tears for it I sang

As the cards are laid out they turn to ashes
I kiss
The light to those who love it it is brief

Goodbye before it is taken away
I have been with it the season could sign for me

The message sang in its bottle it would find me
I knew the king of the moths I knew the watchman's country
I knew where the phoebe lost herself I knew the story
I stepped in the lock I
Turned
My thumb was carved with the one map of a lost mountain

My scars will answer to no one but me
I know the planet that lights up the rings in the hems
I know the stars in the door

I know the martyrs sleeping in almonds
I know the gloves of the hours I know Pilate the fly
I know the enemy's brother

But it will happen just the same goodbye

Heart my elder

My habits of sand
My bones whose count is lost every night every day
The milestones of salt the rain my feet
Memory in its rivers
Goodbye my house my cat my spiders

Goodbye distance from whom I
Borrow my eyes goodbye my voice
In the monument of strangers goodbye to the sun
Among the wings nailed to the windows goodbye
My love

You that return to me through the mountain of flags
With my raven on your wrist
You with the same breath

Between death's republic and his kingdom

SPRING

On the water the first wind
Breaks it all up into arrows

The dead bowmen buried these many years

Are setting out again

And I
I take down from the door
My story with the holes
For the arms the face and the vitals
I take down the sights from the mantle
I'm going to my uncle the honest one
Who stole me the horse in the good cause

There's light in my shoes
I carry my bones on a drum
I'm going to my uncle the dog
The croupier the old horror
The one who takes me as I am

Like the rest of the devils he was born in heaven

Oh withered rain

Tears of the candles veins full of feathers
Knees in salt
I the bell's only son

Having spent one day in his house
Will have your answer

THE HERDS

Climbing northward
At dusk when the horizon rose like a hand I would turn aside
Before dark I would stop by the stream falling through black ice
And once more celebrate our distance from men

As I lay among stones high in the starless night
Out of the many hoof tracks the sounds of herds
Would begin to reach me again
Above them their ancient sun skating far off

Sleeping by the glass mountain
I would watch the flocks of light grazing
And the water preparing its descent
To the first dead

FOR THE ANNIVERSARY OF MY DEATH

Every year without knowing it I have passed the day
When the last fires will wave to me
And the silence will set out
Tireless traveller
Like the beam of a lightless star

Then I will no longer
Find myself in life as in a strange garment
Surprised at the earth
And the love of one woman
And then shamelessness of men
As today writing after three days of rain
Hearing the wren sing and the falling cease
And bowing not knowing to what

LOOKING FOR MUSHROOMS AT SUNRISE

for Jean and Bill Arrowsmith

When it is not yet day
I am walking on centuries of dead chestnut leaves
In a place without grief
Though the oriole
Out of another life warns me
That I am awake

In the dark while the rain fell
The gold chanterelles pushed through a sleep that was not mine
Waking me
So that I came up the mountain to find them

Where they appear it seems I have been before
I recognize their haunts as though remembering
Another life

Where else am I walking even now
Looking for me

WATCHERS

The mowers begin
And after this morning the fox
Will no longer glide close to the house in full day
When a breath stirs the wheat
Leaving his sounds waiting at a distance
Under a few trees

And lie out
Watching from the nodding light the birds on the roofs
The noon sleep

Perhaps nothing
For some time will cross the new size of the stubble fields
In the light
And watch us
But the day itself coming alone
From the woods with its hunger
Today a tall man saying nothing but taking notes
Tomorrow a colorless woman standing
With her reproach and her bony children
Before rain

COME BACK

You came back to us in a dream and we were not here
In a light dress laughing you ran down the slope
To the door
And knocked for a long time thinking it strange

Oh come back we were watching all the time
With the delight choking us and the piled
Grief scrambling like guilt to leave us
At the sight of you
Looking well
And besides our questions our news
All of it paralyzed until you were gone

Is it the same way there

CAESAR

My shoes are almost dead
And as I wait at the doors of ice
I hear the cry go up for him Caesar Caesar

But when I look out the window I see only the flatlands
And the slow vanishing of the windmills
The centuries draining the deep fields

Yet this is still my country
The thug on duty says What would you change
He looks at his watch he lifts
Emptiness out of the vases
And holds it up to examine

So it is evening
With the rain starting to fall forever

One by one he calls night out of the teeth
And at last I take up
My duty

Wheeling the president past banks of flowers
Past the feet of empty stairs
Hoping he's dead

DECEMBER AMONG THE VANISHED

The old snow gets up and moves taking its
Birds with it

The beasts hide in the knitted walls
From the winter that lipless man
Hinges echo but nothing opens

A silence before this one
Has left its broken huts facing the pastures

Through their stone roofs the snow
And the darkness walk down

In one of them I sit with a dead shepherd
And watch his lambs

IT IS MARCH

It is March and black dust falls out of the books
Soon I will be gone
The tall spirit who lodged here has
Left already
On the avenues the colorless thread lies under
Old prices

When you look back there is always the past
Even when it has vanished
But when you look forward
With your dirty knuckles and the wingless
Bird on your shoulder
What can you write

The bitterness is still rising in the old mines
The fist is coming out of the egg
The thermometers out of the mouths of the corpses

At a certain height
The tails of the kites for a moment are
Covered with footsteps

Whatever I have to do has not yet begun

ON OPEN FORM

What is called its form may be simply that part of the poem that had directly to do with time: the time of the poem, the time in which it was written, and the sense of recurrence in which the unique moment of vision is set.

Perhaps this is why in much of the poetry of the high Middle Ages the form seems transparent. Both the role of time in the poem and the role of the poem in time doubtless seemed clear and simple to the Arcipreste de Hita, Dante, Guillaume de Lorris and Chaucer. We can be sure of neither, and we cannot even be certain whether the pretense to such certainty that characterizes some later periods of society (in particular certain phases of neoclassicism) is one of the absurd disguises that can help an art to survive, or merely one of the shrouds that are hardly more than wasted efforts to lend decency to its burial.

The invention of a new form of stanza was a matter of genuine poetic importance to the troubadours. To us it would probably seem scarcely a matter for much curiosity. For the troubadours the abstract form (which certainly they did not hear as an abstract thing) was unquestionably related to that part of the poem that was poetic. For us it is hard to remain convinced that the form, insofar as it is abstract, is not merely part of what in the poem is inescapably technical. For us, for whom everything is in question, the making keeps leading us back into the patterns of a world of artifice so intricate, so insidious, and so impressive, that often it seems indistinguishable from the whole of time.

In a world of technique *motions* tend to become methods. But the undependable life that appears on occasion as poetry would rather die, or so it seems, than follow this tendency, and when a poet himself follows it farther than the source of his gift warrants, his gains of technical facility are likely to render him the helpless master of mere confection.

And yet neither technique nor abstract form can be abandoned, finally. And no doubt neither is dangerous in itself as long as each is recognized as no more than a means, and is not made into an idol and loved for itself. (But it seems to be characteristic of a technological age that means come to dwarf and eclipse or destroy their ends.)

And certainly neither of them automatically excludes or implies the other.

* * *

In an age when time and technique encroach hourly, or appear to, on the source itself of poetry, it seems as though what is needed for any particular nebulous unwritten hope that may become a poem is not a manipulable, more or less predictably recurring pattern, but an unduplicatable resonance, something that would be like an echo except that it is repeating no sound. Something that always belonged to it: its sense and its conformation before it entered words.

* * *

At the same time I realize that I am a formalist, in the most strict and orthodox sense. For years I have had a recurring dream of finding, as it were in an attic, poems of my own that were as lyrically formal, but as limpid and essentially unliterary as those of Villon.

* * *

Much of what appears, or appeared, as great constructive energy in the poetic revolutions of the first half of this century must have been in part energy made available by the decomposition of a vast and finally anti-poetic poetic organism that had become a nuisance even to itself. The original iconoclasts have reared up other anti-poetic poetic monsters that have achieved senility far more quickly since their shapes were less definite and their substance more questionable from the start.

* * *

A poetic form: the setting down of a way of hearing how poetry happens in words. The words themselves do not make it. At the same time it is testimony of a way of hearing how life happens in time. But time does not make it.

* * *

To recur in its purest forms (whether they are strict, as in Waller's "Go, Lovely Rose," or apparently untrammelled, as in The Book of Isaiah in the King James Version) poetry seems to have to keep reverting to its naked condition, where it touches on all that is unrealized.

Our age pesters us with the illusion that we have realized a great deal. The agitation serves chiefly to obscure what we have forgotten, into whose limbo poetry herself at times seems about to pass.

* * *

What are here called open forms are in some concerns the strictest. Here only the poem itself can be seen as its form. In a peculiar sense if you criticize how it happens you criticize what it is.

* * *

Obviously it is the poem that is or is not the only possible justification for any form, however theory runs. The poem is or it is not the answer to 'why that form?' The consideration of the evolution of forms, strict or open, belongs largely to history and to method. The visitation that is going to be a poem finds the form it needs in spite of both.

* * *

The "freedom" that precedes strict forms and the "freedom" that follows them are not necessarily much alike. Then there is the "freedom" that accompanies poetry at a distance and occasionally joins it, often without being recognized, as in some proverbs. ("God comes to see without a bell." "He that lives on hope dances without music.")

W. S. Merwin
France, 1967

JAMES WRIGHT

James Wright was born in 1927 in Martin's Ferry, Ohio, and grew up on a small farm in the Ohio Valley. He was educated at Kenyon, Washington, and Vienna. He lives with his wife in New York City, where he teaches at Hunter College. His books of verse are A Green Wall, Saint Judas, *and* The Branch Will Not Break. *He is also the translator of a book of tales by Theodor Storm, and of many poems from German, French, and Spanish.*

AS I STEP OVER A PUDDLE AT THE END OF WINTER,
I THINK OF AN ANCIENT CHINESE GOVERNOR

And how can I, born in evil days
and fresh from failure, ask a kindness
of Fate? —Written A.D. 819

Po Chu-i, balding old politician,
What's the use?
I think of you,
Uneasily entering the gorges of the Yang-Tze,
When you were being towed up the rapids
Toward some political job or other
In the city of Chungshou.
You made it, I guess,
By dark.

But it is 1960, it is almost spring again,
And the tall rocks of Minneapolis
Build me my own black twilight
Of bamboo ropes and waters.
Where is Yuan Chen, the friend you loved?
Where is the sea, that once solved the whole loneliness
Of the Midwest? Where is Minneapolis? I can see nothing
But the great terrible oak tree darkening with winter.
Did you find the city of isolated men beyond mountains?
Or have you been holding the end of a frayed rope
For a thousand years?

TO THE EVENING STAR: CENTRAL MINNESOTA

Under the water tower at the edge of town
A huge Airedale ponders a long ripple
In the grass fields beyond.
Miles off, a whole grove silently
Flies up into the darkness.
One light comes on in the sky,
One lamp on the prairie.

Beautiful daylight of the body, your hands carry seashells.
West of this wide plain,

Animals wilder than ours
Come down from the green mountains in the darkness.
Now they can see you, they know
The open meadows are safe.

A DREAM OF BURIAL

Nothing was left of me
But my right foot
And my left shoulder.
They lay white as the skein of a spider floating
In a field of snow toward a dark building
Tilted and stained by wind.
Inside the dream, I dreamed on.

A parade of old women
Sang softly above me,
Faint mosquitoes near still water.

So I waited, in my corridor.
I listened for the sea
To call me.
I knew that, somewhere outside, the horse
Stood saddled, browsing in grass,
Waiting for me.

MILKWEED

While I stood here, in the open, lost in myself,
I must have looked a long time
Down the corn rows, beyond grass,
The small house,
White walls, animals lumbering toward the barn.
I look down now. It is all changed.
Whatever it was I lost, whatever I wept for
Was a wild, gentle thing, the small dark eyes
Loving me in secret.
It is here. At a touch of my hand,
The air fills with delicate creatures
From the other world.

A BLESSING

Just off the highway to Rochester, Minnesota,
Twilight bounds softly forth on the grass.
And the eyes of those two Indian ponies
Darken with kindness.
They have come gladly out of the willows
To welcome my friend and me.
We step over the barbed wire into the pasture
Where they have been grazing all day, alone.
They ripple tensely, they can hardly contain their happiness
That we have come.
They bow shyly as wet swans. They love each other.
There is no loneliness like theirs.
At home once more,
They begin munching the young tufts of spring in the darkness.
I would like to hold the slenderer one in my arms,
For she has walked over to me
And nuzzled my left hand.
She is black and white,
Her mane falls wild on her forehead,
And the light breeze moves me to caress her long ear
That is delicate as the skin over a girl's wrist.
Suddenly I realize
That if I stepped out of my body I would break
Into blossom.

A PRAYER TO ESCAPE FROM THE MARKET PLACE

I renounce the blindness of the magazines.
I want to lie down under a tree.
This is the only duty that is not death.
This is the everlasting happiness
Of small winds.
Suddenly,
A pheasant flutters, and I turn
Only to see him vanishing at the damp edge
Of the road.

TWILIGHTS

The big stones of the cistern behind the barn
Are soaked in whitewash.
My grandmother's face is a small maple leaf
Pressed in a secret box.
Locusts are climbing down into the dark green crevices
Of my childhood. Latches click softly in the trees. Your hair is gray.

The arbors of the cities are withered.
Far off, the shopping centers empty and darken.

A red shadow of steel mills.

RAIN

It is the sinking of things.

Flashlights drift over dark trees,
Girls kneel,
An owl's eyelids fall.

The sad bones of my hands descend into a valley
Of strange rocks.

EISENHOWER'S VISIT TO FRANCO, 1959

"... we die of cold, and not of darkness."
—Unamuno

The American hero must triumph over
The forces of darkness.
He has flown through the very light of heaven
And come down in the slow dusk
Of Spain.

Franco stands in a shining circle of police.
His arms open in welcome.
He promises all dark things
Will be hunted down.

State police yawn in the prisons.
Antonio Machado follows the moon
Down a road of white dust,
To a cave of silent children
Under the Pyrenees.
Wine darkens in stone jars in villages.
Wine sleeps in the mouths of old men, it is a dark red color.

Smiles glitter in Madrid.
Eisenhower has touched hands with Franco, embracing
In a glare of photographers.
Clean new bombers from America muffle their engines
And glide down now.
Their wings shine in the searchlights
Of bare fields,
In Spain.

STAGES ON A JOURNEY WESTWARD

1

I began in Ohio.
I still dream of home.
Near Mansfield, enormous dobbins enter dark barns in autumn,
Where they can be lazy, where they can munch little apples,
Or sleep long.
But by night now, in the bread lines my father
Prowls, I cannot find him: So far off,
1500 miles or so away, and yet
I can hardly sleep.
In a blue rag the old man limps to my bed,
Leading a blind horse
Of gentleness.
In 1932, grimy with machinery, he sang me
A lullaby of a goosegirl.
Outside the house, the slag heaps waited.

2

In western Minnesota, just now,
I slept again.
In my dream, I crouched over a fire.

The only human beings between me and the Pacific Ocean
Were old Indians, who wanted to kill me.
They squat and stare for hours into small fires
Far off in the mountains.
The blades of their hatchets are dirty with the grease
Of huge, silent buffaloes.

3

It is dawn.
I am shivering,
Even beneath a huge eiderdown.
I came in last night, drunk,
And left the oil stove cold.
I listen a long time, now, to the flurries.
Snow howls all around me, out of the abandoned prairies.
It sounds like the voices of bums and gamblers,
Rattling through the bare nineteenth-century whorehouses
In Nevada.

4

Defeated for re-election,
The half-educated sheriff of Mukilteo, Washington,
Has been drinking again.
He leads me up the cliff, tottering.
Both drunk, we stand among the graves.
Miners paused here on the way up to Alaska.
Angry, they spaded their broken women's bodies
Into ditches of crab grass.
I lie down between tombstones.
At the bottom of the cliff
America is over and done with.
America,
Plunged into the dark furrows
Of the sea again.

AUTUMN BEGINS IN MARTINS FERRY, OHIO

In the Shreve High football stadium,
I think of Polacks nursing long beers in Tiltonsville,
And gray faces of Negroes in the blast furnace at Benwood,
And the ruptured night watchman of Wheeling Steel,
Dreaming of heroes.

All the proud fathers are ashamed to go home.
Their women cluck like starved pullets,
Dying for love.

Therefore,
Their sons grow suicidally beautiful
At the beginning of October,
And gallop terribly against each other's bodies.

LYING IN A HAMMOCK AT WILLIAM DUFFY'S FARM IN PINE ISLAND, MINNESOTA

Over my head, I see the bronze butterfly,
Asleep on the black trunk,
Blowing like a leaf in green shadow.
Down the ravine behind the empty house,
The cowbells follow one another
Into the distances of the afternoon.
To my right,
In a field of sunlight between two pines,
The droppings of last year's horses
Blaze up into golden stones.
I lean back, as the evening darkens and comes on.
A chicken hawk floats over, looking for home.
I have wasted my life.

RIP

It can't be the passing of time that casts
That white shadow across the waters
Just offshore.
I shiver a little, with the evening.
I turn down the steep path to find
What's left of the river gold.
I whistle a dog lazily, and lazily
A bird whistles me.
Close by a big river, I am alive in my own country,
I am home again.
Yes: I lived here, and here, and my name,

That I carved young, with a girl's, is healed over, now,
And lies sleeping beneath the inward sky
Of a tree's skin, close to the quick.
It's best to keep still.
But:
There goes that bird that whistled me down here
To the river a moment ago.
Who is he? A little white barn owl from Hudson's Bay,
Flown out of his range here, and lost?
Oh, let him be home here, and, if he wants to,
He can be the body that casts
That white shadow across the waters
Just offshore.

POEMS TO A BROWN CRICKET

1

I woke,
Just about daybreak, and fell back
In a drowse.
A clean leaf from one of the new cedars
Has blown in through the open window.
How long ago a huge shadow of wings pondering and hovering
      leaned down
To comfort my face.
I don't care who loved me.
Somebody did, so I let myself alone.
I will stand watch for you, now.
I lay here awake a long time before I looked up
And found you sunning yourself asleep
In the Secret Life of Jakob Boehme
Left open on the desk.

2

Our friends gave us their love
And this room to sleep in.
Outside now, not a sound.
Instead of rousing us out for breakfast,
Our friends love us and grant us our loneliness.
We shall waken again

When the courteous face of the old horse David
Appears at our window,
To snuffle and cough gently.
He, too, believes we may long for
One more dream of slow canters across the prairie
Before we come home to our strange bodies
And rise from the dead.

3

As for me, I have been listening,
For an hour or so, now, to the scampering ghosts
Of Sioux ponies, down the long road
Toward South Dakota.
They just brought me home, leaning forward, by both hands clinging
To the joists of the magnificent dappled feathers
Under their wings.

4

As for you, I won't press you to tell me
Where you have gone.
I know. I know how you love to edge down
The long trails of canyons.
At the bottom, along willow shores, you stand, waiting for twilight,
In the silence of deep grass.
You are safe there, guarded, for you know how the dark faces
Of the cliffs forbid easy plundering
Of their beautiful pueblos:
White cities concealed delicately in their chasms
As the new eggs of the mourning dove
In her ground nest,
That only the spirit hunters
Of the snow can find.

5

Brown cricket, you are my friend's name.
I will send back my shadow for your sake, to stand guard
On the solitude of the mourning dove's young.
Here, I will stand by you, shadowless,
At the small golden door of your body till you wake
In a book that is shining.

THREE SENTENCES FOR A DEAD SWAN

1

There they are now,
The wings,
And I heard them beginning to starve
Between two cold white shadows,
But I dreamed they would rise
Together,
My black Ohioan swan.

2

Now one after another I let the black scales fall
From the beautiful black spine
Of this lonesome dragon that is born on the earth at last,
My black fire,
Ovoid of my darkness,
Machine-gunned and shattered hillsides of yellow trees
In the autumn of my blood where the apples
Purse their wild lips and smirk knowingly
That my love is dead.

3

Here, carry his splintered bones
Slowly, slowly
Back into the
Tar and chemical strangled tomb,
The strange water, the
Ohio river, that is no tomb to
Rise from the dead
From.

YOUTH

Strange bird,
His song remains secret.
He worked too hard to read books.
He never heard how Sherwood Anderson
Got out of it, and fled to Chicago, furious to free himself
From his hatred of factories.

My father toiled fifty years
At Hazel-Atlas Glass,
Caught among girders that smash the kneecaps
Of dumb honyaks.
Did he shudder with hatred in the cold shadow of grease?
Maybe. But my brother and I do know
He came home as quiet as the evening.

He will be getting dark, soon,
And loom through new snow.
I know his ghost will drift home
To the Ohio River, and sit down, alone,
Whittling a root.
He will say nothing.
The waters flow past, older, younger
Than he is, or I am.

IN MEMORY OF LEOPARDI

I have gone past all those times when the poets
Were beautiful as only
The rich can be. The cold bangles
Of the moon grazed one of my shoulders,
And so to this day,
And beyond, I carry
The sliver of a white city, the barb of a jewel
In my left clavicle that hunches.
Tonight I sling
A scrambling sack of oblivions and lame prayers
On my right good arm. The Ohio River
Has flown by me twice, the dark jubilating
Isaiah of mill and smoke marrow. Blind son
Of a meadow of huge horses, lover of drowned islands
Above Steubenville, blind father
Of my halt gray wing:
Now I limp on, knowing
The moon strides behind me, swinging
The scimitar of the divinity that struck down
The hunchback in agony
When he saw her, naked, carrying away his last sheep
Through the Asian rocks.

THE LIFE

Murdered, I went, risen,
Where the murderers are,
That black ditch
Of river.

And if I come back to my only country
With a white rose on my shoulder,
What is that to you?
It is the grave
In blossom.

It is the trillium of darkness,
It is hell, it is the beginning of winter,
It is a ghost town of Etruscans who have no names
Any more.

It is the old loneliness.
It is.
And it is
The last time.

FROM A LETTER

I have only a few brief statements to make about my own practice. I have nothing to say about the theory of prosody. During the past few months I had occasion to read several of Dr. Williams's discussions of prosody pretty thoroughly, and I have yet to make any *usable* sense out of his phrase "the variable foot." He had a perfectly tuned ear; he could write in the "musical phrase" that Pound asked for, though his poems are capable of including many more different kinds of music than Pound; but the unity of his poetry is not to be found in his prosody alone. Perhaps that is why he has had so many bad imitators. In order to write as well as Dr. Williams wrote, one has to have a fine instinctive sense of music in the American language, the music of speech and the music of song; and one must have the character of a great man who loves women, children, the speech of his native place, and the luminous spirit that lurks frightened in the tortured bodies of the sick and the poor. Without these gifts, many new poets have devoted their attention to the art of typewriting; and their poems (to refer to another useful phrase by Pound) look and sound like bad prose hacked into arbitrary linelengths.

For myself, I have never written in syllabics, which sound to me even more tedious than the rhymed iambics which no fashionable poet would be caught dead writing these days. If any principle of structure can be disentangled from the poems that I have written in free verse, it is, I suppose, the principle of parallelism, a term which of course need not be limited to a strictly grammatical application. For the rest, I have been trying to grope my way toward something which I cannot yet describe, but whose interest, if any, is not limited to the concerns of prosody and form.

James Wright
New York City, N.Y.
1967

PHILIP LEVINE

Philip Levine was born in 1928, in Detroit, Michigan. He was educated at Wayne State University, Iowa, and Stanford, and has taught for several years at Fresno State College. He is presently living in Spain with his wife and three sons. His books of verse are On The Edge *and* Not This Pig.

SILENT IN AMERICA

"Vivas for those who have failed . . ."

I

Since I no longer speak I
go unnoticed among men;
in the far corners of rooms,
greeted occasionally
with a stiff wave, I am seen
aslant as one sees a pane

of clear glass, reflecting both
what lies before and behind
in a dazzle of splendid
approximations. They mouth
to each other, and the wind
answers them, while my tongue, furred,

captive, wandering between
contagious wards of the palate,
discovers a foreignness
that is native. One woman,
hearing me grunt for breath, sits
by my side in a green dress,

her hands cupped in the valley
of her life. She would receive
my sympathy and in my
eyes sees—God knows what she sees
in my eyes. Let them have
all they find under the sky.

II

Sometimes on especially
    warm evenings I
take a card chair out under
    the almond tree

and catching the last light, speak
    to myself without

words. I try to catch what is
   behind my throat,

without words, all that exists
   behind and before.
Under the low branches the
   earth's matted floor,

cropped Bermuda and clover
   that the bees attack,
glistens in shade. The sprinkler
   swings out of dark

into light and back again,
   and the water sighs
as though it were suffering
   before my own eyes.

Before my own eyes I am
   almost speaking; my
jaws ache for release, for
   words that will say

anything. I force myself
   to remember
who I am, what I am, and
   why I am here.

III
   When Dr. Leo
addresses me, I pretend
   to be distracted:
   "Look here, Philip, no
damage," and he points his wand
   at a clogged bridge-head

   in the white-on-black
map of my throat. The lights come
   on again. I blink
   like a good patient.
Behind two great stained thumbs
   he advances straight

toward my defenseless
mouth, enters and pries. The hair
   on his hands interests
   me no longer, nor
does his magic power amaze.
   He has his good days

   and his bad. I see
from her gold breast-pin nursey's
   a grade A typist,
   and he, from his acts,
is an existentialist
   with no faith in facts.

   IV

And I, I am the silent
   riser in a house
of garrulous children.
   I am Fresno's

dumb bard, America's last
   hope, sheep in sheep's
clothing. Who names the past
   names me, who sleeps

by my side shall find despair
   and happiness,
a twi-night double header.
   He who loves less

than I, loves no one, who speaks
   more than I, speaks
too much. I am everything
   that is dishonest,

everything under the sun.
   And I say "balls,"
the time will never come
   nor ripeness be all.

   V

     I tell time
by the sunlight's position
   on the bedroom wall:

it's 5:30, middle June.
    I rise, dress,
    assume my name

    and feel my
face against a hard towel.
    My mind is empty;
I see all that's here to see:
    the garden
    and the hard sky;

    the great space
between the two has a weight,
    a reality
which I find is no burden,
    and the height
    of the cot tree

    is only
what it has come to deserve.
    I have not found peace,
but I have found I am where
    I am by
    being only there,

    by standing
in the clouded presence of
    the things I observe.
What is it in the air or the
    water caught
    on the branches

    of the brown
roses hanging toward autumn?
    What is it that moves
when it's still, and strikes me dumb
    when it speaks
    of being alive.

    VI

In a room with no way out,
abandoned by everyone
to something they call my fate,

292 PHILIP LEVINE

with only my squat demon,
my little Bobby, jumping up
and down, demanding women,
demanding more in his cup,
pushing his hand where a hand

should not be pushed, pushing his
shrill voice everywhere, I tried
escape, but the broken stairs
went nowhere. "Police," I cried,
but the phones were off the hook,
and I wasn't, and Bobby
was close behind with a trick
or two up his sleeve, his fly

catching like canvas on the
night wind, crying, "One more, just one."
Knowing he would master me,
I turned to you: "Levine,"
I called softly, and called you
again and again, and it was I who,
given unto Bobby, screamed NO.

VII

For a black man whose
name I have forgotten who danced
   all night at Chevy
         Gear & Axle,
   for that great stunned Pole
who laughed when he called me Jew
   Boy, for the ugly
      who had no chance,

   the beautiful in
body, the used and the unused,
   those who had courage
         and those who quit—
   Rousek and Ficklin
numbed by their own self-praise
   who ate their own shit
      in their own rage;

for these and myself
whom I loved and hated, I
    had presumed to speak
        in measure.
The great night is half
over, and the stage is dark;
    all my energy,
        all my care for

those I cannot touch
runs on my breath like a sigh;
    surely I have failed.
        My own wife
and my children reach
in their sleep for some sure sign,
    but each has his life
        private and sealed.

    VIII

I speak to H. in a bar
        in downtown L.A.
Over a schooner of beer
        he waits out the day
in the anonymous dark.
        Archimbault is here—
I do not have to be drunk
        to feel him come near,

and he touches me with his
        life, and I could cry,
though I don't know who he is
        or why I should care
about the mad ones, imagined
        and real, H. places
in his cherished underground,
        their wounded faces

glowing in the half-light of
        their last days alive,
as his glows here. Let me have
        the courage to live

as fictions live, proud, careless,
    unwilling to die.
We pay for our drinks, rise,
    and enter the city

waiting, impatient and loud.
    Come with us tonight,
drifters in the drifting crowd,
    we shall arrive, late
and tired, beyond the false lights
    of Pasadena
where the living are silent
    in America.

THE CEMETERY AT ACADEMY, CALIFORNIA

On a hot summer Sunday
I came here with my children
who wandered among headstones
kicking up dust clouds. They found
a stone that said DAVI and
nothing more, and beneath the stone
a dead gopher, flat and dry.
Later they went off to play
on the dry dirt hills; I napped
under a great tree and woke
surprised by three teenagers.
They had put flowers in tin cans
around a headstone that showed
the sunrise over a slate sea,
and in the left-hand corner
a new bronze dove broke for peace.
Off in the distance my boys
had discovered the outhouses,
the twin white-washed sentinels,
and were unwinding toilet
paper and dropping whatever
they could find through the dark holes,
and when I found and scolded
them the two younger ones squeezed

my hands and walked stiffly at
my side past the three mourners.

I came here with a young girl
once who perched barefoot on her
family marker. "I will go
there," she said, "next to my sister."
It was early morning and
cold, and I wandered over
the pale clodded ground looking
for something rich or touching.
"It's all wildflowers in the spring,"
she had said, but in July
there were only the curled cut
flowers and the headstones blanked out
on the sun side, and the long
shadows deep as oil. I walked
to the sagging wire fence
that marked the margin of the
place and saw where the same ground,
festered here and there with reedy
grass, rose to a small knoll
and beyond where a windmill
held itself against the breeze.
I could hear her singing on
the stone under the great oak,
but when I got there she was
silent and I wasn't sure
and was ashamed to ask her,
ashamed that I had come here
where her people turned the earth.

Yet I came again, alone,
in the evening when the leaves
turned in the heat toward darkness
so late in coming. There was
her sister, there was her place
undisturbed, relatives and
friends, and other families
spread along the crests of this
burned hill. When I kneeled
to touch the ground it seemed like
something I had never seen,

the way the pale lumps broke down
to almost nothing, nothing
but the source of what they called
their living. She, younger now
than I, would be here some day
beneath the ground my hand combed.
The first night wind caught the leaves
above, crackling, and on
the trunk a salamander
faded in the fading light.
One comes for answers to a
place like this and finds even
in the darkness, even in
the sudden flooding of the
headlights, that in time one comes
to be a stranger to nothing.

SUNDAY AFTERNOON

At first when we saw a girl
hit with a beer can and saw
one so drunk he wet his pants,
we moved back and gave them room,
and what mattered was to be
unnoticed.
                              On the body
of the Angel without teeth
I counted seventeen welts
scored with a bicycle chain.
Another was hunched into
the shape clay might take if it
were battered with pine boughs,
and the third who ran off down
a fire trail crying, "I am King
of Richmond," returned like dirt
in the bed of a pick-up.

This was Sunday afternoon
in America, the quiet
daydream of the Sierras,

the celebrations the land
demands. We left the cold fires
of the barbecue, we left
our homes grumbling in the heat
like beached U-Boats and came by two's
or with the kids up the long
black cut of highway to see
the first great movies made flesh.

BABY VILLON

He tells me in Bangkok he's robbed
Because he's white; in London because he's black;
In Barcelona, Jew; in Paris, Arab:
Everywhere and at all times, and he fights back.

He holds up seven thick little fingers
To show me he's rated seventh in the world,
And there's no passion in his voice, no anger
In the flat brown eyes flecked with blood.

He asks me to tell all I can remember
Of my father, his uncle; he talks of the war
In North Africa and what came after,
The loss of his father, the loss of his brother,

The windows of the bakery smashed and the fresh bread
Dusted with glass, the warm smell of rye
So strong he ate till his mouth filled with blood.
"Here they live, here they live and not die,"

And he points down at his black head ridged
With black kinks of hair. He touches my hair,
Tells me I should never disparage
The stiff bristles that guard the head of the fighter.

Sadly his fingers wander over my face,
And he says how fair I am, how smooth.
We stand to end this first and last visit.
Stiff, 116 pounds, five feet two,

No bigger than a girl, he holds my shoulders,
Kisses my lips, his eyes still open,
My imaginary brother, my cousin,
Myself made otherwise by all his pain.

COMMANDING ELEPHANTS

Lonnie said before this, "I'm
the chief of the elephants,
I call the tunes and they dance."
From his bed he'd hear the drum

of hooves in the bricked alley
and the blast of the Sheenie
calling for rags, wood, paper,
glass—all that was left over—

and from this he'd tell the time.
Beside the bed on a chair
the clean work pants, on the door
the ironed work shirt with his name,

and in the bathroom farther
than he could go the high-top
lace-up boots, the kind the scouts
wore and he'd worn since

he was twelve. To be asleep
hours after dawn, to have
a daughter in school when he
woke, a wife in the same shop

where he'd been the foreman
and said Go, where he'd tripped
the columns of switches and
brought the slow elephant feet

of the presses sliding down
in grooves as they must still do
effortlessly for someone.
"Oh my body, what have you

done to me?" he never said.
His hands surprised him; smelling
of soap, they lay at his sides
as though they were listening.

HEAVEN

If you were twenty-seven
and had done time for beating
your ex-wife and had
no dreams you remembered
in the morning, you might
lie on your bed and listen
to a mad canary sing
and think it all right to be
there every Saturday
ignoring your neighbors, the streets,
the signs that said join,
and the need to be helping.
You might build, as he did,
a network of golden ladders
so that the bird could roam
on all levels of the room;
you might paint the ceiling blue,
the floor green, and shade
the place you called the sun
so that things came softly to order
when the light came on.
He and the bird lived
in the fine weather of heaven;
they never aged, they
never tired or wanted
all through that war,
but when it was over
and the nation had been saved,
he knew they'd be hunted.
He knew, as you would too,
that he'd be laid off
for not being braver,

and it would do no good
to show how he had taken
clothespins and cardboard
and made each step safe.
It would do no good
to have been one of the few
that climbed higher and higher
even in time of war,
for now there would be the poor
asking for their share,
and hurt men in uniforms,
and no one to believe
that heaven was really here.

THE MIDGET

In this café Durruti,
the unnamable, plotted
the burning of the Bishop
of Zaragoza, or so
the story goes. Now it's a hot
tourist spot in season, but
in mid-December the bar
is lined with factory workers
and day laborers as grey
as cement. The place smells
of cement and of urine,
and no one takes off his coat
or sits down to his sherry—
a queen's drink, as thin and dry
as benzine.
              It is Sunday,
late, and each man drinks alone,
seriously. Down the bar
a midget sings to himself,
sings of how from the starving South
he came, a boy, to this terrible
Barcelona, and ate. Not
all the songs are for himself;
he steps back from the bar,

his potbelly pushed out
and wrapped intricately
in a great, somber cummerbund,
and tells the world who is big,
big in the heart, and big down
here, big where it really counts.

Now he comes over to me,
and it is for me he sings.
Does he want money? I try
to buy him off with a drink,
a bored smile, but again
I hear of his power, of how
the Germans, Dutch, English—all
the world's babies—come to him,
and how on the fields of skin
he struts. "Here," he says to me,
"feel this and you'll believe."

In a voice suddenly thin
and adolescent, I tell him
I believe. "Feel this, feel this . . ."
I turn away from him, but
he turns with me, and the room
freezes except for us two.
I can smell the bitterness
of his sweat, and from the cracked
corners of his eyes see the tears
start down their worn courses.
I say, No, No more! He tugs
at my sleeve, hulking now, and
too big for his little feet;
he tugs and will not let go,
and the others along the bar
won't turn or interfere
or leave their drinks. He gets
my hand, first my forefinger
like a carrot in his fist,
and then with the other hand,
my wrist, and at last I can't
shake him off or defend
myself.
        He sits in my lap
and sings of Americas,

of those who never returned
and those who never left. The smell
of anise has turned his breath
to a child's breath, but his cheeks,
stiff and peeling, have started
to die. They have turned along
the bar to behold me
on the raised throne of a torn
plastic barstool, blank and drunk
and half asleep. One by one
with the old curses thrown down
they pay up and go out,
and though the place is still
except for the new rumbling
of the morning catching fire
no one hears or no one cares
that I sing to this late-born freak
of the old world swelling my lap,
I sing lullaby, and sing.

THE BUSINESSMAN OF ALICANTE

He's on my front porch rapping
    like a woodpecker.
No, he will not come in,

this man from Alicante;
    he wants a moment
to unravel the White Coast

from his carved suitcase, "the first
    garden of the world,"
and he points his forefinger

to heaven, May it witness!
    I can buy all this,
the garden, and the children

of the garden, and he winks.
    The towers, the cliffs,
the unchanging blue of sky

and sea tumble through his hands
        all out of focus.
No, I say, this is not my land.

Oh, but it is, he insists,
        and the forefinger
bears witness. It is the last

garden of the world, the last
        slip of land breaking
into the sea, the last crust

of earth we will chew before
        water is our bread.
I don't understand a word.

But I must, he says, and winks
        and winks and won't speak
English and won't be serious.

I go in and slam the door
        and leave him standing
and don't look to see if he's there.

I can hear him, waiting.
        I can hear my breath,
and then the damp chill the day

will pass into and then
        the trees darkening
like clusters of frightened wrens.

WINTER RAINS: CATALUÑA

        I

The Pegasos are steaming
in the rain like scared horses,
and the horses gasp and gasp
to hold their scalding treasures.

Mules, donkeys, women in black,
men in plastic envelopes,
all the unread messages to God
that one cop holds back.

Leathered, gauntleted, and armed;
when the light falls his halo
begins to pulse, and his eyes
behind blank goggles see no

evil they can't master, no
hidden feature they can't place.
The white sword of his raised arm
drops like justice, and we go.

II

His right side drags under the weight
of his tommy gun. He lifts the sling
with his thumb; it is habit,
it is the shrug of a silent man

under the weight of everything.
We stand beneath a tree, side by side,
like two men at a bar, facing the mirror
of the world, he the warrior

with a corked and rusting weapon,
and I the child who has never killed.
Mother is cross. Her boys are huddled
and stamping out in the dark rain.

III

Waiting to go out
I stand with my coat
but the rain doesn't stop.
A lake grows in my street.

Up the hill the rents grow
and the water pours down. The moans
of the drowned stall and start
and stall like a mule cart.

And seen from above
even the sea is abstract,
that corner of his art
which bears the signature.

IV

The unfinished wall
keeps to itself
like a wounded mountain.
The air is unsafe.

Birds are holding
themselves with their brothers,
the stones; they breathe
like carburetors

and glisten in the late light.
The stones have shut
their eyes; if it is night,
if it is the long sigh

of dynamite,
if it is too late
to huddle in flooded cellars
they don't care.

V

In March these fields of nettles
will bear a white scum,
the sour afterthought of heaven,
and the pinpoints of wildflowers

will sprout from nowhere
like the late blossoming
of saints. By a rotting shed,
untethered now, a horse bows

under the fine whippings of rain.
The fields float in his eyes,
the battered arks of husks
spinning and bobbing all day,

until the sky darkens and calms,
and calms the surface of these waters,
weighs down and calms his eyes,
and spreads their darkness like a sigh.

WAKING AN ANGEL

Sparrows quarreled outside our window,
roses swelled, the cherry boughs burst
into fire, and it was spring

in the middle of a bad winter.
We have been good, she said, we have
avoided the fields, tended

our private affairs without complaint,
and this is surely our reward.
I wasn't so sure. There were

hard grey spots on the underbelly
of the ring-tailed coon that died
in the garbage; there was sand

as white as powdered glass overflowing
the vessel of the hyacinth,
there was sand on my own tongue

when I awakened at one or two
in the dark, my nostrils inflamed,
my voice crying out for her.

She wouldn't move. I put my cold hands
on her hips and rocked her gently;
O, O, O was all she said

through set, dry lips. She was slipping
away from me. I was afraid to look
at what dense wings lifted her

out of my bedroom and my one life,
her voice still trailing O, O, O,
like a raiment of victory.

THE SECOND ANGEL

We could be going home.
He sits behind me. The road
breaks over the charred crests
and I follow. I want to speak.
I hear his lips and fingers
meeting in the drained rhythms
of prayer, I hear the pages
fluttering like the voices
of farm wives, like the voices
of onions. Is it money?
He could buy it all, harvests
of dried-out, cured cars, vineyards
of ashes.
       Along the road
the burned gangs of small drawn men
explode into peonies.
In the mirror his face grows—
ancient and smooth and raised,
a face that has never cried,
a face of growing stone, a face
as cold as newsprint. This angel
is my brother. When I turn
he sees all my madness, all
my anger. He sees I'm lost
forever.
       The body is
light as milk, and still I bruise
his head against the doorpost,
and carry him, calm and pliant,
and lay him in the roadside
bones and nettles like a doll,
his eyes still open, seeing,
his wings breathing in and out
in the winds of traffic. What
can I do but turn away,
my chest and arms smeared with dust
and tipped with bloodless feathers.
My brother, the angel, has fallen.

THE CHILDREN'S CRUSADE

Crossbow wanted a child,
a little schoolboy with a red hole
in his brow

like the President. He excited
everyone. They made a brilliant
pair of angel's wings from Kaiser foil

and posterboard, they made a little
tufted box. They would cross his arms
on a single burning peony.

They'd get a glossy Testament,
a blanket tucked in
deep around the sides.

He wanted the little boy who skipped
all the way to school. Eve shook
her red head, and the silver

ignition keys hooked in her
pierced ears chirped. "No, No,"
he was going to be

her lover friend. She wanted
someone like Daddy. Archangel said,
"Daddy."

They took stations.
The night hollered through
the branches and the long grass

like a burned TV.
They bit their hands and waited.
Daddy's car closed.

Everything went quiet and they
had to still their heads like they'd learned
when the bedroom door opened.

After they stabbed him down,
Eve came out from
the shadows. She pulled his beard

but only a little came loose.
She stood so tall in mother's shoes,
and with blue and green chalk

on her lids and cheeks,
he never
knew her. He licked his lips

like when he said important
things, and spread his arms
and made his eyes make tears,

he wanted to talk, he wanted
to help them all, but she just pushed
the knife between his teeth.

When he stopped, they tried
to finish. The box was way too small
and he was too heavy.

So they giggled. When they smelled
what he'd done, they giggled
more. A Daddy going ca ca!

They rolled him over and tore
rags of skin from the eucalyptus
and hid him forever.

Now they ran. The shadows
were all gone, and the air
growing as soft as stone

underwater. Underwater or in moonlight,
the hills rose above the earth,
and they ran shedding their caps and bells,

the little silent bells
they wore at wrist and ankle,
they threw away their names and their no-names.

They cast their knives on the absent waters
and their long bamboo spears.
"Goodbye, rusty can opener, goodbye!"

The houses were snapping.
It was over and they ran. Never
to wait! Now they were free.

Essay by Philip Levine, page 388.

SYLVIA PLATH

Sylvia Plath was born in 1932 in Boston, Massachusetts. She lived for several years in England with her husband, the poet Ted Hughes, and died by her own hand in 1963. Her books of verse are The Colossus *and* Ariel.

TULIPS

The tulips are too excitable, it is winter here.
Look how white everything is, how quiet, how snowed-in.
I am learning peacefulness, lying by myself quietly
As the light lies on these white walls, this bed, these hands.
I am nobody; I have nothing to do with explosions.
I have given my name and my day-clothes up to the nurses
And my history to the anaesthetist and my body to surgeons.

They have propped my head between the pillow and the sheet-cuff
Like an eye between two white lids that will not shut.
Stupid pupil, it has to take everything in.
The nurses pass and pass, they are no trouble,
They pass the way gulls pass inland in their white caps,
Doing things with their hands, one just the same as another,
So it is impossible to tell how many there are.

My body is a pebble to them, they tend it as water
Tends to the pebbles it must run over, smoothing them gently.
They bring me numbness in their bright needles, they bring me sleep.
Now I have lost myself I am sick of baggage——
My patent leather overnight case like a black pillbox,
My husband and child smiling out of the family photo;
Their smiles catch onto my skin, little smiling hooks.

I have let things slip, a thirty-year-old cargo boat
Stubbornly hanging on to my name and address.
They have swabbed me clear of my loving associations.
Scared and bare on the green plastic-pillowed trolley
I watched my teaset, my bureaus of linen, my books
Sink out of sight, and the water went over my head.
I am a nun now, I have never been so pure.

I didn't want any flowers, I only wanted
To lie with my hands turned up and be utterly empty.
How free it is, you have no idea how free——
The peacefulness is so big it dazes you,
And it asks nothing, a name tag, a few trinkets.
It is what the dead close on, finally; I imagine them
Shutting their mouths on it, like a Communion tablet.

The tulips are too red in the first place, they hurt me.
Even through the gift paper I could hear them breathe
Lightly, through their white swaddlings, like an awful baby.
Their redness talks to my wound, it corresponds.
They are subtle: they seem to float, though they weigh me down,
Upsetting me with their sudden tongues and their colour,
A dozen red lead sinkers round my neck.

Nobody watched me before, now I am watched.
The tulips turn to me, and the window behind me
Where once a day the light slowly widens and slowly thins,
And I see myself, flat, ridiculous, a cut-paper shadow
Between the eye of the sun and the eyes of the tulips,
And I have no face, I have wanted to efface myself.
The vivid tulips eat my oxygen.

Before they came the air was calm enough,
Coming and going, breath by breath, without any fuss.
Then the tulips filled it up like a loud noise.
Now the air snags and eddies round them the way a river
Snags and eddies round a sunken rust-red engine.
They concentrate my attention, that was happy
Playing and resting without committing itself.

The walls, also, seem to be warming themselves.
The tulips should be behind bars like dangerous animals;
They are opening like the mouth of some great African cat,
And I am aware of my heart: it opens and closes
Its bowl of red blooms out of sheer love of me.
The water I taste is warm and salt, like the sea,
And comes from a country far away as health.

DADDY

You do not do, you do not do
Any more, black shoe
In which I have lived like a foot
For thirty years, poor and white,
Barely daring to breathe or Achoo.

Daddy, I have had to kill you.
You died before I had time——
Marble-heavy, a bag full of God,
Ghastly statue with one grey toe
Big as a Frisco seal

And a head in the freakish Atlantic
Where it pours bean green over blue
In the waters off beautiful Nauset.
I used to pray to recover you.
Ach, du.

In the German tongue, in the Polish town
Scraped flat by the roller
Of wars, wars, wars.
But the name of the town is common.
My Polack friend

Says there are a dozen or two.
So I never could tell where you
Put your foot, your root,
I never could talk to you.
The tongue stuck in my jaw.

It stuck in a barb wire snare.
Ich, ich, ich, ich,
I could hardly speak.
I thought every German was you.
And the language obscene

An engine, an engine
Chuffing me off like a Jew.
A Jew to Dachau, Auschwitz, Belsen.
I began to talk like a Jew.
I think I may well be a Jew.

The snows of the Tyrol, the clear beer of Vienna
Are not very pure or true.
With my gypsy ancestress and my weird luck
And my Taroc pack and my Taroc pack
I may be a bit of a Jew.

I have always been scared of *you*,
With your Luftwaffe, your gobbledygoo.
And your neat moustache
And your Aryan eye, bright blue.
Panzer-man, panzer-man, O You——

Not God but a swastika
So black no sky could squeak through.
Every woman adores a Fascist,
The boot in the face, the brute
Brute heart of a brute like you.

You stand at the blackboard, daddy,
In the picture I have of you,
A cleft in your chin instead of your foot
But no less a devil for that, no not
Any less the black man who

Bit my pretty red heart in two.
I was ten when they buried you.
At twenty I tried to die
And get back, back, back to you.
I thought even the bones would do.

But they pulled me out of the sack,
And they stuck me together with glue.
And then I knew what to do.
I made a model of you,
A man in black with a Meinkampf look

And a love of the rack and the screw.
And I said I do, I do.
So daddy, I'm finally through.
The black telephone's off at the root,
The voices just can't worm through.

If I've killed one man, I've killed two——
The vampire who said he was you
And drank my blood for a year,
Seven years, if you want to know.
Daddy, you can lie back now.

There's a stake in your fat black heart
And the villagers never liked you.
They are dancing and stamping on you.
They always *knew* it was you.
Daddy, daddy, you bastard, I'm through.

SHEEP IN FOG

The hills step off into whiteness.
People or stars
Regard me sadly, I disappoint them.

The train leaves a line of breath.
O slow
Horse the colour of rust,

Hooves, dolorous bells——
All morning the
Morning has been blackening,

A flower left out.
My bones hold a stillness, the far
Fields melt my heart.

They threaten
To let me through to a heaven
Starless and fatherless, a dark water.

THE APPLICANT

First, are you our sort of a person?
Do you wear
A glass eye, false teeth or a crutch,
A brace or a hook,
Rubber breasts or a rubber crotch,

Stitches to show something's missing? No, no? Then
How can we give you a thing?
Stop crying.
Open your hand.
Empty? Empty. Here is a hand

To fill it and willing
To bring teacups and roll away headaches
And do whatever you tell it.
Will you marry it?
It is guaranteed

To thumb shut your eyes at the end
And dissolve of sorrow.
We make new stock from the salt.
I notice you are stark naked.
How about this suit——

Black and stiff, but not a bad fit.
Will you marry it?
It is waterproof, shatterproof, proof
Against fire and bombs through the roof.
Believe me, they'll bury you in it.

Now your head, excuse me, is empty.
I have the ticket for that.
Come here, sweetie, out of the closet.
Well, what do you think of *that*?
Naked as paper to start

But in twenty-five years she'll be silver,
In fifty, gold.
A living doll, everywhere you look.
It can sew, it can cook,
It can talk, talk, talk.

It works, there is nothing wrong with it.
You have a hole, it's a poultice.
You have an eye, it's an image.
My boy, it's your last resort.
Will you marry it, marry it, marry it.

LADY LAZARUS

I have done it again.
One year in every ten
I manage it——

A sort of walking miracle, my skin
Bright as a Nazi lampshade,
My right foot

A paperweight,
My face a featureless, fine
Jew linen.

Peel off the napkin
O my enemy.
Do I terrify?——

The nose, the eye pits, the full set of teeth?
The sour breath
Will vanish in a day.

Soon, soon the flesh
The grave cave ate will be
At home on me

And I a smiling woman.
I am only thirty.
And like the cat I have nine times to die.

This is Number Three.
What a trash
To annihilate each decade.

What a million filaments.
The peanut-crunching crowd
Shoves in to see

Them unwrap me hand and foot——
The big strip tease.
Gentlemen, ladies

These are my hands
My knees.
I may be skin and bone,

Nevertheless, I am the same, identical woman.
The first time it happened I was ten.
It was an accident.

The second time I meant
To last it out and not come back at all.
I rocked shut

As a seashell.
They had to call and call
And pick the worms off me like sticky pearls.

Dying
Is an art, like everything else.
I do it exceptionally well.

I do it so it feels like hell.
I do it so it feels real.
I guess you could say I've a call.

It's easy enough to do it in a cell.
It's easy enough to do it and stay put.
It's the theatrical

Comeback in broad day
To the same place, the same face, the same brute
Amused shout:

'A miracle!'
That knocks me out.
There is a charge

For the eyeing of my scars, there is a charge
For the hearing of my heart——
It really goes.

And there is a charge, a very large charge
For a word or a touch
Or a bit of blood

Or a piece of my hair or my clothes.
So, so, Herr Doktor.
So, Herr Enemy.

I am your opus,
I am your valuable,
The pure gold baby

That melts to a shriek.
I turn and burn.
Do not think I underestimate your great concern.

Ash, ash—
You poke and stir.
Flesh, bone, there is nothing there——

A cake of soap,
A wedding ring,
A gold filling.

Herr God, Herr Lucifer
Beware
Beware.

Out of the ash
I rise with my red hair
And I eat men like air.

THE MUNICH MANNEQUINS

Perfection is terrible, it cannot have children.
Cold as snow breath, it tamps the womb

Where the yew trees blow like hydras,
The tree of life and the tree of life

Unloosing their moons, **month** after month, to no purpose.
The blood flood is the **flood** of love,

The absolute sacrifice.
It means: no more idols but me,

Me and you.
So, in their sulphur loveliness, in their smiles

These mannequins lean tonight
In Munich, morgue between Paris and Rome,

Naked and bald in their furs,
Orange lollies on silver sticks,

Intolerable, without mind.
The snow drops its pieces of darkness,

Nobody's about. In the hotels
Hands will be opening doors and setting

Down shoes for a polish of carbon
Into which broad toes will go tomorrow.

O the domesticity of these windows,
The baby lace, the green-leaved confectionery,

The thick Germans slumbering in their bottomless Stolz.
And the black phones on hooks

Glittering
Glittering and digesting

Voicelessness. The snow has no voice.

POPPIES IN JULY

Little poppies, little hell flames,
Do you do no harm?

You flicker. I cannot touch you.
I put my hands among the flames. Nothing burns.

And it exhausts me to watch you
Flickering like that, wrinkly and clear red, like the skin of a
    mouth.

A mouth just bloodied.
Little bloody skirts!

There are fumes that I cannot touch.
Where are your opiates, your nauseous capsules?

If I could bleed, or sleep!——
If my mouth could marry a hurt like that!

Or your liquors seep to me, in this glass capsule,
Dulling and stilling.

But colourless. Colourless.

THE MOON AND THE YEW TREE

This is the light of the mind, cold and planetary.
The trees of the mind are black. The light is blue.
The grasses unload their griefs on my feet as if I were God,
Prickling my ankles and murmuring of their humility.
Fumey, spiritous mists inhabit this place
Separated from my house by a row of headstones.
I simply cannot see where there is to get to.

The moon is no door. It is a face in its own right,
White as a knuckle and terribly upset.
It drags the sea after it like a dark crime; it is quiet
With the O-gape of complete despair. I live here.
Twice on Sunday, the bells startle the sky——
Eight great tongues affirming the Resurrection.
At the end, they soberly bong out their names.

The yew tree points up. It has a Gothic shape.
The eyes lift after it and find the moon.
The moon is my mother. She is not sweet like Mary.
Her blue garments unloose small bats and owls.
How I would like to believe in tenderness——
The face of the effigy, gentled by candles,
Bending, on me in particular, its mild eyes.

I have fallen a long way. Clouds are flowering
Blue and mystical over the face of the stars.
Inside the church, the saints will be all blue,
Floating on their delicate feet over the cold pews,
Their hands and faces stiff with holiness.
The moon sees nothing of this. She is bald and wild.
And the message of the yew tree is blackness—blackness and
    silence.

STINGS

Bare-handed, I hand the combs.
The man in white smiles, bare-handed,
Our cheesecloth gauntlets neat and sweet,
The throats of our wrists brave lilies.
He and I

Have a thousand clean cells between us,
Eight combs of yellow cups,
And the hive itself a teacup,
White with pink flowers on it,
With excessive love I enamelled it

Thinking 'Sweetness, sweetness'.
Brood cells grey as the fossils of shells
Terrify me, they seem so old.
What am I buying, wormy mahogany?
Is there any queen at all in it?

If there is, she is old,
Her wings torn shawls, her long body
Rubbed of its plush——
Poor and bare and unqueenly and even shameful.
I stand in a column

Of winged, unmiraculous women,
Honey-drudgers.
I am no drudge

Though for years I have eaten dust
And dried plates with my dense hair.

And seen my strangeness evaporate,
Blue dew from dangerous skin.
Will they hate me,
These women who only scurry,
Whose news is the open cherry, the open clover?

It is almost over.
I am in control.
Here is my honey-machine,
It will work without thinking,
Opening, in spring, like an industrious virgin

To scour the creaming crests
As the moon, for its ivory powders, scours the sea.
A third person is watching.
He has nothing to do with the bee-seller or with me.
Now he is gone

In eight great bounds, a great scapegoat.
Here is his slipper, here is another,
And here the square of white linen
He wore instead of a hat.
He was sweet,

The sweat of his efforts a rain
Tugging the world to fruit.
The bees found him out,
Moulding onto his lips like lies,
Complicating his features.

They thought death was worth it, but I
Have a self to recover, a queen.
Is she dead, is she sleeping?
Where has she been,
With her lion-red body, her wings of glass?

Now she is flying
More terrible than she ever was, red

Scar in the sky, red comet
Over the engine that killed her——
The mausoleum, the wax house.

THE ARRIVAL OF THE BEE BOX

I ordered this, this clean wood box
Square as a chair and almost too heavy to lift.
I would say it was the coffin of a midget
Or a square baby
Were there not such a din in it.

The box is locked, it is dangerous.
I have to live with it overnight
And I can't keep away from it.
There are no windows, so I can't see what is in there.
There is only a little grid, no exit.

I put my eye to the grid.
It is dark, dark,
With the swarmy feeling of African hands
Minute and shrunk for export,
Black on black, angrily clambering.

How can I let them out?
It is the noise that appals me most of all,
The unintelligible syllables.
It is like a Roman mob,
Small, taken one by one, but my god, together!

I lay my ear to furious Latin.
I am not a Caesar.
I have simply ordered a box of maniacs.
They can be sent back.
They can die, I need feed them nothing, I am the owner.

I wonder how hungry they are.
I wonder if they would forget me
If I just undid the locks and stood back and turned into a tree.
There is the laburnum, its blond colonnades,
And the petticoats of the cherry.

They might ignore me immediately
In my moon suit and funeral veil.
I am no source of honey
So why should they turn on me?
Tomorrow I will be sweet God, I will set them free.

The box is only temporary.

GARY SNYDER

Banyan Ashram

Gary Snyder was born in 1930 in San Francisco, California; he was educated at Reed, Berkeley, Indiana, and a Zen monastery in Kyoto. He has worked as a logger, forest ranger, and seaman. His books of verse are Riprap, Myths and Texts, A Range of Poems, Rivers and Mountains Without End, *and* The Back Country.

MID-AUGUST AT SOURDOUGH
MOUNTAIN LOOKOUT

Down valley a smoke haze
Three days heat, after five days rain
Pitch glows on the fir-cones
Across rocks and meadows
Swarms of new flies.

I cannot remember things I once read
A few friends, but they are in cities.
Drinking cold snow-water from a tin cup
Looking down for miles
Through high still air.

HAY FOR THE HORSES

He had driven half the night
From far down San Joaquin
Through Mariposa, up the
Dangerous mountain roads,
And pulled in at eight a.m.
With his big truckload of hay
          behind the barn.
With winch and ropes and hooks
We stacked the bales up clean
To splintery redwood rafters
High in the dark, flecks of alfalfa
Whirling through shingle-cracks of light,
Itch of haydust in the
          sweaty shirt and shoes.
At lunchtime under Black oak
Out in the hot corral,
—The old mare nosing lunchpails,
Grasshoppers crackling in the weeds—
"I'm sixty-eight" he said,
"I first bucked hay when I was seventeen
I thought, that day I started,
I sure would hate to do this all my life
And dammit, that's just what
I've gone and done."

ABOVE PATE VALLEY

We finished clearing the last
Section of trail by noon,
High on the ridge-side
Two thousand feet above the creek—
Reached the pass, went on
Beyond the white pine groves,
Granite shoulders, to a small
Green meadow watered by the snow,
Edged with Aspen—sun
Straight high and blazing
But the air was cool.
Ate a cold fried trout in the
Trembling shadows. I spied
A glitter, and found a flake
Black volcanic glass—obsidian—
By a flower. Hands and knees
Pushing the Bear grass, thousands
Of arrowhead leavings over a
Hundred yards. Not one good
Head, just razor flakes
On a hill snowed all but summer,
A land of fat summer deer,
They came to camp. On their
Own trails. I followed my own
Trail here. Picked up the cold-drill,
Pick, singlejack, and sack
Of dynamite.
Ten thousand years.

PIUTE CREEK

One granite ridge
A tree, would be enough
Or even a rock, a small creek,
A bark shred in a pool.
Hill beyond hill, folded and twisted
Tough trees crammed
In thin stone fractures

A huge moon on it all, is too much.
The mind wanders. A million
Summers, night air still and the rocks
Warm. Sky over endless mountains.
All the junk that goes with being human
Drops away, hard rock wavers
Even the heavy present seems to fail
This bubble of a heart.
Words and books
Like a small creek off a high ledge
Gone in the dry air.

A clear, attentive mind
Has no meaning but that
Which sees is truly seen.
No one loves rock, yet we are here.
Night chills. A flick
In the moonlight
Slips into Juniper shadow:
Back there unseen
Cold proud eyes
Of Cougar or Coyote
Watch me rise and go.

NOOKSACK VALLEY

February 1956

At the far end of a trip north
In a berry-pickers cabin
At the edge of a wide muddy field
Stretching to the woods and cloudy mountains,
Feeding the stove all afternoon with cedar,
Watching the dark sky darken, a heron flap by,
A huge setter pup nap on the dusty cot.
High rotten stumps in the second-growth woods
Flat scattered farms in the bends of the Nooksack
River. Steelhead run now
              a week and I go back
Down 99, through towns, to San Francisco and Japan.
All America south and east,

Twenty-five years in it brought to a trip-stop
Mind-point, where I turn
Caught more on this land—rock tree and man,
Awake, than ever before, yet ready to leave.
                    damned memories,
Whole wasted theories, failures and worse success,
Schools, girls, deals, try to get in
To make this poem a froth, a pity,
A dead fiddle for lost good jobs.
                    the cedar walls
Smell of our farm-house, half built in '35.
Clouds sink down the hills
Coffee is hot again. The dog
Turns and turns about, stops and sleeps.

from Myths & Texts (Logging)

     3

"Lodgepole Pine: the wonderful reproductive
power of this species on areas over which its
stand has been killed by fire is dependent upon
the ability of the closed cones to endure a fire
which kills the tree without injuring its seed.
After fire, the cones open and shed their seeds
on the bared ground and a new growth springs up."

Stood straight
            holding the choker high
As the Cat swung back the arch
            piss-firs falling,
Limbs snapping on the tin hat
            bright D caught on
Swinging butt-hooks
            ringing against cold steel.
Hsü Fang lived on leeks and pumpkins.
Goosefoot,
        wild herbs,
                fields lying fallow!

But it's hard to farm
Between the stumps:
The cows get thin, the milk tastes funny,
The kids grow up and go to college
They don't come back
              the little fir-trees do

              Rocks the same blue as sky
Only icefields, a mile up,
                    are the mountain
Hovering over ten thousand acres
Of young fir.

5

Again the ancient, meaningless
Abstractions of the educated mind.
          wet feet and the campfire out.
Drop a mouthful of useless words.
—The book's in the crapper
They're up to the part on Ethics now

          skidding logs in pine-flat heat
          long summer sun
          the flax bag sweet
Summer professors
          elsewhere meet
Indiana? Seattle? Ann Arbor?
          bug clack in sage
Sudden rumble of wheels on cattle-guard rails.
          hitching & hiking
          looking for work.

"We rule you" all crownéd or be-Homburged heads
"We fool you" those guys with P.H.D.s
"We eat for you" you
"We work for you" who?
          a big picture of K. Marx with an axe,
"Where I cut off one it will never grow again."
          O Karl would it were true
          I'd put my saw to work for you

& the wicked social tree would fall right down.
(The only logging we'll do here is trees
And do it quick, with big trucks and machines)
    "That Cat wobbles like a sick whore"
So we lay on our backs tinkering
                    all afternoon
The trees and the logs stood still
It was so quiet we could hear the birds.

8

Each dawn is clear
Cold air bites the throat.
Thick frost on the pine bough
Leaps from the tree
        snapped by the diesel

Drifts and glitters in the
        horizontal sun.
In the frozen grass
      smoking boulders
      ground by steel tracks.
In the frozen grass
      wild horses stand
      beyond a row of pines.
The D8 tears through piss-fir,
Scrapes the seed-pine
            chipmunks flee,
A black ant carries an egg
Aimlessly from the battered ground.
Yellowjackets swarm and circle
Above the crushed dead log, their home.
Pitch oozes from barked
      trees still standing,
Mashed bushes make strange smells.
Lodgepole pines are brittle.
Camprobbers flutter to watch.

A few stumps, drying piles of brush;
Under the thin duff, a toe-scrape down

Black lava of a late flow.
Leaves stripped from thornapple
Taurus by nightfall.

14

The groves are down
                    cut down
Groves of Ahab, of Cybele
Pine trees, knobbed twigs
        thick cone and seed
        Cybele's tree this, sacred in groves
Pine of Seami, cedar of Haida
Cut down by the prophets of Israel
        the fairies of Athens
        the thugs of Rome
                    both ancient and modern;
Cut down to make room for the suburbs
Bulldozed by Luther and Weyerhaeuser
Crosscut and chainsaw
        squareheads and finns
        high-lead and cat-skidding
Trees down
Creeks choked, trout killed, roads.

Sawmill temples of Jehovah.
Squat black burners 100 feet high
Sending the smoke of our burnt
Live sap and leaf
To his eager nose.

15

Lodgepole
            cone/seed waits for fire
And then thin forests of silver-gray.
            in the void
            a pine cone falls

Pursued by squirrels
What mad pursuit! What struggle to escape!

Her body a seedpod
Open to the wind
"A seed pod void of seed
We had no meeting together"
            so you and I must wait
Until the next blaze
Of the world, the universe,
Millions of worlds, burning
            —oh let it lie.

Shiva at the end of the kalpa:
Rock-fat, hill-flesh, gone in a whiff.
Men who hire men to cut groves
Kill snakes, build cities, pave fields,
Believe in god, but can't
Believe their own senses
Let alone Gautama. Let them lie.

Pine sleeps, cedar splits straight
Flowers crack the pavement.
            Pa-ta Shan-jen
(A painter who watched Ming fall)
            lived in a tree:
"The brush
May paint the mountains and streams
Though the territory is lost."

from Myths & Texts (Hunting)

3

   this poem is for birds

Birds in a whirl, drift to the rooftops
Kite dip, swing to the seabank fogroll
Form: dots in air changing line from line,
            the future defined.

Brush back smoke from the eyes,
            dust from the mind,
With the wing-feather fan of an eagle.
A hawk drifts into the far sky.
A marmot whistles across huge rocks.
Rain on the California hills.
Mussels clamp to sea-boulders
Sucking the Spring tides

Rain soaks the tan stubble
Fields full of ducks

Rain sweeps the Eucalyptus
Strange pines on the coast
            needles two to the bunch
The whole sky whips in the wind
Vaux Swifts
Flying before the storm
Arcing close hear sharp wing-whistle
Sickle-bird
            pale gray
            sheets of rain slowly shifting
            down from the clouds,
Black Swifts.
            —the swifts cry
As they shoot by, See or go blind!

4

The swallow-shell that eases birth
    brought from the south by Hummingbird.
"We pull out the seagrass, the seagrass,
    the seagrass, and it drifts away"
—song of the geese.
"My children
    their father was a log"
—song of the pheasant.
The white gulls south of Victoria
    catch tossed crumbs in midair.
When anyone hears the Catbird
    he gets lonesome.

San Francisco, "Mulberry Harbor"
    eating the speckled sea-bird eggs
    of the Farallones.
Driving sand sends swallows flying,
    warm mud puts the ducks to sleep.
Magical birds: Phoenix, hawk, and crane
    owl and gander, wren,
Bright eyes aglow: Polishing clawfoot
    with talons spread, subtle birds
Wheel and go, leaving air in shreds
    black beaks shine in gray haze.
Brushed by the hawk's wing
    of vision.

—They were arguing about the noise
Made by the Golden-eye Duck.
Some said the whistling sound
Was made by its nose, some said
No, by the wings.
        "Have it your way.
We will leave you forever."
They went upriver:
The Flathead tribe.

        Raven
    on a roost of furs
No bird in a bird-book,
    black as the sun.

6

    this poem is for bear

"As for me I am a child of the god of the mountains."

A bear down under the cliff.
She is eating huckleberries.
They are ripe now
Soon it will snow, and she
Or maybe he, will crawl into a hole
And sleep. You can see

Huckleberries in bearshit if you
Look, this time of year
If I sneak up on the bear
It will grunt and run

The others had all gone down
From the blackberry brambles, but one girl
Spilled her basket, and was picking up her
Berries in the dark.
A tall man stood in the shadow, took her arm,
Led her to his home. He was a bear.
In a house under the mountain
She gave birth to slick dark children
With sharp teeth, and lived in the hollow
Mountain many years.
         snare a bear: call him out:

honey-eater
forest apple
light-foot
Old man in the fur coat, Bear! come out!
Die of your own choice!
Grandfather black-food!
         this girl married a bear
Who rules in the mountains, Bear!
      you have eaten many berries
      you have caught many fish
      you have frightened many people

Twelve species north of Mexico
Sucking their paws in the long winter
Tearing the high-strung caches down
Whining, crying, jacking off
(Odysseus was a bear)

Bear-cubs gnawing the soft tits
Teeth gritted, eyes screwed tight
        but she let them.

Til her brothers found the place
Chased her husband up the gorge
Cornered him in the rocks.

Song of the snared bear:
        "Give me my belt.
        "I am near death.
        "I came from the mountain caves
        "At the headwaters,
        "The small streams there
        "Are all dried up.

—I think I'll go hunt bears.
                    "hunt bears?
Why shit Snyder,
You couldn't hit a bear in the ass
            with a handful of rice!"

7

All beaded with dew
        dawn grass runway
Open-eyed rabbits hang
        dangle, loose feet in tall grass
From alder snares.
The spider is building a morning-web
From the snared rabbit's ear to the snare

        down trail at sunrise

        wet berry brush
        spiderwebs in the eyes
Gray chunk rocks roll down
Splinter pines,
        bark the firs,
                rest in maple shade.

I dance
On every swamp
                sang the rabbit
        once a hungry ghost
        then a beast
        who knows what next?

Salmon, deer, no pottery;
Summer and winter houses
Roots, berries, watertight baskets—
Our girls get layed by Coyote
We get along
                    just fine.
The Shuswap tribe.

8

this poem is for deer

"I dance on all the mountains
On five mountains, I have a dancing place
When they shoot at me I run
To my five mountains"

Missed a last shot
At the Buck, in twilight
So we came back sliding
On dry needles through cold pines.
Scared out a cottontail
Whipped up the winchester
Shot off its head.
The white body rolls and twitches
In the dark ravine
As we run down the hill to the car.

                    deer foot down scree
Picasso's fawn, Issa's fawn,
Deer on the autumn mountain
Howling like a wise man
Stiff springy jumps down the snowfields
Head held back, forefeet out,
Balls tight in a tough hair sack
Keeping the human soul from care
                    on the autumn mountain
Standing in late sun, ear-flick
Tail-flick, gold mist of flies
Whirling from nostril to eyes.

Home by night
                drunken eye
Still picks out Taurus
Low, and growing high:
                four-point buck
Dancing in the headlights
                on the lonely road
A mile past the mill-pond,
With the car stopped, shot
That wild silly blinded creature down.

Pull out the hot guts
                with hard bare hands
While night-frost chills the tongue
                and eye
The cold horn-bones.
The hunter's belt
                just below the sky
Warm blood in the car trunk.
Deer-smell,
                the limp tongue.

Deer don't want to die for me.
                I'll drink sea-water
Sleep on beach pebbles in the rain
Until the deer come down to die
                in pity for my pain.

12

Out the Greywolf valley
in late afternoon
after eight days in the high meadows
hungry, and out of food,
the trail broke into a choked
clearing, apples grew gone wild
hung on one low bough by a hornet's nest.
 caught the drone in tall clover
lowland smell in the shadows

then picked a hard green one:
watched them swarm.
smell of the mountains still on me.
none stung.

16

How rare to be born a human being!
Wash him off with cedar-bark and milkweed
                send the damned doctors home.
Baby, baby, noble baby
Noble-hearted baby

One hand up, one hand down
"I alone am the honored one"
Birth of the Buddha.
And the whole world-system trembled.
"If that baby really said that,
I'd cut him up and throw him to the dogs!"
said Chao-chou the Zen Master. But
Chipmunks, gray squirrels, and
Golden-mantled ground squirrels
                brought him each a nut.
Truth being the sweetest of flavors.

Girls would have in their arms
A wild gazelle or wild wolf-cubs
And give them their white milk,
                those who had new-born infants home
Breasts still full.
Wearing a spotted fawnskin
           sleeping under trees
           bacchantes, drunk
On wine or truth, what you will,
Meaning: compassion.
Agents: man and beast, beasts
Got the buddha-nature
All but
Coyote.

from Myths & Texts (Burning)

4

Maitreya the future Buddha

He's out stuck in a bird's craw
                    last night
Wildcat vomited his pattern on the snow.

Who refused to learn to dance, refused
To kiss you long ago. You fed him berries
But fled, the red stain on his teeth;
And when he cried, finding the world a Wheel—
            you only stole his rice,
Being so small and gray. He will not go,
But wait through fish scale, shale dust, bone
            of hawk and marmot,
            caught leaves in ice,
Til flung on a new net of atoms:
Snagged in flight
Leave you hang and quiver like a gong

Your empty happy body
Swarming in the light

9

Night here,   a covert
All spun, webs in one
            how without grabbing hold it?
—Get into the bird-cage
            without starting them singing.

"Forming the New Society
            Within the shell of the Old"
The motto in the Wobbly Hall
Some old Finns and Swedes playing cards
Fourth and Yesler in Seattle.
O you modest, retiring, virtuous young ladies
            pick the watercress, pluck the yarrow

"Kwan kwan" goes the crane in the field,
      I'll meet you tomorrow;
A million workers dressed in black and buried,
We make love in leafy shade.

Bodhidharma sailing the Yangtze on a reed
Lenin in a sealed train through Germany
Hsüan Tsang, crossing the Pamirs
Joseph, Crazy Horse, living the last free
      starving high-country winter of their tribes.
Surrender into freedom, revolt into slavery—
Confucius no better—
            (with Lao-tzu to keep him in check)
"Walking about the countryside
           all one fall
To a heart's content beating on stumps."

10

    Amitabha's vow

"If, after obtaining Buddhahood, anyone in my land
    gets tossed in jail on a vagrancy rap, may I
    not attain highest perfect enlightenment.

    wild geese in the orchard
    frost on the new grass

"If, after obtaining Buddhahood, anyone in my land
    loses a finger coupling boxcars, may I
    not attain highest perfect enlightenment.

    mare's eye flutters
    jerked by the lead-rope
    stone-bright shoes flick back
    ankles trembling: down steep rock

"If, after obtaining Buddhahood, anyone in my land
    can't get a ride hitch-hiking all directions, may I
    not attain highest perfect enlightenment.

    wet rocks buzzing
    rain and thunder southwest

hair, beard, tingle
wind whips bare legs
we should go back
we don't

13

Spikes of new smell driven up nostrils
Expanding & deepening, ear-muscles
Straining and grasping the sounds
Mouth filled with bright fluid coldness
Tongue crushed by the weight of its flavours
   —the Nootka sold out for lemon drops
(What's this talk about not understanding!
  you're just a person who refuses to see.)

Poetry a riprap on the slick rock of metaphysics
"Put a Spanish halter on that whore of a mare
& I'll lead the bitch up any trail"

(how gentle! He should have whipped her first)

  the wind turns.
  a cold rain blows over the shale
  we sleep in the belly of a cloud.
(you think sex art and travel are enough?
   you're a skinful of cowdung)

South of the Yellow River the Emperor Wu
Set the army horses free in the mountain pastures,
Set the Buffalo free on the Plain of the Peach Grove.
Chariots and armor were smeared with blood
   and put away. They locked up
   the Arrows bag.
Smell of crushed spruce and burned snag-wood.
   remains of men,
Bone-chopped foul remains, thick stew
Food for crows—
   (blind, deaf, and dumb!
   shall we give him another chance?)

At Nyahaim-kuvara
Night has gone
Traveling to my land
      —that's a Mohave night
Our night too, you think brotherhood
Humanity & good intentions will stop it?
As long as you hesitate, no place to go.

Bluejay, out at the world's end
        perched, looked, & dashed
Through the crashing: his head is squashed.
      symplegades, the *mumonkwan*,
It's all vagina dentata
      (Jump!)
"Leap through an Eagle's snapping beak"

Actaeon saw Dhyana in the Spring.

    it was nothing special,
  misty rain on Mt. Baker,
    Neah Bay at low tide.

15

Stone-flake and salmon.
The pure, sweet, straight-splitting
          with a ping
Red cedar of the thick coast valleys
Shake-blanks on the mashed ferns
          the charred logs
Fireweed and bees
An old burn, by new alder
Creek on smooth stones,
Back there a Tarheel logger farm.
(High country fir still hunched in snow)

From Siwash strawberry-pickers in the Skagit
Down to the boys at Sac,
Living by the river
      riding flatcars to Fresno,

Across the whole country
Steep towns, flat towns, even New York,
And oceans and Europe & libraries & galleries
And the factories they make rubbers in
This whole spinning show
                (among others)
Watched by the Mt. Sumeru L.O.
From the middle of the universe
& them with no radio.
"What is imperfect is best"
                silver scum on the trout's belly
                rubs off on your hand.
It's all falling or burning—
        rattle of boulders
        steady dribbling of rocks down cliffs
        bark chips in creeks
Porcupine chawed here—
                                Smoke
From Tillamook a thousand miles
Soot and hot ashes. Forest fires.
Upper Skagit burned I think 1919
Smoke covered all northern Washington.
        lightning strikes, flares,
Blossoms a fire on the hill.
Smoke like clouds. Blotting the sun
Stinging the eyes.
The hot seeds steam underground
        still alive.

17

    the text

Sourdough mountain called a fire in:
Up Thunder Creek, high on a ridge.
Hiked eighteen hours, finally found
A snag and a hundred feet around on fire:
All afternoon and into night
Digging the fire line
Falling the burning snag
It fanned sparks down like shooting stars
Over the dry woods, starting spot-fires
Flaring in wind up Skagit valley

From the Sound.
Toward morning it rained.
We slept in mud and ashes,
Woke at dawn, the fire was out,
The sky was clear, we saw
The last glimmer of the morning star.

the myth

Fire up Thunder Creek and the mountain—
                troy's burning!
The cloud mutters
The mountains are your mind.
The woods bristle there,
Dogs barking and children shrieking
Rise from below.

Rain falls for centuries
Soaking the loose rocks in space
Sweet rain, the fire's out
The black snag glistens in the rain
& the last wisp of smoke floats up
Into the absolute cold
Into the spiral whorls of fire
The storms of the Milky Way
"Buddha incense in an empty world"
Black pit cold and light-year
Flame tongue of the dragon
Licks the sun

The sun is but a morning star

                  Crater Mt. L. O. 1952–Marin–an 1956

from THE MARKET

2

seventy-five feet hoed rows equals
one hour explaining power steering
equals two big crayfish =
        all the buttermilk you can drink

= twelve pounds cauliflower
= five cartons greek olives = hitch-hiking
      from Ogden Utah to Burns Oregon
= aspirin, iodine, and bandages
= a lay in Naples = beef
= lamb ribs = Patna
        long grain rice, eight pounds
equals two kilogram soybeans = a boxwood
        geisha comb.
equals the whole family at the movies
equals whipping dirty clothes on rocks
  three days, some Indian river
= piecing off beggars two weeks
= bootlace and shoelace
    equals one gross inflatable
    plastic pillows
= a large box of petit-fours, chou-crêmes—
    barley-threshing
  mangoes, apples, custard apples, raspberries
= picking three flats strawberries
= a christmas tree = a taxi ride
carrots, daikon, eggplant, greenpeppers,
oregano   white   goat   cheese
   = a fresh-eyed bonito, live clams.
a swordfish
a salmon
  a handful of silvery smelt in the pocket;
    whiskey in cars.   out late after dates.
    old folks   eating cake   in secret
    breastmilk enough.
        if the belly be fed—

& wash-down.   hose off aisles
reach under fruitstands
    green gross rack
       meat scum on chop blocks
       bloody butcher concrete floor
    old knives sharpened down to scalpels
      brown wrap paper rolls, stiff
        push-broom back
wet spilld food
    when the market is closed
      the cleanup comes
        equals

a billygoat pushing through people
stinking and grabbing a cabbage
arrogant, tough,
he took it—they let him—
Katmandu—the market

I gave a man seventy paise
in return for a clay pot
of curds
was it worth it?
how can I tell

FOXTAIL PINE

bark smells like pineapple: Jeffries
cones prick your hand: Ponderosa

nobody knows what they are, saying
"needles three to a bunch."

      turpentine tin can hangers
      high lead riggers

"the true fir cone stands straight,
the doug fir cone hangs down."

—wild pigs eat acorns in those hills
cascara cutters
tanbark oak bark gatherers
myrtlewood burl bowl-makers
little cedar dolls,
      baby girl born from the split crotch
           of a plum
         daughter of the moon—

foxtail pine with a
clipped curve-back cluster of tight
      five-needle bunches
    the rough red bark scale

and jigsaw pieces sloughed off
            scattered on the ground.
—what am I doing saying "foxtail pine"?

these conifers whose home was ice
age tundra, taiga, they of the
         naked sperm
do whitebark pine and white pine seem the same?

       a sort of tree
       its leaves are needles
       like a fox's brush
(I call him fox because he looks that way)
       and call this other thing, a
           foxtail pine.

THE LATE SNOW & LUMBER STRIKE
OF THE SUMMER OF FIFTY-FOUR

Whole towns shut down
        hitching the Coast road, only gypos
Running their beat trucks, no logs on
Gave me rides. Loggers all gone fishing
Chainsaws in a pool of cold oil
On back porches of ten thousand
Split-shake houses, quiet in summer rain.
Hitched north all of Washington
Crossing and re-crossing the passes
Blown like dust, no place to work.

Climbing the steep ridge below Shuksan
       clumps of pine
       float out the fog
No place to think or work
       drifting.

On Mt. Baker, alone
In a gully of blazing snow:
Cities down the long valleys west
Thinking of work, but here,

Burning in sun-glare
Below a wet cliff, above a frozen lake,
The whole Northwest on strike
Black burners cold,
The green-chain still,
I must turn and go back:
    caught on a snowpeak
    between heaven and earth
And stand in lines in Seattle.
Looking for work.

THINGS TO DO AROUND A LOOKOUT

Wrap up in a blanket in cold weather and just read.
Practise writing Chinese characters with a brush
Paint pictures of the mountains
Put out salt for deer
Bake coffee cake and biscuit in the iron oven,
Hours off hunting twisty firewood, packing it all back up
    and chopping.
Rice out for the ptarmigan and the conies
Mark well sunrise and sunset—drink lapsang soochong.
Rolling smokes
The Flower book and the Bird book and the Star book
Old Readers Digests left behind
Bullshitting on the radio with a distant pinnacle,
    like you, hid in clouds;
Drawing little sexy sketches of bare girls.
Reading maps, checking on the weather, airing out
    musty Forest Service sleeping bags and blankets
Oil the saws, sharpen axes,
Learn the names of all the peaks you see
    and which is highest
Learn by heart the drainages between.
Go find a shallow pool of snowmelt on a good day,
    bathe in the lukewarm water.
Take off in foggy weather and go climbing all alone
The Rock book,—strata, dip, and strike
Get ready for the snow, get ready
To go down.

THINGS TO DO AROUND KYOTO

Lie on the mats and sweat in summer,
Shiver in winter, sit and soak like a foetus in the bath.
Paikaru and gyoza at Min Min with Marxist students full
          of China
Look for country pot-hooks at the Nijo junk store
Get dry bad red wine to drink like a regular foreigner from
          Maki's,
Trudging around with visitors to Gardens.

Pluck weeds out of the moss. Plant morning-glories.
Walk down back alleys listening to looms.
Watching the flock of sparrows whirling over
          trees on winter sunsets;
Get up at four in the morning, to go meet with the Old Man.
Sitting in deep samadhi on a hurting knee.
Get buttered up by bar-girls, pay too much.
Motorcycle oil-change down on Gojo,
Warm up your chilly wife, her big old feet.

Trying to get a key made
Trying to find brown bread
Hunting rooms for Americans
Having a big meeting, speaking several tongues.

Lose your way in the bamboo brush on Hiei-zan in winter
Step on a bug
Quiet weeks and weeks, walking and reading, talking and
          weeding,
Passing the hand
   around a rough cool pot.
Throwing away the things you'll never need
Stripping down—
Going home.

FOR THE WEST

        1
Europa,
      your red-haired
      hazel-eyed
      Thracian girls

your beautiful thighs
everlasting damnations
and grave insouciance—

a woman's country,
even your fat little popes.
              groin'd temples
              groov'd canals
    —me too, I see thru
    these green eyes—

the Cowboys and Indians all over Europe
sliding down snowfields on shields.

what next? a farmer's
corner of the planet—
                        who cares if you are White?

    2

this universe—"one turn"—turnd over.
                    gods of revolution.
sharp beards—fur flap hats—
                    kalmuck whip-swingers,

hugging and kissing
white and black,
men, men,
girls, girls,

wheat, rye, barley,
        adding asses to donkeys
        to fat-haunch horses,
it takes tractors and the
        multiple firing of pistons
to make revolution.
still turning.   flywheel heavy
        elbow-bending awkward
        flippety drive goes
on, white   chicks;

dark skin
        burns the tender lobes.
foggy white skin bleacht out,

pale nipple,
pale breast never freckled,

    they turn and
slowly turn away—

    3

    Ah, that's America:
the flowery glistening oil blossom
      spreading on water—
it was so tiny, nothing, now it keeps expanding
all those colors,
            our world
      opening inside outward toward us,
each part swelling and turning
who would have thought such turning;

as it covers,
      the colors fade.
and the fantastic patterns
      fade.
I see down again through clear water.

    it is the same
ball bounce rhyme the
        little girl was singing,
        all those years.

SOME YIPS & BARKS IN THE DARK

A Notable Utterance

The linguist Bloomfield once defined literature as "notable utterances."
A poem is usually distinguished from other sorts of utterances by some
characteristic arrangement of syllabic stress, pitch, vowel length,
rhyming words, internal tone patterns, syllable count, initial or final
consonants and so forth. In some cases there is a peculiar vocabulary
the poem is couched in. All this is what critics call form. Another
distinction is made on the basis of the nature of the message. Perhaps
something other than "words" is being communicated. Straight from
the deep mind of the maker to the deep mind of the hearer. This is
what poets call the Poem.

The grain of things

For me every poem is unique. One can understand and appreciate the
conditions which produce formal poetry as part of man's experiment
with civilization. The game of inventing an abstract structure and then
finding things in experience which can be forced into it. A kind of
intensity can indeed be produced this way—but it is the intensity of
straining and sweating against self-imposed bonds. Better the perfect,
easy discipline of the swallow's dip and swoop, "without east or west."
   Each poem grows from an energy-mind-field-dance, and has its own
inner grain. To let it grow, to let it speak for itself, is a large part of the
work of the poet. A scary chaos fills the heart as "spir"itual breath—
in"spir"ation; and is breathed out into the thing-world as a poem.
From there it must jump to the hearer's under"stand"ing. The wider
the gap the more difficult; and the greater the delight when it crosses.
If the poem becomes too elliptical it ceases to be a poem in any usual
sense. Then it may be a mantra, a kōan, or a dhāranī. To be used as part
of a larger walking, singing, dancing, or meditating practice.

The Poet

The poet must have total sensitivity to the inner potentials of his own
language—pulse, breath, glottals nasals & dentals. An ear, an eye and a
belly.
   He must know his own unconscious, and the proper ways to meet
with the beings who live there. As Confucius said, he should know the
names of trees, birds, and flowers. From this knowledge and practice
of "body, speech, and mind" the poem takes form, freely.

It is a mistake to think that we are searching, now, for "new forms." What is needed is a totally new approach to the very idea of form. Why should this be? The future can't be seen on the basis of the present; and I believe mankind is headed someplace else.

Gary Snyder
Kyōto 22. VIII. 1966

STEPHEN BERG

C. K. Williams

Stephen Berg was born in 1934 in Philadelphia, and educated at the University of Pennsylvania, Boston, Iowa, and Indiana. He is the author of two books of poems, Bearing Weapons *and* In the Blood; *editor of* Other Tongues: Poems in Translation, The Enemies of Man: Poems of the American Apocalypse; *co-editor of* A Book for Open Learning; *and holder of a National Translation Center Commission Grant to co-translate Miklos Radnoti's* Cloudy Sky. *He lives in Philadelphia with his wife and two daughters, and teaches at the Philadelphia College of Art.*

OLLIE, ANSWER ME

When I pictured you
lifting the old people out of bed,
emptying their pans and glasses,
wheeling them down the hall
and reading to them until their eyes
drifted upward like bubbles,
it was impossible to explain
how you got there.
I began by imagining myself
buying everyone daffodils,
sneaking into the fluorescent ward
after curfew to watch them sleep
and listen as they wheezed
and kept you awake.
And even when I created their dreams
about streets that no longer exist,
and yours about cows and a drowsy father,
that was no answer.
Were you a sentinel
called there to report death
and cancel it somehow,
and if you were God's replacement
what can you say about it?

Late one night, visiting you
with friends, I pushed open the door
where you were staying
and a chalk lady
saw someone who looked back at her
and for no reason said Hello.
Tell me, did I speak to a face
or to nature? Who was I trying to reach?
I will go on asking you
what we were doing there
and what you learned
because I am everyone who was not there
and could not feel your thin hands
cup his head into the air
for transparent food
or bunch pillows under his neck,
or see you kneel at the side of a bed

barely dented with the weight
of a human body.
And explain this—each night since then
I have heard the stupidity of the words
you sang out of good books
so they would rest and understand.

A WIFE TALKS TO HERSELF

A few days ago
my father sent me a box
of wintergreen to replant
so I won't forget him.
I wonder if he saw
the rims of the short notched
leaves get brown
or missed much of the deep odor
before he mailed them,
and thought they might look scorched
by the hot passage
from his yard in South Carolina
to this room of mine.
Today, among other things,
I bought soil
and packed it against the roots
of his gift. If that fails,
I'll write him that
there is still nothing more
I can say than this to the message
he gave me through
these wild masks: it is natural
to be shy with one's daughter,
but when I see those curled,
lost faces trying to live,
I feel my back stiffen
and remember that once,
passing a stranger
whose thin coat brushed the ground,
I couldn't find

my way home
or recognize myself
in the tiny person
looking at me out of his eyes.

PEOPLE TRYING TO LOVE

step into my room tonight
their hands float ahead of them
their legs move apart
in answer to the many

For thirty-two years I have lived
and known the black iron
railings of houses
instead of you

Now even that part of me
I will never know knows
I have stayed between my own fingers
too long
believing I did not need you there

It is dark between our bodies
as we open ourselves
to the one shame
and feel what we lose
the wire stems of poppies

Trying so hard to remain
now even hatred is a false petal
shaking under the rain
sacrificed
to the many

For thirty-two years my hands
have wanted to be other things
cups pliers hammers hooks
wings belonging to a child
they touch you.

BETWEEN US

It is snowing heavily again.
I have been watching it for a long time
the way a blind man looks at the world
on the back of his eyelids.
Something I wanted in my hands
is not there, and I hear
the soft cry of the flakes approaching.
Trapped among branches,
it sounds as if I have lost someone
and have reached up to find
that same whiteness on my mouth,
plunging into itself without me.

A GLIMPSE OF THE BODY SHOP

They are inspecting hearts again.
One slips a fat needle into the left side
to judge the color,
another weighs it, one with goggles on bends
over the scars and black coins
and cuts off ragged strands for the analyzer.
For years they have known about the region
called Moon Breakage,
but grow silent when asked.
Nevertheless it haunts them.
And today, with the tables dripping
and because so many brought theirs in
to be checked,
one of them presses his to his cheek,
one begins chewing the large artery,
one kneels and holds his up to the sky,
one jams his fingers into each hole.
But among all these I stand
aside, doodling with chalk, trying
to bring together the sad details.
Suddenly a wall of the garage
is filled with the weird cry of chalk,

many letters and signs appear.
The one man capable of this sits down,
exhausted and proud.
His helpers wash and bow, laughing.

GOOSEBERRIES

(after reading the Chekhov story)

I can't sleep tonight, can you?
It is the voice of Gooseberries whispering
we are not good enough to be happy.
Near sleep, when your face gazes at itself
through a window or against a pale floor,
I hear you scratching on the wall of my room.
Forget about happiness. Tomorrow, when we
meet outside on the steps of our houses,
show me how to kiss your sad lips, tell me
what I can give you.
The fat owner who is happy is not you,
eating jam near the glue factory, drinking
tea, bathing in the river,
his wet hands lifted to the dying sun.
In a dish the gooseberries do not wait
and the doctor who did not believe in God
still asks forgiveness, and he is you.
I can smell the clean sheets where Burkin lay down,
suspicious of burnt tobacco.
He thought the stink came from something else.
It was hours before he could sleep and touch you.
Rain beat against the window panes all night.

DREAMING WITH A FRIEND

Your brother is dead.
His breath is one of those lost autumn days
you love.
Your mother works in the kitchen again,
beating eggs.

Ashes drift in from factories,
brush fires
cling to the door.
I see you crossing a field toward me,
not knowing
whom you will find,
kicking weeds.

The dream you told me about is a place
where I touch your head
and you turn.
But I could be anyone.
Your brother sits on the porch again,
crying.
Your mother comes down in the rain.
You see me crossing a field toward you,
not knowing
whom I will find,
following the cracked weeds,
turning as you turn

toward someone.

TO MY FRIENDS

Holding its huge life open to the sky,
snow fringes the scaly cones on this hilltop;
I can see it cupped and pierced by the rich needles.
This far from the city, it takes weeks to melt,
and nothing passes on the road that reaches me here
at the back of my house, planted above the river
of headlights. Do you remember that sad movie
where Bogart loses everything and begins
a new life after his plane takes off through the fog,
where he becomes an underground fighter, and poor?
It haunts me tonight because I am not myself
and, wedged between ceilings and floors,
I can feel the tight path of my hands over the keys
get wider. Because those bare, lasting pines
are understandable, because I am here

and not here, because of the silent breath
rising from different lungs,
because these hands are yours, I remember
something no one will ever tell us. Our life,
more like those trees than we are, is the snow;
the stars know it, the dirt road says it again
each time I stop for a minute and listen to the strange
human words of the hedges scraping together, and go in
where the moonlit weedy spaces continue.

from Entering the Body

THE SURVIVOR

Rising without names today
I want to be a fat man in America
and carry a gun,
I want to sit for the rest of my life
looking at the walls, collecting,
thinking about those terrible images
of dissection I burst
out of my mother with, dreaming.
If my face melts off like wax,
if I am beaten across the thighs
until they stick together,
if I find myself drunk in a strange town
looking for a stranger to be my friend,
if I wake with the sea in my mouth
and the wrong father,
if they take one piece of me each year—
the lobe, the glans, the lid, the cap,
the pit—
I would still want to be as fat
as an elephant, and rule, and demand
all others fall to their knees
and serve me.
Rising without names
or wonder in this country,
my fists hardened many days
in the last ovens.

THE HOLES

Suddenly I remember the holes,
suddenly I think of a man with no entrances,
no exits, the closed man, with feelers or claws
so sensitive that he can tell
what rock is, or flesh, water or flame.
Where does everything go when it comes in?
What should I do with the pure speech of cells
where we find ourselves?
The river flies, the dusk crawls into the ground,
the moon has our nose backwards,
the streets get up and leave,
the sun recklessly feeds our blood.
We could be crouching on the branch, we could be
gnawing the brown feathers and thighs of a new animal,
we could be plotting under the ice while others dream.
But I want the infinite man who sleeps
in my veins to rise, I want to hear
the thin buzzing that floats out of my chest
like an arm of locusts making terrible decisions.
Sometimes I want to die because of this.

THE ANIMALS

I'm a pig, I'm a seagull,
I'm the man nature chose to be broken.
These bristles and feathers
could have been thoughts, these wings and hooves
could have been the failures of sleep.
Sometimes I nose under the mud, grunting
about pain and weightlessness,
sometimes I cut the water,
imagining myself fat and motionless.
I'm both of these because of my deaths,
I'm a wing because your eyes beg me,
I'm diving into your birth because it's needed,
I'm sinking into the ground because it helps.
When you follow me over a hill
or along a cold stretch of sand

my soft husks of celery and bread scar your face,
you remember leaving yourself behind,
like the moon, calling
"Give me back! Give me back!"
But it was the thought that spoke,
it was the sleep without skin that lifted you,
it was the dream about acts choosing like water,
it was your mouth closed over the words
of the last God,
the spine, the tail, the mercy
of dark clothing and work.

ROBERT MEZEY

Robert Mezey was born in 1935 in Philadelphia, Pennsylvania. He was educated at Kenyon and Iowa, and has taught briefly at several universities. He lives with his wife and children in the Sierra Nevadas. His books of verse are The Lovemaker, White Blossoms, *and* Favors; *he is also the author of a chapbook,* The Mercy of Sorrow: Ten Poems of Uri Zvi Greenberg.

Douglas Hall

TOUCH IT

Out on the bare grey roads, I pass
by vineyards withering toward winter,
cold magenta shapes and green fingers
and the leaves rippling in the early darkness.

Past the thinning orchard the fields
are on fire. A mountain of smoke
climbs the desolate wind, and at its roots
fire is eating dead grass with many small teeth.

When I get home, the evening sun
has narrowed to a filament. When it goes
and the dark falls like a hand on a tabletop,
I am told that what we love most is dying.

The coldness of it is even on this page
at the edge of your fingernail. Touch it.

A CONFESSION

If someone was walking across
your lawn last night, it was me.
While you dreamt of prowlers, I was
prowling down empty lanes, to breathe
the conifer coolness of just
before dawn. Your flowers were closed,
your windows black and withdrawn.

Sometimes I see a square of
yellow light shining through the trees,
and I cross the grass and look in.
Your great body on the bed
is nude and white, and though I'm starved
for love like everyone, the sight
of your black sex leaves me cold.

What would I say to a squad car
if it came on its noiseless tires
and picked me out with its lights, like

a cat or a rabbit? That I
only wanted to see how people
live, not knowing how? That I
haven't had a woman in months?

Therefore I stay out of sight
and do not speak. Or if I speak,
I make small animal sounds
to myself, so as not to wake you.
They were tears full of seed. What
I wanted to do was enter
and bend and touch you on the cheek.

IN THE SOUL HOUR

Tonight I could die as easily as the grass
and I can't help thinking
whenever the light flickers along the finished
                              blood red boards

how just the other side
of the fiery grain
the skull of the house is clapped in darkness

The joys of our lives tonight
the dance sweat the shining sidelong eyes
the faint sweet cuntsmells
hiding in perfume

music from another planet

voices at night
carried across the blowing water

THERE

It is deep summer. Far out
at sea, the young squalls darken
and roll, plunging northward,
threatening everything. I see

the Atlantic moving in slow
contemplative fury
against the rocks, the frozen
headlands, and the towns sunk deep
in a blind northern light. Here,
far inland, in the mountains
of Mexico, it is raining
hard, battering the soft mouths
of flowers. I am sullen, dumb,
ungovernable. I taste myself
and I taste those winds, uprisings
of salt and ice, of great trees
brought down, of houses and cries
lost in the storm; and what breaks
on that black shore breaks in me.

NIGHT ON CLINTON

The bar is closed and I come
to myself outside the door,
drunk and shivering. The talking
champions, the bedroom
killers, the barroom Catholics
have all drifted away and I
am standing in a yellowish
wound of light. Above the blot
my breathing makes on the glass,
I look down the darkened bar
where the bottles are out of breath,
the stale tumblers bunched, and white
glistening webs in the pitchers
dry up and break and shrivel.
The plastic stools turn
in the hot light that bubbles
from the big Sea Bird, silent now,
and a shape vaguely human
moves with a rag and a limp
among the empty tables
piled high with surrendered chairs.
Nailed on the back wall, a great

Canadian elk fixes me
with his glazed liquid eyes and
the last lights go out. What I see
is important now, but I see
only the dim half-moon
of my own face in the black
mirror of space, and I lay
my cheek against the cold glass.
Snow is beginning to fall,
huge wet flakes that burst from
the darkness like parachutes
and plunge past the streaming light
and melt into the street.
Freeze, die, says the veteran wind
from the north but he goes on
with his work, the night and the snow,
and was not speaking to me.

MY MOTHER

My mother writes from Trenton,
a comedian to the bone
but underneath, serious
and all heart. "Honey," she says,
"be a mensch and Mary too,
its no good to worry, you
are doing the best you can
your Dad and everyone
thinks you turned out very well
as long as you pay your bills
nobody can say a word
you can tell them to drop dead
so save a dollar it can't
hurt—remember Frank you went
to highschool with? he still lives
with his wife's mother, his wife
works while he writes his books and
did he ever sell a one
the four kids run around naked
36 and he's never had,
you'll forgive my expression

even a pot to piss in
or a window to throw it,
such a smart boy he couldnt
read the footprints on the wall
honey you think you know all
the answers you dont, please try
to put some money away
believe me it wouldn't hurt
artist shmartist life's too short
for that kind of, forgive me,
horseshit, I know what you want
better than you, all that counts
is to make a good living
and the best of everything,
as Sholem Aleichem said
he was a great writer did
you ever read his books dear,
you should make what he makes a year
anyway he says some place
Poverty is no disgrace
but its no honor either
that's what I say,
                    love,
                        Mother"

THE UNDERGROUND GARDENS

for Baldasare Forestiere

Sick of the day's heat, of noise
and light and people, I come
to walk in Forestiere's
deep home, where his love never
came to live; where he prayed to Christ;
slept lightly, put on his clothes,
clawed at the earth forty years
but it answered nothing.
Silence came down with the small
pale sunlight, then the darkness.
Maybe the girl was dead. He
grew accustomed to the silence

and to the darkness. He brought
food to his mouth with both
invisible hands, and waited
for night's darkness to give way
to the darkness of day. If
he held his breath and his
eyes closed against the brown light
sifting down by masonry and roots,
he could see her spirit among
his stone tables, laughing and
saying no. When he opened
them to emptiness, he wept.
And at last he kept them closed.
Death gripped him by the hair and
he was ready. He turned and slept
more deeply.
                    There were many
rooms, tunnels and coves and arbors,
places where men and women
could sit, flowering plazas
where they could walk or take food,
and crypts for the tired to rest.
He could almost imagine
their voices, but not just yet.

He is buried somewhere else.

from THERESIENSTADT POEMS

In your watercolor, Nely Silvínová
your heart on fire
on the grey cover of a sketchbook
is a dying sun or
a flower
youngest of the summer

the sun itself
the grizzled head of a flower
throbbing
in the cold dusk of your last day
on earth

There are no thorns to be seen
but the color says
thorns

and much else that is not
visible it says also
a burning wound at the horizon
it says Poland and winter
it says painful Terezín
SILVIN VI 25 VI 1944
and somehow
above the light body on its bed of coals
it says spring
from the crest of the street it says
you can see the fields
brown and green
and beyond them the dark blue line of woods
and beyond that smoke
is that the smoke of Prague
and it says blood
every kind of blood
blood of Jews
German blood
blood of Bohemia and Moravia
running in gutters
the blood of children
it says free at last
the mouth of the womb it says
SILVIN VI 25 VI 1944
the penis of the commandant
the enraged color
the whip stock the gun butt
it says it says it says

Petrified god
god that gave up the ghost at Terezín
what does it say but itself
thirteen years of life
and your heart on fire
                    Nely Silvínová!

THE FRIENDSHIP

What we looked for always remained
in the blue haze drifting behind
our wheels, into the distance.
But our motors roared in concert;
we went into the wind,
faces distended by the wind,
drinking and mouthing in a kind
of brute ecstasy or thirst.
Deafened, with chinese eyes,
we asked what there was to ask
of the onrushing fields, of
the blurred white lines arrowing past
and turned to look at each other,
helmeted, strange, and apart.

2

In the late spring we looked for
snow, and found it in long
rounded patches under the pines.
It was cold in the sunlight
at that height, as we straddled
warm metal and smoked, facing
the timbered slopes where the winter
had come to be. Down below
the river rushed green and white
over the rocks, and a hawk
drifted overhead. Each was there
for the other, and our cheeks burned
in the raw piney darkness
as we raced the downward turns
between big trees, heading home.

3

Tonight the kitchen is warm
and brightly lit and quiet.
I drink his whisky, he buys
my silence and delicacy.
He drinks and his tongue grows loose.
He loves me up with his lies.
The night cannot end unless

he spills himself, breaks a glass
or falls down, his agony
almost visible, like fumes.
When I reach out to touch him,
there is the empty chair
and the bottle, and he is wheeling
drunkenly down this banked
narrowing space, as if his feet
could say what it is he feels,
or his wet face. I can't speak
or think of what he must want,
and his eyes, behind sungoggles,
turn on me like a blind man's
fervent and terrified—
there is an animal loose
in his house, ripe with the scent
of mania, murderous, bloody, full
of blame, a grown creature walking
at last and beyond his power
to love, pacify, or kill.

AFTER HOURS

Not yet five, and the light
is going fast. Milky and veined
a thin frost covers the flooded
ruts of the driveway, the grass
bends to the winter night. Her face
is before me now; I see it

in the misted glass, the same
impossible smile and I can feel
again on my bare shoulder
the dew of her breath. We made
a life in two years, a sky
and the very trees, lost in thought.

I know what it is, to be
alone, to have asked for everything
and to do without, to search
the mind for a face that dances away,

to wait, and what it exacts.
I don't fear it, I say,

but I do, and this night
the wind against my window
and the top branches thrashing about
enter my life and I see
the coming time loose and dark
above me, with new strength

YOU COULD SAY

Yesterday rain fell in torrents,
stripping the branches of leaves and
deepening the arroyo. Now,
although the sun glances like flint
at the edges of cars, houses,
antennas, the water remains.
It lies in the hollows of rocks
and in lakes on the roads. Last night
it signaled a great change; today
winter breathes at my window and
a few last flies, stunned by cold
into fearlessness, nestle close
to my skin. Summer is burned out.
Why does this season with its joy
in killing and its hard iron breath
always find me alone? You could say
but you won't, and I am slowly
drifting away, I am growing
oblique like the sun, striking out
feebly at what is gone.
                    My love,
it was my nature to want you,
lascivious, aloof, a body
fresh as new-fallen snow, and as
cold. Like other men in my
desire, I asked for it and now
I have it—the wind, the black trees,
scum of ice on the roadside pools—
all that the rain promised, and more.

TO HER

Risen above the uncertain
boughs in the last breath of daylight,
so near she seems that you can
touch her with your hand, she rides
in the tall blue silence.
Her light falls across the fields
like drifted snow. The shadow
of the pale barn is like something
alive, softer than fur.
                No one
acknowledges what is happening,
it has happened so many times
and it means nothing. The city
lights flare against the night sky
far off and headlights enter
and leave the dark. All have their own
or other lights to follow,
all have their place.
                Only a dog
gives tongue in this outer dark,
and the insect nations keep
their high-pitched vigil. The gaunt
illiterate sheriff, scratching his nose,
looks upward and is reminded
of other nights, things done
by hands and knives, the flesh laid open
in a seizure of country lust;
and the young boy and girl give up
their first nakedness to her
as they struggle with their mouths
to come together. Things fight and sleep.
But this one, stumbling alone
in a thicket of wishes, feeling
the new bristles on his face,
confesses her power from his knees.

How else can he explain
the inexplicable? When he drove
a thousand miles without rest,
when he pleaded with his girl, when
he drove away, broke his hand, went down

on someone's wife, drank and was sick,
stole money, walked in the woods,
came here to change—if he dare
make his voice heard in this
luminous darkness, who is there
to hear? Only the full moon,
and to her all sounds are music.

WHITE BLOSSOMS

Take me as I drive alone
through the dark countryside.
As the strong beams clear a path,
picking out fences, weeds, late
flowering trees, everything
that streams back into the past
without sound, I smell the grass
and the rich chemical sleep
of the fields. An open moon
sails above, and a stalk
of red lights blinks, miles away.

It is at such moments I
am called, in a voice so pure
I have to close my eyes, and enter
the breathing darkness just beyond
my headlights. I have come back,
I think, to something I had
almost forgotten, a mouth
that waits patiently, sighs, speaks
and falls silent. No one else
is alive. The blossoms are
white, and I am almost there.

REACHING THE HORIZON

Once it was enough simply
to be here. Neither to know
nor to be known, I crossed

in the full sight of everything
that stood dumbly in sunlight
or drank the standing water
when it was clear. I called them
by their names and they were what
I called them. In the low glare
of afternoon I advanced
upon my shadow, glancing
at the grass unoccupied,
into the wind and into
the light. What I did not know
passed shuddering toward me
over the bowed tips of the
grass and what I could not see
raced sunward away from me
like dust crystals or a wave
returning to its yellow source.

This morning the wet black eye
of a heifer darkens with the
passing seconds, holding my gaze.
It has grown cold. Flies
drop from the walls; guinea fowl
roost in the sycamore. Old
dog in the corner, the day
ripples into its fullness.
Surrounded by eyes and tongues,
I begin to feel the waste
of being human. The rose
of the sky darkens to a wound
and closes with one question
on its lips, and the million
stars rise up into the blackness
with theirs. If I spoke to this
formerly it was as one
speaks to a mirror or scummed
pond, guessing how deep it is—
Now I see what has no name
or singularity and
can think of nothing to say.

NEW YEAR'S EVE IN SOLITUDE

Night comes to the man who can pray
only on paper
He disappears into paper
with his old mouth shaped to say no
and his voice is so tiny
in all these miles of silence and cold grass

As I write
the fog has eaten away the mountains
the princely hills and the fields
everything but this house
and this hand
and the few feet of light it throws out against the dark

I try to talk
to the drunken god who sleeps in my arms and legs
tell him god knows what
but what's the use he won't listen
or else he listens in his sleep

and the dead listen in theirs
up on the hill
up past the drifting
iron gates the dead leaves
listen and the frozen
water pipes

And at last I know what to ask
of the new year blowing at my teeth
I know what I really want
and it hurts me

Nothing any more against the darkness
nothing against the night
nothing
in which the bright child is silent and shines very dimly
cover me with your arms
give me your breast

that will make me forgetful and slow
so I can join him in sleep—
Hurry down now good mother give me
my life again
in this hand that lives but a moment and is immortal
cover my eyes and I will see them
those companions clothed head to foot in tiny fires
that I said goodbye to when I first opened my eyes

Give me my robes of earth
and my black milk

APRIL FOURTH

I throw open the door
And someone like the night walks in

A moist wind in the doorway
A breath of flowers
In the wake of this august presence

I was sitting for hours
Watching the coal
Of the cigarette rising and falling
Finally one must do something

The evening I thought
The evening was the last evening
As usual

I was thinking of heroes
Whose knuckles shine as they curl round a rifle
I was thinking of my brother
Who brings me my head in a basket
None of it will do

Let me make myself empty
I can live without sleeping tonight

I can live without dreams of the King
Awash on his balcony
Half of his neck and face in another kingdom

In the morning I will not understand

Mountains surfacing from their mortal darkness
A scum of yellow flowers
The great oak crying with a thousand voices

All that
Wrinkles like heat and disappears into thin air

AN EVENING

The sun blazing slowly in its last hour

A horse motionless on a knoll
His long neck and mouth plunged toward the earth
His tail blowing in filaments of fire

Tuft of grass that bends its illuminated head over its own shadow
The grass sleepy after the long feast of light

And the new leafed figs dancing a little in the silence
Readying themselves for the night

An evening

Understood
By those who understand it not

A FEW WORDS ABOUT NOTHING

When I am sitting alone late at night, with a sheet of paper on the table or in the typewriter, one thing I am not thinking about is what sort of poetry I write, or others write, or ought or ought not to be written. I am thinking about a word or line in a poem, if I'm into one. I am thinking about horses, and war, and dawn, about my wife, my friends, my own enchanted, disenchanted life.

The poems in this book, with a few exceptions, were all written some time ago. In the past two years I have written little. I had many thoughts about The Art of Poetry and My Contemporaries and Whither? etc, but I was not writing and the thoughts were worthless to me. Now I'm beginning again, trying to summon poems such as nothing in my education or early years of poetizing ever led me to expect or even long for. When I was quite young, I came under unhealthy influences— Yvor Winters, for example, and America, and my mother, though not in that order. Winters was easy to exorcise; all I had to do was meet him. My mother and America are another story and why tell it in prose?

Once in Iowa City, a friend said, "Why do you write in rhyme and meter? Your poetry is nothing like your life." What do we know of another's life, I thought, but I had nothing to say. I no longer write in rhyme and meter, and still my life is not much like my poetry. At least, I don't think so. It is possible I'm not a poet at all. But I am a man, a Piscean, and unhappy, and therefore I make up poems.

Robert Mezey
Tollhouse, California
December, 1968

LOOKING FOR AN OPENING

As early as my 24th year, that is to say long before I became tolerably proficient at traditional meters, I had an idea for a poem in free verse and conversational English, a poem which would be harsh, natural, and somehow powerful without employing a heightened vocabulary or a single word suggesting the presence of an idea. The poem was largely sponsored by a phrase from Williams, the "twiggy stuff of bushes," and I suppose the reason I never wrote it, though I tried a dozen different times, was that Williams had already done it.

One poem in particular haunted me, and each week I would collect material for it. I was living at the time with my brother, and on Sunday mornings, the only morning we didn't work, we would walk through the alleys of the neighborhood of our childhood in Detroit, in the alleys because there we were free to drink beer without offending anyone and without being bothered by anyone. Either because they were beautiful or because the night before made them seem so, I wanted to capture the quality of those alleys and the quality of the communion I felt with my brother, who at that time was the only person I knew who didn't suggest I was either wasting my life or drinking too much or both. I was in the alleys of my home town, I was 24 years old, healthy, strong, hungover, and I had a good brother. And when I tried to capture it I always wrote the "twiggy stuff of bushes."

Later that same year I went to Iowa to study under Robert Lowell. I discovered prosody, and the "twiggy stuff of bushes" never got written. I put my brother poem aside, I put my brother aside, I put the alleys of Detroit aside, I put drinking aside, I married, fathered children, and became a professor.

Whatever the faults of my poetry at least I was writing it, and by teaching I was staying alive in the dreary fifties. Occasionally I was even able to get some of the experiences of my life into the poetry without raising it to the level of the emotions of princes. At the same time I so mastered the poetry of princes that Yvor Winters awarded me a fellowship in the creative writing at Stanford.

I don't exactly know why I took up the "twiggy stuff of bushes" again at Stanford. Perhaps it was because of something Winters did or didn't do, but I doubt it, for the Master was a big, awkward man who asked only that I work hard and not write trivial poems. (For him the range of the trivial was enormous, from Charlie Chaplin to Franz Kafka.) He showed me syllabic poetry, though he didn't really admire it or know much about it; he didn't know, for example, that no one could hear syllables, that almost no one could hear the rhymes in syllabic poems, and that the process of writing such poems was something else, that the poems either came in large, nearly complete passages or they didn't come at all. I would show him one of my new poems, and he would read me something by Corbière that turned my tongue to stone. He neither understood nor valued what I did, and he said so.

The poem I wanted most to write at this time was a variation on my "brother-communion" poem, but instead of my brother, who I hadn't seen much of in years, it involved a friend, a big, silent, knowing fellow who had taken me hunting back in Iowa, and it involved all those brittle, "twiggy" details native to an Iowa autumn. I tried again and again in traditional meters, and I got nothing that even hinted at the experience. On Winters' suggestion I was reading the dull, ladylike poetry of Elizabeth Daryush; it was very easy to see the technique in her syllabic poetry because there was almost nothing else there, and so after two hours in the rare book room at Stanford, where Daryush was housed, I was ready to write, but instead of dealing with the relationship with my quiet hunter friend, about which I knew nothing, I wrote about the one time I went out hunting alone and scared myself half to death and never went hunting again. Whatever intensification I gave to the experience did not come from a falsely elevated diction, for with the exception of one slip in the first stanza I had written in the language I used when I spoke. Rhythmically I had used Mrs. Daryush as a base, put her line and stanza down as a norm, and then had broken through it as quickly as I could. And as violently. "Small Game" was the first poem I tried in syllabics; I never handled the form as well again:

SMALL GAME

In borrowed boots which don't fit
and an old olive greatcoat,
I hunt the corn-fed rabbit,
game fowl, squirrel, starved bobcat,
anything small. I bring down
young deer wandered from the doe's
gaze, and reload, and move on
leaving flesh to inform crows.

At dusk they seem to suspect
me, burrowed in a corn field
verging their stream. The unpecked
stalks call them. Nervous, they yield
to what they must: hunger, thirst,
habit. Closer and closer
comes the scratching which at first
sounds like sheaves clicked together.

I know them better than they
themselves, so I win. At night
the darkness is against me.
I can't see enough to sight
my weapon, which becomes freight
to be endured or at best
a crutch to ease swollen feet
that demand but don't get rest

unless I invade your barn,
which I do. Under my dark
coat, monstrous and vague, I turn
down your lane, float through the yard,
and roost. Or so I appear
to you who call me spirit
or devil, though I'm neither.
What's more, under all, I'm white

and soft, more like yourself than
you ever would have guessed before
you claimed your barn with shot gun,
torch, and hounds. Why am I here?
What do I want? Who am I?
You demand from the blank mask
which amuses the dogs. Leave me!
I do your work so why ask!

I showed the poem to Winters, who thought it sounded fine, though he couldn't see that it was about anything except details. In those first poems I wrote in syllabics I needed a rigid count of syllables and rhyme, but within a few years I was able to grow much laxer. I don't know that this produced better poetry, but it did mean that I could more often get a first draft within a few hours rather than a few days. By the time I wrote "The Cemetery at Academy, California" (1962) I was able to let almost everything go and decide line by line what I wanted and where I wanted it.

I tired of the quality of ordinariness in the music of my syllabic poetry, I tired of it even before I achieved it, and as early as 1959 I started working toward a different poetry, highly lyrical, heightened, with driving, unrelenting rhythm. Again and again I got the music well enough but was unable to write decent poetry because I'd let the music run off with me and was unable to match it with theme or details or tale or what have you of sufficient intensity or complexity or tenderness; the only thing I was using was my ear. When I did get a good poem, or one that satisfied me, it looked very traditional. It was; it was simply accentuals; I remember I was reading Dos Passos's *USA* for the first time in twenty years, and to my shock it was at times enormously lyrical. I remember also that a passage of his fell perfectly into kooky kind of accentuals which employed a line ending and rhyming effects much more like that of syllabics. The next day I wrote a poem which excited me enormously even though it wasn't good. Again I was dominated by music, but within a few months I did much better with more imaginative material ("Heaven"). When I went back to syllabics I went back with a heightened sense of lyricism.

The next step was to go back to traditional meters and simply violate them, let the material break them open. Then suddenly, without realizing it, I got my "brother-communion" poem, and without the "twiggy stuff of bushes," though to be sure my brother was my imaginary brother, "Baby Villon." And I got as well a sense, probably a false sense, that I could do what I wanted with meters, I could have them or not, and I could have just so much of a rigid syllabic count as I might want, and I could have meter, rhyme, syllables, accents all at once or none at all.

I thought I was a marvelous poet that autumn of 1965 when I went to Spain. I hadn't traveled in seven years, I had never traveled with a wife and three kids, and I'd never voluntarily gone to a police state. In Spain I discovered to my surprise that I didn't know what was going on inside me or around me. I had lived for years under the same unchanging pale sky and in the same glass and plaster house and among the same bland people. I hung on to poetry for dear life, or to the idea of it, for I confess I had the courage to not write for four months. When I did I began by searching for and finding my old voice, and when I found it I threw it away and wrote some poems, like "Winter Rains," that shocked me with their willingness to admit my terror before the new grasses, the weather, the sky, and the heavy stone houses.

It would be dishonest to pretend I've gone my own way, that I haven't read what my fellow poets were writing. In 1957 just after everyone else, I began to turn away from the frozen poem. The next year on North Beach in San Francisco I gave a poetry reading with Gary Snyder. I liked his presence, I liked it better than my own, and so did the audience. In order to defend myself to myself, I said that the house was stacked in his favor, but I knew he gave them more, that his poems were more readable, more eloquent and looser at the same time, and more consistently in our common American language. He was writing for and about the people who were listening; I had technique. By 1963 I began to think seriously about all that Robert Bly was urging. I can't recall the exact date, sometime I think in the spring of 1965, I knew that he was right and that I had to surrender the poem for better or worse to those forces within me able to produce writing outrageous enough to be relevant and to be American.

Philip Levine
Fresno, California